Four Seeds Wisdom Path:
Teachings and Practices
for Personal & Communal Healing

by Sophia Wise One

Copyright © 2025 by Sophia Wise One

All rights reserved. You may photograph, post, or share up to 2 pages or a single image from this work for noncommercial promotion, classroom use, or personal study, provided each excerpt includes this exact attribution line:
Sophia Wise One, *Four Seeds Wisdom Path: Teachings and Practices for Personal & Communal Healing*, © 2025, sophiawiseone.com. Public posting of larger excerpts, commercial use, or creation/distribution of derivative works is prohibited without prior written permission.

Please tag @sophiawiseone @fourseedswisdompath when sharing
--
I love to see and reshare your posts.

Collaboration Invitation: Collaboration and conversation are welcome. If you'd like to share more publicly or propose a project, please contact me -- I'm a real person and grateful for our joyful cocreation.

For Copyright Permissions requests and Booking Inquiries contact: connect@sophiawiseone.com SophiaWiseOne.com

First Edition 2020
Third Edition 2025

ISBN: 978-1-7344862-6-1 (Hardback)
ISBN: 978-1-7344862-7-8 (Paperback)
ISBN: 978-1-7344862-8-5 (ebook)

Dedication

For love.

For the children.
May this world be prepared to receive the gift you are and what you have brought to this realm with the kindness, beauty, health, and deep true joy you deserve. Limitless.

For the water. For the air.
For our planet.
I am grateful you heal as we heal. May we listen and act in alignment with true wisdom of what it is to live well here.

For the resurrection of the Temples we lost or hid or burned. For the wisdom hunted, stolen, skewed. May it all rise, ignite in each and every being it's true embodiment. May the medicine be honored, restored, celebrated, respected, appreciated, enjoyed, true. May the guardians awaken and tend us in this potent time.

For my mother who built my body with her body. May all the joys of my life reverberate blessings in your bones and soul song.

For my father who gave me the entrepreneurial spirit, showed me faith, midnight and early morning friendship. May you know that I follow my heart and that God's love fills me every step, may you smile and feel joy more truly wit every passing day.

For my brother, blood of my blood, flesh of my flesh. You taught me dreams come true by your life and made me the love warrior I am. May this tend your tender soul and feed your dreams which are holy and wonderful.

For my sister, I stand because you stand with me. May your life be ever more joyous and kind with every year you are here, and may you feel my love everyday of it.

For all those who created this with me. Your holding and loving of me, your wiping of my tears, your feeding of me, your listening, your laughing with me. May everything you gave to me come back to you in the ways you need to fulfill your visions, with grace and ease and joy.

For all my Kickstarter backers, you are dream manifestors. May your faith and contribution to this project come back to you at least 100 fold.

For you in acknowledgment and gratitude, my transcription and editorial team, this simply would not have happened without your love, care, and skills. Emily Jean Benson, Diane Levenson, Sharon, Caitl Davis, Leah Moon, Grace Browne, and Joe Graff, your focus, gifts, and time were bridges over immense canyons in my journey. Thank you from all of me. May all your endeavors be blessed in pleasurable and aligned support, joy and delight, always, all ways. May your medicine path be clear and may all the calls of your spirit be fulfilled.

I give thanks to my ancestors blood, spirit, and land and all our lineages.
    May this honor all our lineages.
    May this honor all my teachers throughout the ages.
    May this bring joy and remembering to those who touch it.
    I am grateful.
    Thank you.
    Be blessed and know you are a blessing.

The Table Of Contents

Honoring .... *xxi*

On Loving Life .... *xxiii*

Four Seeds Wisdom Path App & Wisdom Deck .... *xxvi*

INVITATION & PROCLAMATION .... *xxvii*

How to Play the Medicine Circle Game .... *xxviii*

Oracle & Wisdom Deck Layouts .... *xxxii*

Part One - Teachings *1*

 Ancestors (No Words) *3*

 Alignment Check *5*

 All Fear Is the Fear of Death, All Death Is the Death of the Ego *7*

 Ascend onto the Planet *9*

 Ask A Different Question *11*

 Attend To Your Little *13*

 Balm of Forgiveness *15*

 Be Still *17*

 Become *18*

 Becoming Enlightened: Watching Yourself Make Mistakes *20*

 Breathe, Remember, Beauty, Know, Infinite, Love *23*

 BURNOUT! Sustainability *24*

 Cleanse Through Nourishment *27*

 Congrats You Survived *29*

 Don't Go Dancing In the Dark Alone *31*

 Earth *33*

Ego's Last Stand	34
Embodied Enlightenment	36
Ether	38
Everybody's Best Is A Mess	40
Expand. Embrace.	42
Fire	44
Flip It	46
Give Yourself Permission	48
Go Inside and Call On Spirit	50
Healing Happens In A Moment	52
Help	54
Hug It Out	56
I Am So Grateful	57
I Am Whole Just As I Am	59
Incarnation Is the Jam	60
It's All You	62
Know Thyself Know God	64
Life Is Ridiculous	66
Make An Offering	67
Money Issues Are Expressions of Root Issues	69
Need≠Wrong Need=Need	71
No. Stop. Not In My Space.	76
No. Yes.	78
Open Your Eyes	80

PLAY *82*

Practice *84*

Question Everything *86*

Radical Acceptance *88*

Reveal to Heal *90*

Silence *92*

Space *93*

Start Where You Are *94*

Stay the Course *95*

Tend Your Altar *97*

The Monster Carries a Gem *100*

The Truth May Be Harder to Swallow, But it's Easier to Digest *102*

There Is Nothing To Fix *104*

These Are My Feet *106*

Trade Vigilance for Boundaries *107*

Trust the Body's Wisdom *109*

Trust Truly *111*

Truth Is Relative *114*

Turn Poison Into Medicine *116*

Under Stress More Communication Not Less *118*

Use Your Breath As Your Ally *120*

Water *122*

We Are Creatures of Habit *124*

When We Learn to Mother/Father/Parent as Children We Mother/Father/

- Parent Like Children ... 125
- Who You Are Is What You Teach ... 128
- Wind ... 130
- Witness, Witnessed ... 132
- You Are On Time ... 134
- You Existed Long Before This Life, and Will Exist Long After ... 137
- You Make You Orgasm ... 139
- Your, My, Our, The Healing ... 141
- Your Story Is Medicine ... 143

Part Two - Practices ... 147
- Round Robins ... 149
  - Instructions ... 149
  - Alignment ... 149
  - Congrats You Survived ... 150
  - Confession Session ... 150
  - Commitment and Course Reflection ... 150
  - Ether ... 150
  - Receiving and Expressing Burnout/Sustain ... 151
  - Hard to Hear ... 151
  - Healing In A Moment Reflection ... 151
  - Heard Medicine Story ... 152
  - Personal Medicine Story ... 152
  - Naming Foundational Belief Systems ... 152
  - Needs List Identification ... 152

    Ownership Prompt 152

    Processing Feedback 153

    Seasonal Wisdom 154

    Two Minutes of Silence Then Share 156

    Wisdom Circle 157

Games 158

    Instructions 158

    Alternatives 159

    Ascending Off and On 160

    Clearing Delusion 161

    Contact Movement with Wrists 161

    Gibberish Convo 162

    High Fives! 162

    The Funny Face Game 163

    Fuels of Improv 163

    Freeze 165

    Make The Room 166

    My Little! 167

    Monster Is My Teacher 168

    Physical Storytelling 169

    Trust Fall 170

    Word Association 172

    YES I AM! YES YOU ARE! 173

Medicine Songs 175

- Instructions ... 175
  - I Am Whole Just As I Am ... 176
  - Goddess Chants ... 176
  - Rise up, Rise up, Rise up! ... 177
  - Stampede of the Elephants ... 178
  - Stardust ... 179
  - Peace Now ... 179
  - We Are In This Together ... 180
- Writing Prompts ... 182
  - Instructions ... 182
  - Admitting a Truth ... 183
  - Healing Systemic Conditioning ... 184
  - Becoming ... 185
  - Belief Traders ... 185
  - Boundary Patterns Modeled ... 186
  - Brain Dump ... 186
  - Brain Equations ... 187
  - Charting You ... 188
  - Clarity on Offerings/Gifts ... 189
  - Dear Little ... 189
  - Design That Match Your Intent ... 190
  - Desire Admittance ... 190
  - Forgiveness Letter ... 191
  - Journaling ... 191

Habit Identification 194

Love Letter 195

Money Sorting 195

Mind Mapping 196

More Communication 197

Naming the Gifts of Your Lineage 197

Naming and Loving Coping Patterns 198

Observing 198

Responsibility Charting 198

Thank You Note 199

Truth Sorting 200

Hyper Vigilance Sorting 200

Where I Am 201

What I Want In Sexy Time 201

Yes/No Sorting 201

Meditations 203

Instructions 203

Organic Movement Meditation 204

Flame Meditation 205

Still Meditation 205

Walking Meditation 206

Guided Practices 207

Instructions 207

Ancestors Re-weaving 208

Balm of Forgiveness ... 214
Body Wisdom Approach Practice ... 214
Bone Breathing Meditation ... 216
Calling In Spirit ... 218
Calling The Directions ... 220
Communing with Elementals ... 220
Communing with your Sacred Warrior Guide ... 222
Dance of Sustainability ... 224
Despair & Radiance ... 226
Eye Gazing ... 228
Expanding to Hold Pain ... 232
Fear/Little Meditation ... 237
Grounding Cord ... 240
Mirror Meditation ... 241
Nourishment Identification ... 244
Observation Bias ... 246
Pelvic Bowl Meditation ... 246
Restoring Our Inner Temple ... 250
Simple Moontime Practice ... 257
Soul Unification Healing Meditation ... 258
Space In Joints Meditation ... 264
Stealing From Ourselves ... 267
Visiting Our Inner Temple ... 268

Breath Practices ... 274

    Instructions 274
    Alternate Nostril Breathing 274
    Audible Exhale 275
    Breath of Fire 276
    Breathe to Stretch 276
    Cooling Breath 276
    Mindful Breathing 277

Offerings 278
    Instructions 278
    Make an Offering 279
    Make an Offering to Yourself 280
    Meditation Gift 280
    Sing a Song or Play Music 281

Rituals 282
    Instructions 282
    Break The Chain of Familial Abuse 282
    Death and Rebirth Ritual 284
    Fire Ceremony 284
    Grief Ritual 285
    Healing With Big Ancestors 287
    Healing with Recent Ancestors 289
    Healing the Hunted Wound 290
    Warrior Vows 292
    Water Healing Ceremony 292

- Wind Ceremony ... 293
- Healing Hands ... 294
  - Instructions ... 294
  - Healing Hands Circle ... 295
  - Healing Hands On Self ... 295
  - Healing Hands Shared ... 295
- Hugging ... 297
  - Instructions ... 297
  - Hugging Yourself ... 298
  - Hugging with Extremities ... 299
  - Hugging Sitting Down ... 300
  - Hugging over Time and Space ... 300
  - Hugging Standing Up ... 301
  - Group Hugging Exercise ... 302
- Visual and Crafting Healing Arts ... 303
  - Instructions ... 303
  - Collaging or Vision Boarding ... 304
  - Non-Dominant Hand Drawing ... 304
  - Pain Recognition and Self Expansion ... 304
  - Finger Painting ... 305
- Chanting ... 306
  - Instructions ... 306
  - Fuck It ... 307
  - I Do What I Can When I Can ... 307

I Am On Time	307
Permission Invocation	307
Sat Nam	308
These Are My Feet	308
Practices	**310**
Four Corners of Your Foot	310
40 Day Practice	310
A Fall-Apart-y	311
Adult Rocking	311
Ask a New, Pull a New	316
Begging for Help	316
Birth the World	317
BLESS IT	317
Build an Altar	319
Clear Objects and Tools with Resonance	321
Constructive Feedback	321
Cosmic Shuffle	322
Cosmic Shuffle Dance Party	322
Little Check-In	323
Declutter	324
Deep Clean	326
Discernment Prayer	327
Following the Thread	329
Financial Transparency	330

Go Ahead - Get Heady Convo ... 331

Go Swimming in Living Water ... 332

Group Process Format ... 332

Habits for Feeling Your Feelings ... 335

Habits for Completing Goals ... 335

Help Through the Crack ... 337

How to Accept a Compliment ... 337

How to Manifest What You Really Want ... 338

I Am Willing to Admit ... 340

Internal Bodywork ... 342

Learn Something New ... 344

Record a Story and Listen to Yourself ... 345

Inversions ... 345

Ironic to Sincere "Thank you" Prayer Practice ... 346

Nature Bath ... 346

"Yes" and "No" ... 347

Nourishment Practices ... 348

Pendulum Practice ... 349

Players Choice ... 350

Professional Assistance ... 350

Pro-Active Listening ... 352

Prayer Practice ... 353

Reverse the Question ... 357

Savoring ... 357

Self Swaddling … 358
Sensitivity Scanning … 360
Take a Bath … 361
Tour of the Pelvic Bowl … 362
Warrior Pose and Teachings by Grace Perkins … 371
We Are Whole, Together Circle … 372
Wind Prayer … 373
Unwinding Group Exercise … 373

Honoring

The lineages are innumerable.
Known and unknown.
Named and unnamed.
The lives are countless.
The teachers precious.
I am as I am because of all of you.

You know who you are, when you read a line, feel a wave, see a card.
It is because of you that I am here.
I bless you.
I am vibrating gratitude for your existence.
I bow to each and every mystery that has brought this to and through me.

It is of you, Sacredness.

It is for you, Sacredness.

You have taken form, time and time again, to share your wisdom and healing with me.
May each and every being who has blessed me
be known and blessed in ways
that most fulfill their hearts,
bring joy to their life,
light up every sacred thread of their holy being.

I praise.
I celebrate.
I bow.

I am carved and carving.

Bless this.
Bless each in their own sacred way.
Thank you.

On Loving Life

There is an infinite amount of wisdom that pours forth through people, animals, traditions, books, poetry, music, land, silence, sound, and story. I looked for and hungered, from the start of my being, to hear that wisdom around me. I found it everywhere. Everywhere I have walked, the wisdom throughout the ages has been felt and shared with me.

The Four Seeds Wisdom Path is how we allow the wisdom, love, fun, and peace that await and call from within to move out into our body, mind, lives, and relationships. Calling Medicine is what happens when we say, "yes" to the healing that is knocking. When we learn how to say "yes" to the inner inkling and are skillful in our action of thought, heart, energy, and action we turn these moments into the mystical doorway of coming home to ourselves. When we live in the sanctuary of our own soul we naturally love our life.

Loving Your Life is about being internally resourced and capable in a way that allows us to feel appreciative and present during external situations that are less than ideal and those that are blissful. Loving our life is about radically accepting and loving what is. This is generated by an underlying foundation of life being an adventure which allows the various situations to be "just the thing at hand" rather than being "the problem" or "the answer". I believe that loving is our nature, and it is by being in a participatory relationship with loving, combined with integritous effort and action, that real and lasting enjoyment of life becomes the result.

The hope and prayer for this book (and Four Seeds Wisdom Path Oracles Cards and App), and Medicine Circle Game format are to pass on the teachings and practices that led me into rooted and lasting enjoyment, true pleasure and peace. I've witnessed these things lead countless clients, students, and friends into an experience of knowing and loving themselves, knowing and loving their lives, and knowing and loving the people and places they are in. I believe when we are well taken care of on all levels of our being, we want the people and places we interact with to be well taken care of as well.

The chapters, the imagery, the descriptions, and the practices are meant to remind you of your own knowing and wisdom. They are offered here to validate what you know to be true, and to question the limitations which inhibit you from knowing the beautiful reality that is available to you.

There are times in our lives when we need to see beyond what we are already seeing. That is the point of all divination. There are times in our lives when we just don't know what to do, when we lack the optimal and satisfying skills to navigate a situation we are in. The purpose of self and professional development is the cultivation of skills needed to accomplish your visions.

Everything here is inviting you to ask, notice, and listen. To relate to your body, your life, and your visions in deep intimacy. To enter a timespace to treasure and enjoy the beauty of you and your life as it is right now. To take the time to heal the disconnect, the othering, and stories that have ripped at the faithful, vision having, loved and loving darling precious being you are.

When you are really you and embrace everyone and, indeed, everything, people and the natural world of which we are a part, as we are, needing and expressing in our unique ways, miracles happen. When we respect and find true compersion in our sameness and differences then the very foundations of how we think, feel, and collectively make decisions as families, communities, businesses, societies shift into one of enhancing mutual benefit.

Calling medicine and doing healing and medicine practices can be inspiring, intimidating, or even a little daunting and that is why I outline how to do a medicine circle in the form of a game. The most powerful thing I have learned is to relax, trust, and *play* in the face of wild life. The format of playing at healing takes us into a less serious mindset and into the landscape of safe risk-taking and adventure. The potency is only increased when we deepen our breath and let the mystery unfold. You can use the format inside a sacred space with candles and as a high ritual in a group, or as a daily practice with yourself, or as a pickup game out in the park, or however you dream. You are invited to use this however you are called. Allow it, in all its forms and formats, to nourish you and those with whom you play and practice.

Many of the teachings and practices are meant for the strong of heart, courageous of the mind, and dedicated of spirit. These are summonings and requests to meet yourself in the depths and love what is there. These are invitations to enter your body and embody your soul and then make choices about your life. These are callings to enjoy your own majesty. All your bodies, all your minds, and all your lives, from the deep subtle to the overt and material. This is a charge to make empowered choices about the very vibrational existence you inhabit.

The teachings and practices are all from my lived experiences, both as a child mystic who has always spoken with the divine, my ancestors, angels, and spirit guides, and as one who has been blessed with initiations, blessings, and healings from innumerable lineages and teachers across the globe. I bow in deep honor and respect to each and every one who has contributed to the reclaiming of my bloodline and spiritual ancestral lines of wisdom, and the ways that are expressed and shared here.

At the core of loving your life is the power you have to create your life. Do you know what you are creating? Are you interested in seeing that honestly? When you see what you contributed to creating, you are reminded of what you are capable of, and here is a potent place for all of us in this time of great, fast, and needed cultural and cosmic change.

Love your life by knowing it. Know it by being here. Being here isn't always easy, and yet it is always sacred. Love what is here while it is happening so we can be in this world and create the one we want together.

I love my life. It is magnificent.

May you trust your wisdom and you path and may you truly love your life.

Four Seeds Wisdom Path App & Oracle Cards

Digital Library of curated additional information that *grows*.

There are a multitude of multimedia materials!

- 72 Transmission videos for the cards
- You can virtually pull a card, roll a die, go deeper into the practices
- Audio recording of all the Guided Practices & More
- Call and Response recordings of the medicine songs
- Supplemental instructional videos
- In depth curated subject specific content

You can order your copy of *Four Seeds Wisdom Path Oracle Cards*, get the *Four Seeds Wisdom Path App*, become a member, or access your membership here:
sophiawiseone.com/member-access

INVITATION & PROCLAMATION

Each Chapter that is matched to a card from the companion deck, *Four Seeds Wisdom Path Oracle Cards* and carries a teaching and a list of practices which are activities to do when you resonate with a card.

The teachings do not carry the answer, they hope to carry you to *your* answer.

The purpose is to reflect back to you and acknowledge some part of you in a way that illuminates your own inner wisdom and grants you access to your own guidance.

Take what serves you and leave the rest.

This is a tool to help you open up and have deep and sincere conversation and communication with your true self. That is sacred communication and no one knows better than you.

This information is not meant to tell you what your own truth is. Knowing and living your truth is yours to discover.

Practice, take risks, stretch beyond the familiar, and then from your own awakened and lived experience.

Trust what you truly know.

How to Play the Medicine Circle Game

The medicine circle game format utilizes the power of play, optimized with the power of community.

- My favorite definition of the word healing is "to become more whole"
- I believe healing comes from having our experiences altered, and in the new experience finding love and acceptance for both ways of being, and from that acceptance feeling empowered and compassionate, while moving forward in choice with the preferred perspective
- Healing is the true force of our human potential! We can and will be healed by experiencing ourselves alone, in community, in relationship, by process and ritual, by play, and inadvertently.
- Healing includes the uncovering of what is there, be it precious gifts, desires, or wounds, and accepting it in its wholeness, without judgment and with love

You can play with game with the whole set up, or with just the book.
    Pulling Cards or using Pick a Number between 3 and 143 Instructions for using this book, the oracle cards, die, and the App, to play:
The Medicine Circle Game

    ITEM NEEDED: The game calls for a six sided die. You can use any method to allow random and divination space to select 1-6. Some ideas:
- A six sided die
- Make six pieces of paper each with the number 1-6 and a cup or hat to mix them in
- A dice rolling app
- Use a standard deck of playing cards and pull out Ace-6

- Roll an imaginary die
- Make something up

STEP 1: Aiming for Safety and Vulnerability in Shared Space

Read aloud the guide below, and then have everyone give a physical or verbal signal that they are in agreement. No one can create a safe space for anyone else. These agreements, and any you add or changes you make, are aiming towards creating a space in which everyone who is present wants to fully participate.

- At all times, we will have respect for one another & respect for ourselves. We agree to respect each other's space, feelings, individual experiences, & physical bodies to the best of our ability.
- Everyone here is valued as wise.
- Each of us is responsible for our experience together. This means each of us taking ownership for our own actions, needs, & feelings.
- We acknowledge the courage it takes to ask questions & express ourselves & our feelings. It is healthy to be vulnerable. We are all here to support each other.
- We will ask permission to discuss something that someone shared inside the space before assuming they want to talk about it or have it talked about afterwards.
- We invite each other to ask for help when we need it.
- Does anyone else have a request or need before starting?

STEP 2: Identify your Statement of Curiosity

This is where you name what is on your heart-mind-consciousness. Identify an issue or question you want greater insight on.

If you're thinking of a Yes/No question, shift it to be more open ended.

If you don't have something in particular, you can always use something like:
"What will serve me in this moment?"
"What do I need to hear right now?"
"I am showing up to grow and expand in loving presence, I am open to help and guidance."

Who are you saying this to? Whomever makes sense to you.

If you are looking for insight on something you know you may have resistance to hearing openly about it helps to name it. If you are aware of resistance to hearing a certain thing, you can speak directly to it like this, for example:

"Tell me about [insert your Statement of Curiosity], and I am aware of my resistance and fear that says now is not a good time. I acknowledge my attachment to hearing a particular message, and even so, I really am willing to hear and be guided past that. Help me really hear."

STEP 3: Pull A Card, "Pick a Number Between 3 and 143", or "Flip to a Page" and let people flip through the pages until they land on their chapter, mark it.

Each person takes a moment with the book or deck. Hold the book or shuffle the cards while you focus on your question, contemplation, Statement of Curiosity. Then Pull A Card from the top or anywhere in the deck, "Pick a Number" or "Flip to a Page" Whatever your pleasure.

When playing with cards, after you select your card place it face down without looking.

STEP 4: It's Always Your Turn

This isn't really a step as much as a framework.

This concept is two fold. The first is that when someone else heals and has insights, we all receive the benefit, so when someone else is sharing their card, they are doing your healing work for you. The more you can support their process, the more you are supporting your own healing as well.

Secondly, welcome any insights that are revealed on anyone's turn towards your own Statement of Curiosity, or associations and feelings that come up while you are witnessing.

In essense, it is always your turn. And every card is also for you.

STEP 5: Order and Sequencing

Roll the die. The person who rolls highest goes first (unless someone knows they are the one who is supposed to start).
Then go around the circle, doing Step 6 with each player and card.
Play each round until all cards are played, read, and practiced.

STEP 6 - Play the Cards
1. Share the Statement of Curiosity while leaving the card face down.
2. Roll the die to pick which practice will be done.
3. Flip the card over.
4. Player reads the Teaching aloud from the book or asks someone to read it to them.
    - If the player wants you can watch the Transmission Teaching for the card in the Temple Times Membership

5. Do the practice that matches the die roll.
6. Some of the practices give specific instructions on sharing in closing the practice. If there are no specific instructions, share as a group in a way that feels right before transitioning to the next person. It can be nice for the person whose pulled the card to share insights gained after the practice, and sometimes there is nothing to say.
7. Take a moment before moving on to the next person. Examples are: Ring three bells, take a group breath, or everyone shake for 15 seconds, give a round of high fives, sit in silence for a moment, choose something to mark the transition.

STEP 7 : Closing the Game

Everyone is given a moment to have the floor to share closing and transitional comments. 2 minutes is a good amount of time if you want the container.

The last person who speaks or the host says, "Any closing comments?"

And then when closing comments are complete they say, "I hereby motion to bring this game to close. All in favor say, *[insert closing exclamation]*!" Closing exclamation can be anything: "*SHENANIGANS"* Or *"Shenanigans be blessed."* Or *"Thank you!"* Or *"Snapperdoodle."*

In a chorus of playful and sincere voices or action let the game complete!

"Drink Water. Fear Nothing." Grace Perkins

Oracle & Wisdom Deck Layouts

For those of you who will work with this book with its companion deck, *Four Seeds Wisdom Path Oracle Cards*, I offer these Wisdom Deck Layouts.

Do a layout by yourself or for an other.
Below are just a few options to get you started.
Remember this deck is not here to tell you what you should do or who you are, it is intended to give you guidance and insight on you, and your power and the choices being presented to you. Ask and listen. Play and enjoy.

Before pulling your card or cards take a moment decide what layout you are going to use. Then hold the deck or shuffle the cards while you focus on your question, contemplation, statement of curiosity, or anything that is on your heart and mind. Then pull your card from the top, anywhere in the deck, fan the cards out and pick, pick the card from one of these methods or however you feel called. You may find you have one way you like to do it, you may find you like different ways at different times.

Place the cards in the chosen layout, and review them individually by looking and feeling intuitively first, what does the card immediately tell you? Then read the teaching for each of the cards.

If you would like a do a practice you can roll the die to select or choose any practice from one of the card's teaching page.

May you remember peace and wellbeing.

Singular Insight
Pull 1 card, this is the card that is showing you the fundamental core issue at hand.

3 Petals
A version of the classic Three Card Pull
Card 1: One card on the left, is where you are coming from, your past
Card 2: One card in the center, is where you are, what is current

Card 3: One card on the right, is where you are headed without a change of the current momentum or path you are on.

Seed, Bud, and Bloom
Seed: One card, this is the center issue, starting gestating point

Bud: Three Cards, these are the things you are experiencing internally around the issue and what needs to be addressed

The Bloom: Five cards, showing you the ways this is showing up in your external life and what needs to be addressed and the gifts you will be sharing when you address them

What do I choose? YES or NO Questions
If you have a choice to make or a "yes" "no" to address, identify the options you are choosing from, it will be at least two (yes and no) and there may be more options that that.

For each choice option pull two cards. One card with the question: "what will be the challenge for this choice?" and the second, "what will be the gift?"

Look to see what is being reflected to you.

Choose you path now with your added insight.

Other Options
You can also use other classic Tarot deck or Oracle deck layouts with this deck to find more meaning and insight.

You can also make up your own layout. Imagine a number of cards, where they go, and how they relate to one another. Then pull the cards and place them in arrangement you imagined.

You can order the Four Seeds Wisdom Path: Oracle Cards at sophiawiseone.com/member-access

PART ONE

TEACHINGS

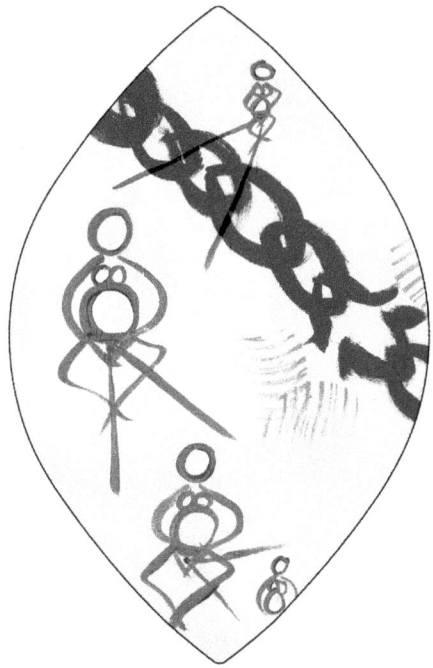

Ancestors (No Words)

We are deeply woven through time. We are the combination of breath, blood, pain, joy, courage, love, stardust, stories, and the innumerable infinite.

We are the prayers of our ancestors being answered. The prayers of the ancestors who endured violence, suffering, and silencing. We are the prayers of our ancestors who survived and continued to heal and evolve. We are the continuation of their dancing, singing, and ecstatic knowing. We are their prayer that someday their kin will have it better. That at some point there would be a chance to remember the lost ceremonies, revive the hidden wisdom, and release the inherited and reasonable paranoia and fear of being our true, wise selves. Every moment before this is blessed. Honored. Not hated, not cursed. Blessed, because we are weaving, living in, building, and creating a blessed, peaceful, and kind world.

The prayer that we will break the chains of familial abuse, cultural amnesia, spiritual dissociation, and patterns that keep us and the planet as a whole from our scared potential.

We are the echo of what was, and we are singing what will be echoed from now. We are our future kin's ancestors.

My ancestors have taught me that this is not a journey of going back to when they knew everything. They have been learning and healing with me, leading up to me now. Yes, it is important to learn and remember their wisdom, and it is also important to access and share our *living and currently being-birthed* wisdom and sacred medicines. We are healing and evolving together with our ancestors.

Wisdom is not a set, still, static thing which must be uncovered and shared as a stationary object. Wisdom, and the wisdom of our ancestors, is a living, vibrant experience. We are here as we are now because of what was, and we are the determining factors in what will be. When we walk through life consciously remembering all of this with our ancestors, we have greater knowledge and the greatest potential for healing.

You are not alone. Your ancestors are not alone. We are in this together.

⚀ Restoring Our Inner Temple on page 250
⚁ Naming the Gifts of Your Lineage on page 197
⚂ Ancestors Re-weaving on page 208
⚃ Break The Chain of Familial Abuse on page 282
⚄ Roll Again
  ⚀⚁⚂ Healing with Recent Ancestors on page 289
  ⚃⚄⚅ Healing With Big Ancestors on page 287
⚅ Roll Again
  ⚀⚁⚂ We Are In This Together on page 180
  ⚃⚄⚅ Peace Now on page 179

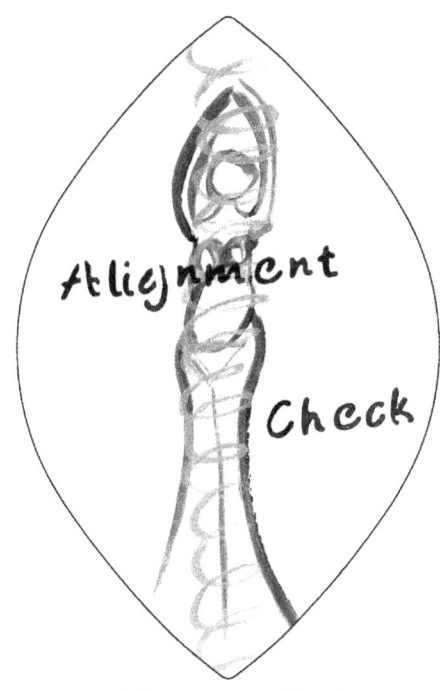

Alignment Check

Because there are no fundamentally good or bad decisions, and all decisions have results we cannot control, the question changes from, "Is this a good idea or bad idea?" to, "Is this choice in alignment with me as I am right now?"

There are many things that can cause misalignment, including but not limited to:

- Innocent miscommunication
- Chronically unhealthy relationships
- Chronic lying
- Repetitive use or misuse of the body
- Internal self-hate and abuse
- Cultural stigma
- Perceptions of who and what we are supposed to be

It's time to get clear on who you are and your own unique alignment. You can look for alignment in your:

- Physical form -- meaning posture, body ease and pain, muscle structure, and/or bone structure
- Physical space you are responsible for -- i.e. your bedroom, your home, your desk, the inside of your purse, book bag, suitcase,

wallet, etc.
- If you are attuned to your subtle body, or energetic body, you can notice alignment and misalignment there as well, both in the locations of the pathways and in the flow through them
- Mental functioning
- Emotional coherence -- Are you feeling your feelings? Do you know where they are originating from? Can you feel them in your body? Are they moving and expressing or are they stuck and repeating or being repressed?
- Consciousness of your actions -- meaning, do you choose to do things, or do you just do things without thinking?
- Actions themselves

Each one of these are perspectives from which you can see yourself and your alignment. The act of looking at these parts of yourself and their relationships to one another can offer a very specific picture about who and how you are.

The process of knowing yourself and your alignment continues as you evolve, because as you change, so changes what is in or out of alignment for you.

It takes diligence, compassion, and fortitude to know yourself well. Be patient and keep kind while you discover the thoughts you think, sense your subtle self, get to know the structure of your body, find the rhythm and roots of your emotions, and become aware of the actions you take and choose in your life.

⚀ Following the Thread on page 329
⚁ Discernment Prayer on page 327
⚂ Walking Meditation on page 206
⚃ Still Meditation on page 205
⚄ Alignment on page 149
⚅ Body Wisdom Approach Practice on page 214

All Fear Is the Fear of Death, All Death Is the Death of the Ego

If you follow a fear down its rabbit hole and ask yourself, "What are you afraid is going to happen, if this actually happens?" eventually you will find yourself at the edge of survival. For instance, "If I don't belong or am rejected, I will die without my community", also known as, "I'll end up on the street." Fear is our number one tool in maintaining survival.

Survival of what?

The ego is your identity, who you think you are, who you have valued yourself to be, and who people perceive you as. Because who you are in essence is space and matter, light and vibration, and components of other mysteries, the only thing that can truly die is who you think you are.

Ego death is the obliteration of your identity as you know it to be. Many people only experience this death of identity upon the physical end of their life. As a result, people think this is the only time death happens. The only fear that is driving you, subtly or overtly, is fighting for the survival of your current identity. All change and transformation threatens to end your identity as it is.

The only thing to do in the face of fear is to slow down inside of yourself by breathing. The element separating fear from excitement is whether we are breathing or not. When we are afraid, our consciousness -- our soul, energetic, and spiritual self -- can leave the body as a way to step out of an actual or potential soul-damaging situation. By breathing, we stay in our bodies and can usher ourselves through changes and transformations gracefully.

Ego death is immediately followed by a new ego birth. The door of transformation does not lead into an abyss, but instead leads into a revolution. The ego is not an enemy to be slain. The ego is a companion to release when their work is done, which then makes space to receive a new kind of companionship.

It's time to find a new source of strength, and that source is your ability to stay present.

Courage is being afraid and doing it anyway.

Allow yourself to die as you allow yourself to be reborn.

Breathe, breathe, breathe.

⚀ Fear/Little Meditation on page 237
⚁ Roll Again
      ⚀⚁⚂ Grief Ritual on page 285
      ⚃⚄⚅ Death and Rebirth Ritual on page 284
⚂ Stardust on page 179
⚃ A Fall-Apart-y on page 311
⚄ Organic Movement Meditation on page 204
⚅ Roll Again
      ⚀ Alternate Nostril Breathing on page 274
      ⚁ Audible Exhale on page 275
      ⚂ Breath of Fire on page 276
      ⚃ Breathe to Stretch on page 276
      ⚄ Cooling Breath on page 276
      ⚅ Mindful Breathing on page 277

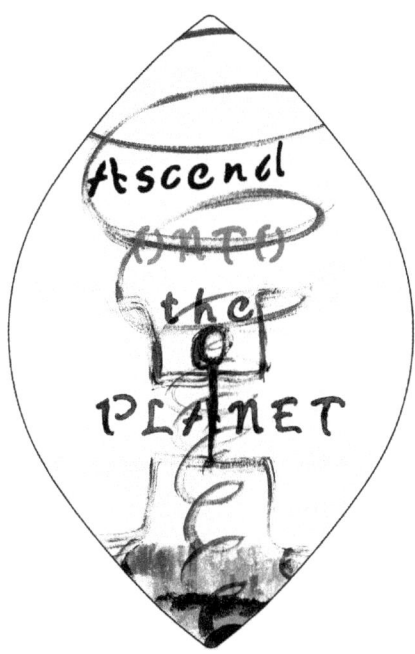

Ascend onto the Planet

    Ascension, in this context, is referring to the remembering that we are one with everything. It is the embodied knowing that we *are* the potential that creates form as well as the form itself. Knowing that we are space, matter, and the invisible, ascension teaches that each of theses things are limitless and continuous.

    Ascending is the process of being conscious and deciding to be in or out of form, on purpose. Ascending off the planet can be described as the process of becoming so conscious that you choose to release your physical form and disperse your consciousness into the cosmos. This can be thought of as dropping the body or even dispersing the body's entire atomic structure.

    Ascending onto the planet is an invitation to bring the power of consciousness into form. From that space, you can use all of that presence of influence to create and heal the body, the human collective consciousness, and Mama Earth herself, to name just a few possibilities. This awareness allows you to simultaneously know yourself as temporary and manifested, while also knowing yourself as infinite.

⚀ Stardust on page 179
⚁ Soul Unification Healing Meditation on page 258
⚂ How to Manifest What You Really Want on page 338
⚃ Ascending Off and On on page 160
⚄ Sing a Song or Play Music on page 281
⚅ Breathe to Stretch on page 276

Ask A Different Question

When we're not receiving an answer or the guidance that we're seeking, it is most often because the wrong question is being asked. This is not to say that the question is a wrong question in and of itself. Rather, it is just not the question that is addressing or connecting to the place where we can have the greatest insight, access, or influence for what's happening now. We repeatedly get preoccupied with what needs to be done, what is going to happen, or who is to blame. Often, these are thoughts sitting on top of subtler and more core issues at hand. Pivot your perspective and ask a different question.

Sometimes, we are not getting answers because we are asking questions back to back without sufficiently leaving room or space to hear a response. Other times, we are not getting answers because we are unwilling to hear what's actually coming up.

Zoom out. Decide you're ready to listen. Get clear and connected to your next question. Then make space to receive a response, insight, or guidance.

The practices below are different ways to explore where you are, and open up to another perspective on what you are contemplating.

⚀ Word Association (Written) on page 172
⚁ Word Association (Verbal) on page 172
⚂ Reverse the Question on page 357
⚃ Prayer Practice on page 353
⚄ Where I Am on page 201
⚅ Ask a New, Pull a New on page 316

Attend To Your Little

You are precious, you are dear, you are innocent. Each of us was once a tiny, perfect, and lovable child. In fact, each of us remains that way. Just as we are the wise experienced person we are yet to become, so too are we the continuation of the children we once were. This child is your Little.

Many of us did not get all that we needed as children. Some of us were also abused and neglected. We walk around, running patterns from our wounds. It is not too late to heal the wounds we experienced as children. We do that by finding, validating, and listening to the wisdom and aches of this innocent, precious being.

Being a victim is generally viewed as an unenlightened perspective. When working with your Little, it is essential and liberating to recognize that you were only a child. That it was, in fact, someone else's job to show up and protect or provide for you. Although it is understandable, and even forgivable, that adults are human and imperfect, it is also amply just to recognize the ways in which you were failed.

At the same time, many people may find a soulful comfort in recognizing the gifts that struggle has brought into their lives. Allowing your inner child, your Little, the pain of being a victim is not inherently contrary to having gratitude for, and fully recognizing, the complexity of your life.

Attending to your Little means you get to know them, play with them, cry with them, and heal with them. We also heal our Little by becoming the adult we always needed and still need now. You are now the grown up who is capable of knowing exactly what your Little needs and then finding ways to provide those things at long last and continually.

If you already have a relationship with your Little, it is time to check in. If not, it's time to start cultivating this relationship.

You are capable of being the caregiver you always needed.

If you are a child or a teen or in the process of learning true adulting, I have an important recommendation. In order to avoid a child raising a child, call on your Wise One -- the wiser, more healed version of yourself to help tend, support, and love your Little -- to guide you in how to do this work.

- ⚀ Hugging Yourself on page 298
- ⚁ Fear/Little Meditation on page 237
- ⚂ My Little! on page 167
- ⚃ Little Check-In on page 323
- ⚄ Cosmic Shuffle Dance Party on page 322
- ⚅ Dear Little on page 189

Balm of Forgiveness

I've always appreciated the theory of forgiveness. Yet, in application, it felt mysterious and elusive. As the body has taught me that wounding and hurt is stored physically, I have also discovered points in the process where forgiveness is asked for and necessary for the body's healing.

The body has taught me a very basic understanding of forgiveness. I visualize a bottomless bucket of a healing balm. I dip a brush inside and then coat the places in my being that need forgiveness. I allow forgiveness to be an organic, natural process of accepting, nourishing, and releasing anything that has been holding out for a different past.

As you apply the Balm of Forgiveness to your being, watch it penetrate places that you don't know how to soften. Witness the balm become absorbed into these spaces within yourself, as a topical application would interact with dry skin, and keep applying more until the area is saturated, assuring that you get what you need.

Forgiveness is a balm that can tend grief, disappointment, impatience, and resentment caused by myself, others, and/or circumstances.

There is a particular experience of back pain, which is characterized by the sensation of being stabbed in the back. This is, more often than not, paired with an emotional experience of betrayal. That sense of betrayal may require communication and amends made between people.

Frequently the person who first created the perceived "knife in the back" was our own self. In retrospect, we may see that we missed an opportunity.

We might run stories that we "should have known better" or that we "should have done things differently." That is an unreasonable weight to put on ourselves.

So, in order to heal this pain and fully reconcile, we must first address the betrayal of self, and realize that the healing is in essence the forgiving of one's self. In this circumstance, as well as many others, forgiving others and yourself is partnered with growing trust in your intuition. You did the best you could at the time. Everyone did. Sometimes everyone's best is disappointing -- sometimes tragic. As heartbreaking as it can be, whatever occurred was still your or their best.

Coat it all in the limitless Balm of Forgiveness.

⚀ Balm of Forgiveness on page 214
⚁ Organic Movement Meditation on page 204
⚂ Forgiveness Letter on page 191
⚃ Two Minutes of Silence Then Share on page 156
⚄ Audible Exhale on page 275
⚅ Ownership Prompt on page 152

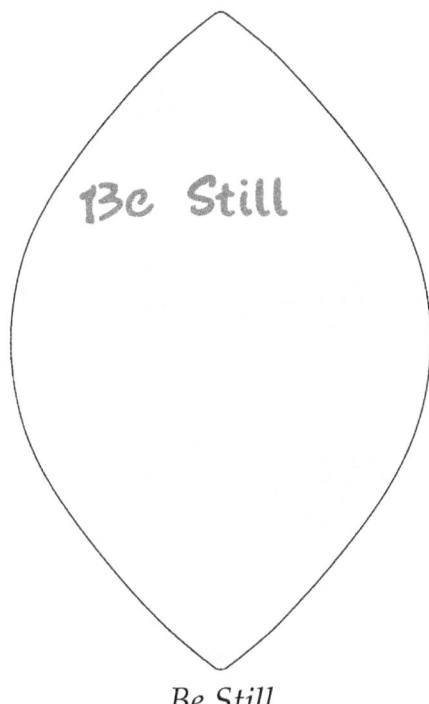

Be Still

Through profound stillness, we can remember that movement and change is a sign of life and vibrancy.

Stilling, in and of itself, is a process of allowing momentum to run out and come into the presence of potential. In turn, this potential makes space to birth consciousness, creation, and movement. As you come into stillness, do so from a place of releasing initiation, rather than from a place of restraint.

Often, we create new movement habitually as a way to avoid sensations or experiences that are uncomfortable. Be mindful of any tendency to battle your movement into captivity caused by fearful freezing and control. Stillness is not meant to be catatonic. It is the practice of letting go of unconscious perpetuating, interruption or starting new movements of the mind, body, and identity.

Soften into stillness with courage, curiosity, forgiveness, and wonder.

- ⚀ Still Meditation on page 205
- ⚁ Organic Movement Meditation on page 204
- ⚂ Healing Hands On Self on page 295
- ⚃ Healing Hands Circle on page 295
- ⚄ Read the Witness, Witnessed teaching on page 132
- ⚅ Unwinding Group Exercise on page 373

Become

I release who I was, to become what I am.

We can so easily get fixated on external results and in seeking validation. Many of us don't even know that looking to external results or seeking validation is problematic. We are taught to value it, so much so that we don't even think of it as fixation. We think that we are simply doing what we are supposed to. Thinking that when we *have* something we will *be* something. When we *do* something we will be *worthy* of something.

Take a moment to see if you have confused the outcome of a circumstance to be the same as your worthiness or your quality as a person. Now, make space to see past this perspective and explore another possibility.

We can reverse engineer the mindset of external results equaling personal satisfaction, or value, to identify what it is we want and once we know what we want, we indeed have the power to *become* it.

This concept is often talked about in terms of giving what we want. For example, if you want love, give love. Although that is often a good starting point, a deep freedom comes when we step out of an exchange model and into embodiment. Becoming love results in giving love. It also means we radiate, receive, get filled with, and are nourished by love. What follows is a continuous stream of what we once looked outside for, now in perpetual flow. Becoming love is about surrendering the aspects of yourself that have side-stepped the truth of the love that you already are.

The thing you are longing for is that which you are called to become. When we allow ourselves to become what we long for, the giving and receiving of this element in our daily and concrete lives is a joyful side effect.

Each and every one of us is a cosmos -- vast space with countless galaxies. We are already everything. It is by invitation and allowance that we summon and then embody that which we want. That which we deeply long for, we are.

Be it love, wisdom, courage, sexiness, safety, peace, fierceness, beauty, healing, medicine, knowing...it goes on and on. If you want something, you can become its birthplace, the origin point of what you are searching for. Nothing is any more outside of you than it is already within you.

It is time to Become the manifested answer to your prayers, and from there, you will see this reflected in the life you live.

- ⚀ Soul Unification Healing Meditation on page 258
- ⚁ Becoming on page 185
- ⚂ Stardust on page 179
- ⚃ I Am Whole Just As I Am on page 176
- ⚄ Grief Ritual on page 285
- ⚅ Organic Movement Meditation on page 204

Becoming Enlightened: Watching Yourself Make Mistakes

Enlightenment is not about being perfect. It does not make someone right all of the time, and it certainly does not include a requirement to look good.

What enlightenment does consist of is profound awareness. Enlightenment, from a brief moment to a sustained state, is a place of consciousness in which you, a limitless expansive essence, is aware of the human experience that is happening. Human experience, in this context, is referring to both the personal physical sensations of your body, mind, emotions, spirit, as well as the contextual acknowledgement of the societal, geopolitical, cultural, and environmental world in which you are existing. All the while, embodying the infinite truth that is always present that is beyond articulation and yet also within your experience.

Many of us know the results of our actions after the fact and with reflection. One of the most potent aspects of becoming enlightened is recognizing the patterns we are running and the recurring results we get from them. This process -- identifying an action, recognizing a pattern, and changing the habitual behavior -- is often uncomfortable and awkward. Frequently, the journey goes something like this:

1. We realize the ramifications of an action -- **way after the fact.**
2. With increased reflection, we then realize that we repeated an action that has certain ramifications -- **immediately after we do it.**

3. Now we're so aware -- that while we are repeating the action we know what the ramifications will be -- **we are watching ourselves do it.** If the results are unsatisfying, we might call that action a mistake or have remorse or conflicting feelings while it's happening.
4. With all this self-awareness, **we notice the moment before** we take the action due to habit and momentum, **and we watch ourselves do it anyway.**
5. After experiencing what's described above, many, many times, we can see yourself moving towards the habituated action and **we can see a potential different path**. Then, due to habit, comfort, or whatever else, **we still do the same thing we did before**.
6. With enough distance, self-awareness, and diligence upon seeing the habituated pathway and alternative options, **we choose something new.**

For results, you've just gotta stick with yourself through the journey. It is a humbling process, revealing the power of habit, comfort, and self involvement. Enlightenment exposes the various prices we are willing to pay, including emotional struggle, financial burdens or stress, ineffective work habits, and a denial of one's own needs to attempt to maintain control over existence.

It takes vulnerability, exposure, and kindness to have the courage and resilience to see this process happening time and again, and be willing to bring your consciousnesses so deep into a moment that you can see where it is going before it goes there. Please note that without kindness, the vulnerability at play here usually turns into shut down.

There is no choice without consciousness. Until you discover space where you previously did not know there was space, you are just running a habit of being. It is through the excruciating practice of staying present after, during, and eventually before we do the regretted, or even just misaligned things, that we discover the space in which decision making occurs.

It is the journey of forgetting and then remembering, over and over again, that leads us to a state where even as we forget, we are reminded. This is a moment-to-moment surrender of what we once knew in order to make space for what actually is or could be now. The process of enlightenment is an invitation to cultivate the courage and focus required to be more interested in what *is* happening than what could be happening.

To enlighten means to shine light. This practice is most dramatic when it takes place in the dark. Voluntarily becoming enlightened is about climbing into dark spaces where you, your ancestors, and our world have shoved things away into hiding.

If instead of feeling better at times, you feel worse, do not be surprised.

The effect of enlightenment is not about feeling better or worse. The result of this path is to feel *more*. Although, as you feel more and truly, the urge to control existence becomes less.

Enlightening the dark is worthwhile. The return on investment includes freedom, divine love, and the ability to co-create the world as you would like.

- ⊡ Habit Identification on page 194
- ⊡ Forgiveness Letter on page 191
- ⊡ Alternatives on page 159
- ⊡ Soul Unification Healing Meditation on page 258
- ⊡ I Am Willing to Admit on page 340
- ⊡ Little Check-In on page 323

Breathe, Remember, Beauty, Know, Infinite, Love

It is time for creativity. Time for allowing the magical, kind mysteries of breathing, remembering, beauty, knowing, infinity, and love to reveal themselves in and around you. It is time to revel and savor. Take a moment to appreciate the unfolding beauty and infinite interconnectedness of all things. All that you want you already have. You are limitless. You are the dancing majesty of stardust. All is well. The movement of light, matter, and waves *is* life. Celebrate this.

- ⚀ Cosmic Shuffle Dance Party on page 322
- ⚁ Trust Fall on page 170
- ⚂ Non-Dominant Hand Drawing on page 304
- ⚃ Alternate Nostril Breathing on page 274
- ⚄ Players Choice on page 350
- ⚅ Roll Again
    - ⚀ ⚁ Healing Hands On Self on page 295
    - ⚂ ⚃ Healing Hands Shared on page 295
    - ⚄ ⚅ Healing Hands Circle on page 295

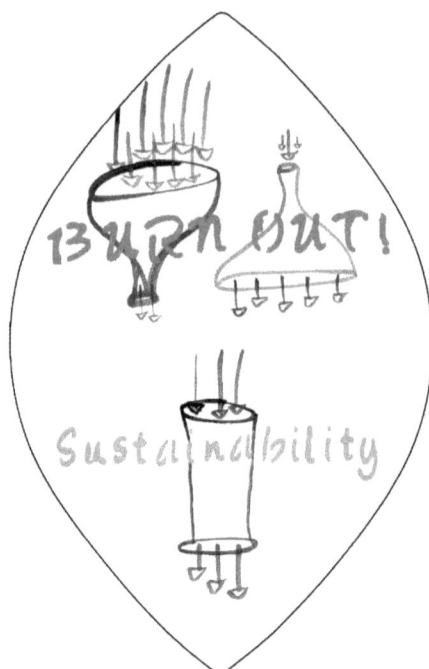

BURNOUT! Sustainability

Life is a current or a pathway. When you receive, you fill up. You have to empty yourself in order to maintain an ability to be inspired and in a state of reception.

Ideas, visions, resentments, belongings, and muscle tensions are all examples of things we might be holding on to that we need to let go of in order to make space for new dreams, ease in our relationships, money, and health.

The stream of life is flowing constantly. A radical place of trust, while practicing self-care, is leaning into the knowing that all we need is ALWAYS available to us. Always. No exceptions. All is flowing.

So, self-care practices are less of a way to *give* us something we need, than a method to get us into a state where we *allow* our needs to be met. We let the need to empty, the need for affection and support, or the need for play -- whatever the needs are that we're making space for in ourselves -- to be satisfied. The real challenges are opening yourself up to receiving and finding the courage needed to let what is coming out of you go.

I see giving and receiving as a nourishing cycle. My body and life are like the wall of a spiraling hose. Life force and presence are the water running through it. Self-care helps me to keep the hose unkinked. It is your job to make sure that both your receiving and giving pathways are expanded to create a steady and nourishing flow for yourself.

If you're constricted on either the giving or receiving end, your hose begins to look more like a funnel. This is not an I-give-this-much therefore I-need-this-much formula, but rather a matter of maintaining an ease of flow. Although, that false equation can be a useful place to look for information about your patterns of receiving and giving.

Look to the images on the card.

Top-left funnel: Easy to fill, constriction causes congestion so it's hard to empty, which in turn means it's too congested to keep receiving, which results in labored stagnant exhaustion.

Top-right funnel: Easy emptying, but constriction makes it hard to fill, which in turn means resistance to new resource, which results in depletion and unavailability.

Bottom: Easy come, easy go, which means creative inspiration and expression, receiving full nourishment, and releasing of what's no longer needed, which results in vibrant, expansive, available, energized experience.

As we are human, we are less like hard ceramic or plastic, and more like putty. We are dynamic, ever changing beings. Self-care is about being supported to expand, receive, and let go, so that there is movement. In the movement, we can fully receive what we want, and share what we want to give the world. We are giving something of meaning to life when we can fully take in our inspirations, digest them, and then let them out.

Make your self-care a regular daily and weekly priority, as important as your other work and commitments. Use a combination of your own practices, as well as being taught by others, to fully nourish and replenish your resources. Sustainability requires taking responsibility to get the support you need to receive more and to let go more. This card may be a call to get guidance on building a structure that can provide consistency in your internal form, thus creating an ease of flow within.

I observe that every additional layer of support I provide for others requires a deeper level and more consistent amount of self-care. The wider I expand to give, the more I need to make sure I am open and receiving to keep that current flowing. If I don't get the care I need, or don't let go of the heavy emotions that I have been carrying or creative inspirations stirring my heart, I get irritable with those closest to me. If I don't catch it there, then I burn out quickly.

The current of life moving through us changes us. That change, or the potential of change, can cause us to restrict the flow out of fear. And yet, that change is life and health. Get to know yourself and what you need to breathe -- inhaling and exhaling, metaphorically and literally. This equilibrium will shift over time for most people, so return to yourself with curiosity.

Go with the flow.

⚀ Roll Again
　　⚀⚁ Declutter on page 324
　　⚂⚃ Brain Dump on page 186
　　⚄⚅ Nourishment Practices on page 348
⚁ Grief Ritual on page 285
⚂ Professional Assistance on page 350
⚃ Roll Again
　　⚀⚁⚂ Expanding to Hold Pain on page 232
　　⚃⚄⚅ Bone Breathing Meditation on page 216
⚄ Receiving and Expressing Burnout/Sustain on page 151
⚅ Dance of Sustainability on page 224

Cleanse Through Nourishment

We often associate cleansing with elimination or removal. In contrast, we can see profound cleansing and releasing of toxins by providing ourselves with what we actually need.

Across the board -- spiritually, physically, mentally, and emotionally -- we often take what we can get, trying to get our needs even partially met. Our expectations are often based on what we have had in the past. When we are nourished with what we actually need, not just something that gets close to it, a detox process begins in our bodies and lives of that which we were holding onto simply because we thought it was the best we could have.

Instead of eliminating what you know you don't need, focus on adding in what you really do need. Watch as craving and attachments change. You may notice that you long less for what you have been trying to detox from or eliminate. Pay attention to notice if there are things you didn't even know you were holding onto, because you experienced them as the best you could get. Things that, perhaps, you no longer want, now having something more satisfying. See what happens when you are truly nourished.

⚀ Love Letter on page 195
⚁ Nourishment Practices on page 348
⚂ Nourishment Identification on page 244
⚃ Collaging or Vision Boarding on page 304
⚄ Mindful Breathing on page 277
⚅ Savoring on page 357

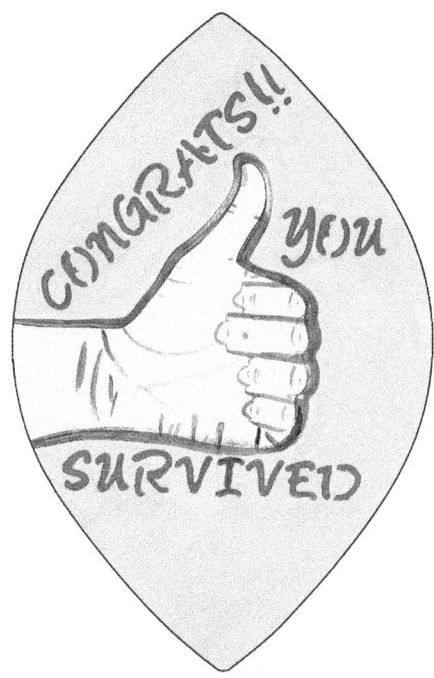

Congrats You Survived

The purpose of coping mechanisms is to keep you from dying. If you are alive and reading this now, then you are a 100% success. When we are in less than ideal circumstances, from horrific tragedies to subtle neglect, from ourselves and from others, we find a way to make it through. We use the skills that we have innately and those that are taught to us, to navigate survival until we learn how to use more efficient tools in more effective ways.

Congrats, you survived! HOORAY! You are totally not dead!

You got to this point using a range of 100% successful habits and tactics. Now it's time to name and own the coping mechanisms that you have used, like manipulation, avoidance, isolation, dominance, and submission.

Sometimes these behaviors are shrouded as functional, normal, or welcome ways of being. An example is being a charming conversationalist who controls a social scene or private conversation. Or bullying. Or not using your voice or standing up for yourself.

Some survival habits are more visible and easy to identify. For instance, tantrums are a survival tactic, which can look like a lot of different things in adults. Being emotionally volatile until you get what you want from another person counts. So does refusing to speak or participate in conversation or a previous agreement.

Intimidation can be, but is not limited to, verbal or written threats, aggressive body language, and blackmail.

Substance misuse and abuse is also a survival coping mechanism.

So is spiritual bypassing, which is when you use spiritual practices to relieve stress without ever owning or changing the life that creates your tension. This also includes using spiritual practices to get high and try to bypass feelings, accountability, and responsibility.

The list of coping mechanisms as survival tactics goes on and on. I don't know anybody who hasn't done, or who doesn't do, some or all of these things, myself included. This teaching is not here to shame us. This invitation is about recognition. These are the ways that we survive, and in fact, I am grateful for them.

What's true is that now you are at a crossroads, because now you have consciousness about these ways of being, and consciousness allows for choice. We cannot make choices when we are unconsciously living in habits. We must first know that we are running patterns. That knowing is the gateway to creating *new* habits and patterns. The good news is, you can do something new. You can replace survival oriented habits with optimal life-giving habits. You now get to learn alternative ways of being, in order to integrate survival skills with thrival skills.

⚀ Naming and Loving Coping Patterns on page 198
⚀ Roll Again
      ⚀⚀⚀ I Am Willing to Admit on page 340
      ⚁⚄⚂ Cosmic Shuffle Dance Party on page 322
⚀ Organic Movement Meditation on page 204
⚄ Stardust on page 179
⚄ Alternatives on page 159
⚂ Congrats You Survived on page 150

Don't Go Dancing In the Dark Alone

When I was a teenager, I was guided on a drum and didgeridoo soul journey. I blacked out. When I woke up, I couldn't remember anything. I was unsatisfied that I did not get a clear answer to my question. So that night, I laid down with my feet above my head and asked Grandmother and Grandfather Spirit to answer my question again. The next thing I knew there was a crowd of people around me. The Medicine Caller that had led the journey earlier that day was blowing my soul back into my body. It took ten minutes to get me to wake up. My first memory was looking at a crowd of people around me from above and then I was in my body again, being drawn and directed back inside. It took over two minutes for me to be able to stand up with help. After sitting with a tree and receiving some very skilled assistance from a number of people, I was able to stand on my own two feet.

When I told my teacher what I had done, he said, "Don't go dancing in the dark alone." This card is about relationship building with a teacher, Medicine Caller, healer or with your spirit guides. Traveling in between and among the worlds is a very real business. It is perfectly safe to travel with guidance, and that guide can be in human or in spirit form. So find a guide. It is just as important to have one take you out as it is to have one bring you back.

If you naturally do this kind of traveling, it is essential that you strengthen your relationships with your spirit guides. If you're new to this practice, the first step is meeting and building relationships with your guides.

⚀⚁⚂ Soul Unification Healing Meditation on page 258
⚃⚄⚅ Professional Assistance on page 350

Earth

Nourishment. Seasons and cycles. Deep rest. Composting. New life. Abundance. Generosity. Connection. Heart communication. Womb wisdom. Patience. Willingness. Leaves, roots, buds, blossoms, and fruit. Dirt, stones, sand, and crystals. Potentiality. Mother energy. Home. Presence. Grounded.

The Earth element is as abundant and diverse as our dear Mother Earth herself. It is time for you to lean into this element's nourishing, patient, fierce, life-giving, death, and composting wisdom. Lean into your connection and reach for your practices. It's time to accept responsibility for the Earth that you are. Cultivate awareness of your ever present interconnectedness. Bring your Earth element into balance, for yourself and for Mama Earth. If you don't have a relationship with Mama Earth or Earth elementals, now is the time to start your journey.

- ⚀ Make an Offering on page 279
- ⚁ Walking Meditation on page 206
- ⚂ Communing with Elementals on page 220
- ⚃ Goddess Chants on page 176
- ⚄ Seasonal Wisdom on page 154
- ⚅ Organic Movement Meditation on page 204

Ego's Last Stand

There comes a time when a certain habit, or an ingrained way of being, really starts to change. Things are moving forward, you are receiving all the signs that you're on track, and then The Ego's Last Stand happens. You can call it a test. You can call it an initiation. Or you can call it just good old stubborn humanness. Right as you sit on the precipice of real transformation, an old habit or pattern gets activated, and there you are in the middle of a mess, feeling just like you used to feel.

You know it's the Ego's Last Stand when the pain and drama of the situation is excruciating in its redundancy. With time, practice, or a gift of good humor, the experience can also become laced with a ridiculous thread of hilarity. You may feel a touch of terror that you're doomed to forever repeat this pattern. You're not. It's possible that you can see the old, new, and changing behaviors all at the same time: how you used to do it, how you've done it differently, and how you'll do it from now on.

It will take effort, a good sense of humor, and your practices to get beyond the tantrum your ego is throwing, as that old way of being thrashes its way towards death and rebirth. This is a good time to stay the course and remember you are bigger than your identity and habits. You are loved. Now's the time for a hug, a dance party, a flow of tried and true tears, and many deep breaths.

⚀ Adult Rocking on page 311
⚁ A Fall-Apart-y on page 311
⚂ Cosmic Shuffle Dance Party on page 322
⚃ Still Meditation on page 205
⚄ Grief Ritual on page 285
⚅ BLESS IT on page 317

Embodied Enlightenment

Embodied enlightenment is actually a redundant statement. It's a common misconception that enlightenment is this state of being that is beyond physical form.

Embodied enlightenment speaks to the journey of profound consciousness through the connection and experience of manifested human form. It speaks to the perspective that your body, your fear and pain, its needs, and your creative desires, are not inhibiting your spiritual growth, but are indeed essential to your spiritual consciousness. The deeper the roots, the farther and wider the branches can grow and go.

It is time to fall in love with your body, your blood, menstrual blood, your sexuality, and your desires. By becoming intimate with your experience, you bring consciousness and sanctity to your time on earth. You will find power and peace in embodying your humanness. Celebrating the mess allows you to keep your eyes open and your focus clear. We are perpetually manifesting from our conscious and unconscious desires, which means to be consciously connected to your desires is to be aware and take responsibility for that which you are creating.

Being conscious in your body while knowing you are vibration and light is spiritual awareness.

⚀ Simple Moontime Practice on page 257
⚁ Desire Admittance on page 190
⚂ Birth the World on page 317
⚃ Organic Movement Meditation on page 204
⚄ Tour of the Pelvic Bowl on page 362
⚅ Internal Bodywork on page 342

Ether

    The elemental breakdown of the cosmos is varied and dynamic. In this book and in the oracle cards, I share with you five elements. Ether is space and it is also the light lattice that constructs space. It is space and matter before anything becomes form, as well as space and matter that hold form.

    Ether knows that the time space continuum is not linear, meaning it is the element of immortality and infinity. Ether is spirit and soul, it is consciousness and that which holds consciousness. Ether is the elemental truth of vulnerability, that which is as profoundly powerful and strong as it is gentle and subtle. Ether is the element of synchronicity. Working with Ether is another way to talk about notions of weaving reality, manifesting, sourcing, and the energetic structures of all things.

    This card has shown up as a reminder to get into conscious relationship with Ether. Perhaps you think it's a fictional or theoretical concept. This is an invitation to see if you can have a more personal, experiential understanding of Ether. Or, perhaps, you have been overusing this particular element in your incarnation. Either way, it is time to get connected and be curious about being in a new relationship with Ether.

    Ether is also... well... "really out there, man, way out there, man... but you know what man? Totally right here, man."

⚀ Birth the World on page 317
⚁ Ether on page 150
⚂ Still Meditation on page 205
⚃ Sensitivity Scanning on page 360
⚄ Pendulum Practice on page 349
⚅ Make The Room on page 166

Everybody's Best Is A Mess

    We are all lovable and human. By our nature we are imperfect, not in control, and wired to keep ourselves from dying. We eat and we poo, all of us bleed, many of us monthly, and everyone is doing the best they can.

    We are creatures who long for intimacy and connection, while also needing autonomy and independence. Each and every one of us is our own complex galaxy. Even if we lived in complete isolation, at times we would make mistakes. When you place everyone's inconsistencies together, you get life as we know it.

    We do our best and it's messy, imperfect, complicated, and most often rooted in survival and love. Be gentle and forgiving with others and yourself.

    When dealing with other humans, bear in mind that most likely, other people are not trying to hurt your feelings, they are trying to manage their own.

    Choose to give up pretending there is a right way. Give up the stories of how someone should do it better. Release the thoughts and conversations of "if they only..." and "if I would just...".

    Breathe deeply and remember: we are all a bit of a wreck, and all a lot of beautiful.

⚀ Cosmic Shuffle Dance Party on page 322
⚁ The Funny Face Game on page 163
⚂ Unwinding Group Exercise on page 373
⚃ Roll Again
 ⚀ ⚁ ⚂ A Fall-Apart-y on page 311
 ⚃ ⚄ ⚅ I Am Willing to Admit on page 340
⚄ Mirror Meditation on page 241
⚅ I Do What I Can When I Can on page 307

Expand. Embrace.

Expand to hold the pain.

We do not need to change the pain or alter the feelings we experience. Yes, even when they are consuming or destructive. What we need to do is expand our presence enough to spaciously hold the feeling. Feelings will pass without damage when we give them enough space to be fully expressed. Pain, and all intense sensations, are opportunities to grow past our previous limited perspective of self. If the feeling is consuming you, *you*, this amorphous and yet very real *you*, must grow bigger so that the feeling is smaller in comparison.

This idea may feel abstract and unlikely when we are living with pain, or are used to being overcome by emotions and sensation. Consistently working with this concept transforms it into a tangible and practical tool.

Look to the image on the card. See the person curled into a ball in the center of the chest; that is the feeling, the sensations. The outline of the person is you; it is your awareness, your wisdom, your presence.

Another image: this is a journey of letting waves move into and through you, without confusing yourself with being the wave. You are the ocean, waves and currents are how you live.

Denying, resisting, and repressing feelings does not work for peacemaking. Expanding our presence and embracing our humanness with love, compassion, patience, and affection does lead to experiences of peace. Expand. Embrace.

⚀ Expanding to Hold Pain on page 232
⚀ Roll Again
⠀⠀⠀⠀⚀ ⚀ ⚁ Ascending Off and On on page 160
⠀⠀⠀⠀⚂ ⚄ ⚅ Bone Breathing Meditation on page 216
⚁ Pain Recognition and Self Expansion on page 304
⚂ Sat Nam on page 308
⚃ Becoming on page 185
⚅ Despair & Radiance on page 226

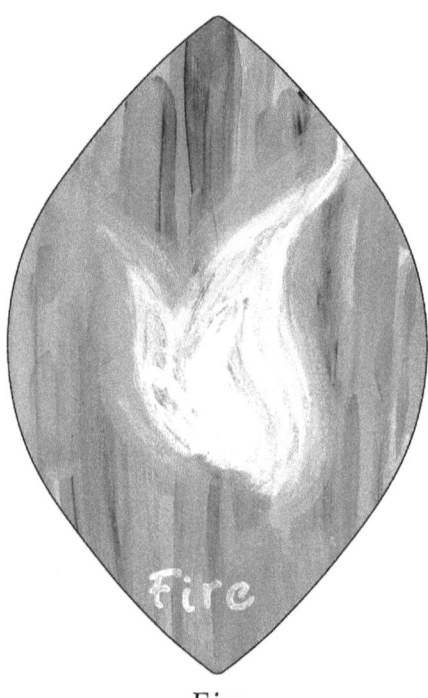

Fire

    The Fire element. Passion. Transformation. Transmutation. Heat. Ecstasy. Sensuality. Power. Purpose. Soul. Sexuality. Creative expression. Alchemy. Prayer carrier. The Fire element speaks to that which will destroy you unless it is respected.

    Around the globe, Fire has had a plethora of meanings for millennia. If you do not already have a relationship with Fire, consider this a call to begin one. If you do have an established connection, Fire is here to be your ally. In excess or with carelessness, Fire will burn you. Literally, or through exhaustion and the consumption of all your resources. In it's absence or diminished presence, you will lack drive, appetite for pleasure, and inspiration. In extreme cases, you could experience apathy, numbness, and vacuousness. As your partner, Fire wants you to claim your desires, to find and trust your passions and body.

    Fire wants to teach you alchemy.

    Take all of your prayers, concerns, dreams, and visions to the Fire. Allow this element to illuminate, transform, and bring into being a miracle.

⚀ Flame Meditation on page 205
⚁ Fire Ceremony on page 284
⚂ Communing with Elementals on page 220
⚃ Collaging or Vision Boarding on page 304
⚄ Desire Admittance on page 190
⚅ Cosmic Shuffle Dance Party on page 322

Flip It

Be it a cultural belief or personal story, *it is not what it seems.*
Flip It and explore it.
We are bombarded daily by cultural norms and expectations. These colonized norms are the standard for a culture that has been both homicidal and suicidal. The dominant culture is destroying our resources faster than we can understand the impact of what we're doing. Unchecked, this results in killing one another, and eventually, ourselves. Although this may seem heavy-handed, it is intended to illustrate the importance of reconsidering these norms. If we aim for a life-giving and life-sustaining culture, we have to create different standards. The starting point here is to flip it on its head. For example:

Menstruation is dirty and needs to be kept a secret. When actually: **Menstruation is sacred and needs to be honored.**

Being afraid and isolated will keep me safe. When actually: **Being vulnerable and interconnected will keep me well.**

Polluting the water is just a unavoidable consequence of industry growth and can be dealt with later. When actually: **Protecting the water and natural resources is essential and when standards are set for industry then growth includes better care of resources and the the time to deal with pollution is the moment is its realized either before it takes place or once it is discovered.**

Our hearts have been manipulated into believing that these irrational behaviors are justified. It is far too easy to "teach" by providing limited information repetitively, filtering the intellect, and establishing an upside-down sense of "right". By flipping these beliefs, we can engage and connect with our hearts and intellects, becoming more difficult to control or "teach" into a sense of domination. When our intellect reveals emotions as part of a whole, larger context, we cannot be manipulated.

It's time to reconsider the very foundations of the questions or concerns at hand.

⚀ Belief Traders on page 185
⚁ Inversions on page 345
⚂ Still Meditation on page 205
⚃ Clearing Delusion on page 161
⚄ Where I Am on page 201
⚅ Mirror Meditation on page 241

Give Yourself Permission

Give Yourself Permission to be you. To feel. To heal. To change.

In the face of change, we all get a tingle of "ugh!" Explicit permission can be really helpful. Healing happens with change.

As much as we may want the permission to heal to come from outside of us, at the end of the day, we won't even believe it from the outside until we can allow permission from the inside. Once we have access to that, even just a little bit, we have the capability to experience profound and whole healing.

You don't need permission from nobody but you.

And I offer you permission as a bonus, too!

Because we are all in this together.

Allow yourself to *feel* whatever you are feeling.

Resisting or trying to change your feelings, instead of experiencing them, only drags out the experience longer. This tactic often pushes your feelings deeper in the body, which can lead to the emotions settling on the dense physical layer, waiting to be processed later.

Feelings will pass. Whether they are ecstasy and giddiness, or sadness and fatigue. If we surrender into our experience, the feelings will shift.

So often we are told to avoid and not give in to or even admit "bad" or "negative" feelings such as grief, anger, rage, sadness, fear, and hate. However, that kind of control over, resistance to, and guilt or shame for a feeling is counterproductive. Even self-hate is just a feeling. Admit what is happening so you can give yourself the compassion and acceptance you'd want to offer to another person, and then watch the feelings pass through.

Feeling a feeling is not the same as dwelling in the story. The story which has it's time and place, can be distracting from the information the feelings are trying to communicate. When we dwell in a story or feed the drama of circumstance we are stepping out of our center and creating a constructed landscape. This card is about giving yourself permission for evening going into the drama of circumstance or the high of a story, and yet the invitation is to come to your own trueness and allow yourself to change through being who and as you are.

Feelings are body based, so if you are not sure if you are being with what is or revolving around ideas of what is, was or will be try the following: Either stand up, breathe, and move your body, or sit very still and slow your breathing into an even rhythm and then feel what's happening. Try movement if stillness is swirling, sit down if movement is distracting . Whichever option is a little more uncomfortable is probably the one that can best connect you to the feelings you are resisting

Give yourself explicit permission to explore. A feeling is just a feeling. When I feel joy, love, hate, anger, or exhaustion with compassion, I get to live a compassionate life!

Give Yourself Permission to be you, right now. Be as you are, as you were, and as you will be. To want what you want, feel what you feel, know what you know, to not know what you do not know, to be stubborn, to be free, to be. Give Yourself Permission.

- ⚀ Permission Invocation on page 307
- ⚁ Cosmic Shuffle Dance Party on page 322
- ⚂ Desire Admittance on page 190
- ⚃ We Are In This Together on page 180
- ⚄ I Am Whole Just As I Am on page 176
- ⚅ Organic Movement Meditation on page 204

Go Inside and Call On Spirit

There are some things for which no advice is the best advice. Times when our journey is between self and self and self and Spirit. Moments when the only thing to do is Go Inside and Call On Spirit.

If you don't know how to call on spirit or how to go inside, bring yourself into a quiet and comfortable space. Close your eyes and look into the darkness. Honestly begin your relationship by saying something to the effect of, "I know I've never done this before, I'm not sure how this works, and yet I'm willing to try. Self and Great Mystery that has a lot of names I'm asking for your help."

If you do this, and know how, it is time to retune to this knowledge with clear sight and fervor. We can support ourselves by returning to the place of power within ourselves where we remember our ability to make choices in our lives and the courage we must gather to go inside to heal and change again. Take this moment to do what you must so you are able to travel into your depths and engage with the medicine that is waiting for you.

You can use or take inspiration from Calling In Spirit (page 218) as part of any of the practices below.

- ⚀ Still Meditation on page 205
- ⚁ Walking Meditation on page 206
- ⚂ Organic Movement Meditation on page 204
- ⚃ Soul Unification Healing Meditation on page 258
- ⚄ Internal Bodywork on page 342
- ⚅ Take a Bath on page 361

Healing Happens In A Moment

Picture a river with a tree and a rope swing. The river is a constant cosmic flow that carries and knows all things. Healing is the moment when you let go of the rope swing, trusting that the river will catch you.

Let's be clear, to get to the moment of healing, which is the complete surrender and letting go into change, you have to first make it to the jumping off place. Spiritual practices, therapy, art, and really the mastery of anything, can take you from the highway of common life, down to the riverside.

For most of us, making it to the healing moment -- the journey to the riverbank, climbing up the tree, grabbing the rope, and jumping off to swing out -- requires commitment, persistence, and diligence. Often it takes work, or at least effort. The healing itself does not. The healing is the leap, the release, and it just takes a moment.

I think of miracle workers and healers as humans standing next to the river. People choose to trust them, for whatever reason, and so run full speed to the healer. The healer has the ability to lift the person and throw them with their own momentum into the river. This is to say that there's many entry points to the miracle moment of flying, holding on to nothing, towards the river.

Wherever you are, there is a river and a way in.

- ⚀ Trust Fall on page 170
- ⚁ Healing In A Moment Reflection on page 151
- ⚂ Healing Hands On Self on page 295
- ⚃ Healing Hands Shared on page 295
- ⚄ Healing Hands Circle on page 295
- ⚅ Roll Again
    - ⚀⚁⚂ Freeze on page 165
    - ⚃⚄⚅ Bone Breathing Meditation on page 216

Help

My favorite prayer is the four letter word HELP. There's no great preoccupation with who it is that I am praying to. There's no predetermined attachment to the outcome. "Help" fully communicates a surrender that makes space for change, admitting I don't want to do it alone, and that I want a different experience.

I learned the power of this prayer when I woke up one morning and was so heavy with grief I could not lift a limb. My face was thinned. I did not have clarity or energy for a long prayer. In fact, I was hopeless. From the stillness of my body, I opened my mouth and an honest word fell out, "Help." Fifteen minutes later, I noticed that I was standing up. There I was getting dressed and had moved from the depths of hopelessness. When all I could offer was begging, I was lifted and carried from the edge, back into the seat of my life.

Your prayers don't need to be poetic or long to work. Prayers simply need honesty, rawness, and an opening; a crack in your structure that allows assistance to come in.

⚀ Help Through the Crack on page 337
⚁ Mirror Meditation on page 241
⚂ Prayer Practice on page 353
⚃ Begging for Help on page 316
⚄ Healing Hands On Self on page 295
⚅ Cosmic Shuffle on page 322

Hug It Out

Put the words aside. Open your arms and allow patient, honoring, and forgiving love to come to you and through you in embrace. The matter at hand needs to be held and loved, hugged and rocked, embraced and treasured. Establish or reestablish connection in this basic and profound way. Let the love and healing that is possible, happen.

It usually takes at least twenty seconds for oxytocin to release from a hug. This helps ease stress, deepen breathing, stabilize excitement, and heal hurt.

- ⚀ Hugging Yourself on page 298
- ⚁ Hugging Sitting Down on page 300
- ⚂ Hugging over Time and Space on page 300
- ⚃ Hugging with Extremities on page 299
- ⚄ Hugging Standing Up on page 301
- ⚅ Group Hugging Exercise on page 302

I Am So Grateful

Take a moment to breathe in and appreciate that which you are easily grateful for.

Gratitude can look and feel like many different things. It can be an open heart pouring forth, weakness in the knees, or a tearful experience. Gratitude can be felt as excitement, celebration, deep peace, and ecstatic exhilaration. Many different things can activate an experience of gratitude.

This card is inviting you to get connected and use the power of gratitude. Open your eyes and see all that's around and through you. Notice what you already treasure and adore.

Being theoretically grateful for difficulties in your life is a common way to spiritually bypass uncomfortable feelings. It takes a fair amount of courage to be grateful for something without needing it to be okay. If there are things you're having trouble being grateful for, take some time to get really close to those feelings inside yourself, and stay with this discomfort. Breathing and bringing your presence to this place will eventually, naturally, and without rationalization or explaining away hardship, move you into gratitude. The key to this advanced gratitude process is to find gratitude for the discomfort, not to be grateful in spite of it. This is the moment when you say, "Thank you," for your life in as a whole. It is what happens when you connect to and appreciate all the dynamic elements that compose your sacred journey the strife and struggle, the relief and lessons learned , and for the pleasure.

Authentic gratitude is a physical and emotional experience. Allow thankfulness to enter your whole being, like a cup or a well filling with clear, clean water. Keep its nourishing movement filling inside you until the cup overflows. The overflow is gratitude you can share with others.

This life is a mystery and it's yours! Allow yourself the gift of gratitude by practicing it.

One way to grow your habit of gratitude is to review experiences that brought you pleasure., physical pleasure. "That felt good." And to exclaim internal and externally when something is happening that you are enjoying in the moment, "This feels good." "I am enjoying this feeling." Try naming the specific sensations you are feeling: Where in your body? What is it like? What happened and how do you feel? "As I hold this cup of tea my hands are warm breathed in the sweet smell of the plants, and my heart softened and opened and I felt my face warm up and now I am smiling." It may sound silly to narrate your life, and silliness is highly rewarded when it comes to cultivating new habits. So review and savor the sensually satisfying.

The final game changing element to gratitude after feeling it is expressing it. Thank you! I appreciate it! I appreciate you. "Thank you hot water and mug and plants and everything that made this moment possible."

Take some time for the next day to thank everything you can. People, objects, ideas, and memories. Inside your mind and out loud. It changes things, potentially everything, go see for yourself what that does for you.

⚀ How to Accept a Compliment on page 337
⚁ Cosmic Shuffle Dance Party on page 322
⚁ Savoring on page 357
⚂ Ironic to Sincere "Thank you" Prayer Practice on page 346
⚄ Journaling (Gratitude) on page 191
⚄ Thank You Note on page 199

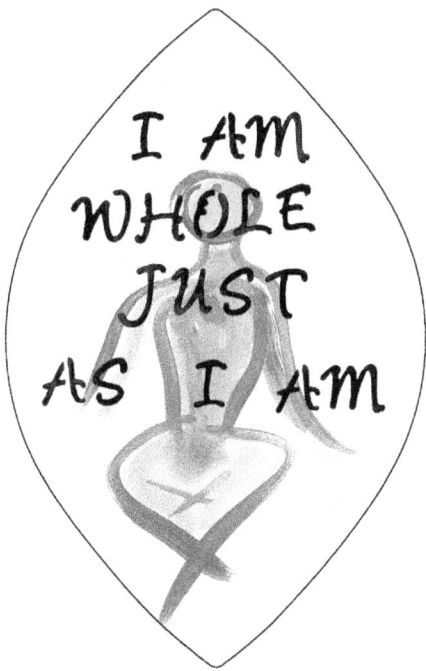

I Am Whole Just As I Am

My favorite definition of "healing" is to become more whole. The implied truth in this statement is that we are already whole. You are already whole.

Breathe deeply, feel your heartbeat, sense your blood and breath moving through your body. You are worthy of your existence today because you are here. You are a sacred mystery that contains universes. You are a majesty of wonder.

In this moment, no matter the experience you are having of your existence you are still whole. No matter how fragmented or shattered you feel, no matter how broken or hopeless you may appear, no matter how dejected or lost you are, you are still here. Just as you are, without changing a single thing, you are complete, and you are loved.

Move into the part of you that knows the truth: I Am Whole Just As I Am.

- ⚀ I Am Whole Just As I Am on page 176
- ⚁ Soul Unification Healing Meditation on page 258
- ⚂ Mirror Meditation on page 241
- ⚃ Make an Offering to Yourself on page 280
- ⚄ Unwinding Group Exercise on page 373
- ⚅ We Are Whole, Together Circle on page 372

Incarnation Is the Jam

WHAT A TRIP!

We've come all the way into form, from the great cosmic soup, into this incarnated, manifested miracle of human shape. Here we can sense one another and know birth and death. Incarnated, we can witness beauty because it is separate enough from us that we can behold its majesty. From this viewpoint, we can know the profound sensations of loss, and the fiery passions of justice and joy.

Any way you look at it, life, in all of its complexities, is incredible. The opportunities for fun, laughter, connection, and belonging are so delicious and exquisite because we have edges. These edges allow us to feel the beauty of being contained as well as the ecstasy of traveling beyond limitation.

You came all the way here. Be it from a spiritual perspective, or in the sense of pregnancy and birth, it's time to celebrate your humanness including all of its ups and downs.

Incarnation is a miracle in and of itself. Life's a party of molecules!

- ⚀ Cosmic Shuffle Dance Party on page 322
- ⚁ Non-Dominant Hand Drawing on page 304
- ⚂ High Fives! on page 162
- ⚃ Freeze on page 165
- ⚄ These Are My Feet on page 308
- ⚅ Physical Storytelling on page 169

It's All You

It is all about you. There is no mind/body split. From every direction, this is all an expression of you. Your mental landscape, your emotional life, your spiritual experiences, and your body itself are all expressions of YOU. They are connected, mutually and simultaneously exposing who you are. They are not separate. They are different perspectives on the same being. There's no need to master one so as to control the other. It is a natural process that the more connected and empowered you are in one area, the more connected you are with yourself across the board. Take a moment to consider how knowing oneself is different than using aspects of oneself. This is about knowing and being in honest relationship and ownership of yourself.

This means that trauma or damage done on any front -- emotional, physical, mental, or spiritual -- is going to affect all the rest. For example, a damaged physical body is going to impact the mental, emotional, and spiritual landscapes. The same is true for all the rest. Although this may seem like bad news, the inverse is true as well. When there is healing through any of these perspectives, improvement is also simultaneously happening for all of your other landscapes.

When you pull this card it may be time for you to come to terms with the fact that whatever symptoms you're experiencing are not separate from the rest of you.

There may be an easier way into changing your patterns than wherever the issue is most obviously appearing. Sometimes physical injury can't fully heal until anxiety from a trauma has been addressed and supported. Sometimes talk therapy has gone as far as it can, and it is time to bring the body's knowledge into the picture, with yoga, bodywork, or movement studies. Sometimes a mental blockage or struggle with focus can be alleviated with physical training or spiritual practice.

If you have hit a growth plateau or a stagnant spot, maybe it's time to try a different approach. Even if the new approach doesn't help immediately, it may help bring a fresh set of eyes when you return to your previous methods.

It may also be time for you to consider the status you might be giving to certain parts of yourself over others. Do you take better care of some parts of yourself than? Do you honor or acknowledge certain aspects and disregard others? Do you say you treasure one, but always prioritize another? Most of us do that in some way or another. Take this time to consider what possibilities you may be missing. Importantly, please be careful and avoid using this as an opportunity to be mean to yourself.

⚀ Still Meditation on page 205
⚁ I Am Willing to Admit on page 340
⚂ Grief Ritual on page 285
⚄ Roll Again
      ⚀ ⚁ Healing Hands Circle on page 295
      ⚂ ⚄ Healing Hands On Self on page 295
      ⚄ ⚄ Healing Hands Shared on page 295
⚄ Stampede of the Elephants on page 178
⚄ Body Wisdom Approach Practice on page 214

Know Thyself Know God

    Within each of us, there is a Temple. Truth be told, each of us *is* a Temple. On the walls of your Temple, there are inscriptions or depictions of your sacred truth. This is your compass as well as the path itself. It is both the destination to which you are headed as well as the way you will get there. This is both what you are here to learn and embody as well as teach and share; what you need to experience to be healed and the medicine you offer.

    Your own gifts and character flaws are the passage to understanding and communing with Divinity. It is through dissolving into the mystery that we expand our perceptions and have a greater understanding of who we are as human beings. Here we can experience the mystery of self that is beyond explanation. It is in knowing the depth of our humanity that we can touch, know, and remember the limitless potential of the sacred.

    Receiving this card is a summoning for your own intimate knowing of your limited human self and your timeless, limitless self. By knowing and loving yourself, you will know and love God.

- ⚀ Restoring Our Inner Temple on page 250
- ⚁ Visiting Our Inner Temple on page 268
- ⚂ Collaging or Vision Boarding (Your Temple Inscription) on page 304
- ⚃ Roll Again
  - ⚀ ⚁ Healing Hands On Self on page 295
  - ⚁ ⚃ Healing Hands Shared on page 295
  - ⚄ ⚅ Healing Hands Circle on page 295
- ⚄ Wisdom Circle on page 157
- ⚅ Mirror Meditation on page 241

Life Is Ridiculous

Let me repeat, Life Is Ridiculous. The root of the word ridiculous is laughable. Between the sheer improbability that our human body functions at all, combined with the stories we tell ourselves, mirrored with the astounding beauty of our planet, compounded by the pain and suffering of billions...life is ridiculous. Life is rich. It is beyond comprehension. It is outside our conceivable ability to understand, and yet we are gifted experiences which take us beyond our limited understanding into oneness.

This card is an invitation to relax. No one gets out of this alive. No matter what we do, someday our planet will be stardust again. And yet, everyone is accurately the center of their own universe. Lighten up, laugh about it, lean back, put your feet up, and realize that it's just a wild ride, any which way you do the journey.

- ⚀ Cosmic Shuffle Dance Party on page 322
- ⚁ The Funny Face Game on page 163
- ⚂ Gibberish Convo on page 162
- ⚃ Fuck It on page 307
- ⚄ Hugging Yourself on page 298
- ⚅ Hugging Standing Up on page 301

Make An Offering

It's time to say thank you by giving something of yourself. The practices of making an offering are as diverse as the oceans. The magic of making an offering comes when the offering is the sharing of your life force.

Some examples of include:

- **Things that nourish your life** such as staple and luxury foods or medicines
- **Expressions and use of your life force** such as song, dance, blood, art, your time, emotional support, labor and skills
- **Representations of manifested life force** such as money and valuables

Pick something that pulls a thread on your own personal tapestry. Weave it into what you are giving to, thus your offering becomes nourishment for that which you are grateful. Offerings are not meant to diminish you, so listen for the things to offer that connect and invest without depleting you. This may seem vague at first, but with practice and deep listening, you will be able to discern the differences.

Sometimes we make an offering before things happen. Other times an offering occurs during or in the midst of an experience. Upon completion is also an opportune time to make an offering. Wherever you are, now is the time to identify something you have to offer that pulls you enough that you can feel its impact while the giving does not also undermine your true wellbeing.

Give a gift that sings the song of thanksgiving.

⚀ Make an Offering on page 279
⚁ Sing a Song or Play Music on page 281
⚂ Cosmic Shuffle Dance Party (Offering Style) on page 322
⚃ Meditation Gift on page 280
⚄ Clarity on Offerings/Gifts on page 189
⚅ Mindful Breathing on page 277

Money Issues Are Expressions of Root Issues

Here, the root, is referring to the generative base of our own being held in the pelvis, hips, space between our legs and lower abdomen. It includes and is not limited to the physical organs and it holds the energetic centers of material plane, our sense of belonging, sensuality, eros, worthiness and safety. The root taught me: "I am made of space and matter. I take up space and I matter." It is the center of human creation and the interplay between the mysterious and the manifested.

One day I decided that if I was so committed to love that I had to find a way to love our oppressors (internal and external, one and the same), I also had to find a way to love something as neutral as money.

Money is a cultural agreement about how we share life force and potential life force. It is not, in and of itself, a big thing that will solve all of our problems or the source causes of them. Money is, however, massively loaded with associations and experiences of self worth, quality of life, health, and power. How we relate to our worth, life choices, and an experience of power can usually be seen in our relationship with money. These issues do not inherently rest in money; they rest in our root. And they will express themselves through habits of avoidance, controlling behaviors, abuse, bullying, coping, and in the same manner they will transparently reveal as integrity, equitable behaviors, consistency, honesty, and kind maturity.

Transparency of your money habits will expose both vulnerable wounds and how much power you are already wielding, your patterns of privilege, systemic poverty, abuse, and addiction. By getting unapologetically honest with money and resources -- an act that engages and requires extreme exposure -- you have access, through awareness, to make change. That exposure, when treated with love, compassion, and creativity, becomes a strong and trustworthy foundation. Here you can build new habits and heal, first yourself, and then your relationship to money and other resources.

⚀ Alternatives on page 159
⚁ Confession Session on page 150
⚂ Healing the Hunted Wound on page 290
⚃ Financial Transparency on page 330
⚄ Roll Again
    ⚀ ⚁ ⚂ Stealing From Ourselves on page 267
    ⚃ ⚄ ⚅ Pelvic Bowl Meditation on page 246
⚅ Roll Again
    ⚀ ⚁ ⚂ Money Sorting on page 195
    ⚃ ⚄ ⚅ Healing Systemic Conditioning on page 184

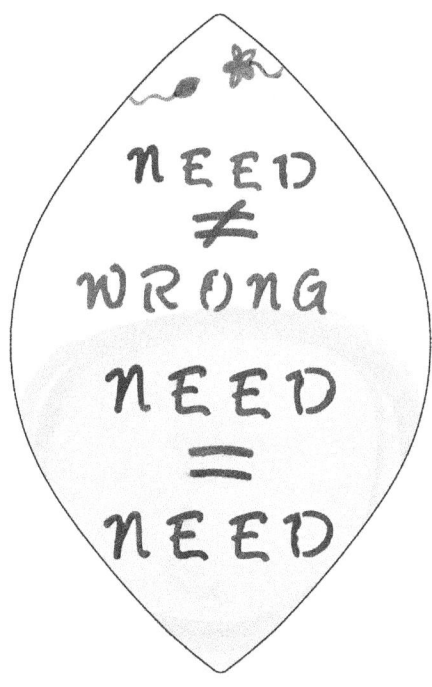

Need≠Wrong Need=Need

Having a need does not equal being wrong. Having a need equals having a need.

When you have a need, it does not mean you've done something incorrect. Many of us have been conditioned to believe that we should be entirely self-sufficient, not ever requiring assistance from anything or anyone else. For some of us, this belief system goes even deeper, and is experienced as thinking we should have no needs at all -- except possibly the need to be of service to others. If this way of being is internalized, when we have a need for space, rest, expression, acknowledgement, or anything else, we feel as though we have failed and thus done something wrong.

Turns out, having a need does not make you wrong or prove that you have messed up, and it is not a mark of failure. Having a need does indicate that you are a human and you have needs.

Having a need means you have a need. According to Marshall Rosenberg, the creator of Nonviolent Communication, all humans have the same needs. As individuals, we prioritize or value those needs differently, and yet we still share them all.

To get a fuller understanding, I have provided a list of needs and a list of feelings. Looking at them together can help clarify an approach to self awareness and empathy.

Needs Inventory[1]

The following list of needs is neither exhaustive nor definitive. It is meant as a starting place to support anyone who wishes to engage in a process of deepening self-discovery and to facilitate greater understanding and connection between people.

Needs List:

CONNECTION
acceptance
affection
appreciation
belonging
cooperation
communication
closeness
community
companionship
compassion
consideration
consistency
empathy
inclusion
intimacy
love
mutuality
nurturing
respect/self-respect
safety
security
stability
support
to know and be known
to see and be seen
to understand and
be understood
trust
warmth

PHYSICAL WELLBEING
air
food
movement/exercise
rest/sleep
sexual expression
safety
shelter
touch
water

HONESTY
authenticity
integrity
presence

PLAY
joy
humor

PEACE
beauty
communion
ease
equality
harmony
inspiration
order

AUTONOMY
choice
freedom
independence
space
spontaneity

MEANING
awareness
celebration of life
challenge
clarity
competence
consciousness
contribution
creativity
discovery
efficacy
effectiveness
growth
hope
learning
mourning
participation
purpose
self-expression
stimulation
to matter
understanding

---

[1] Needs Inventory from Nonviolent Communication © 2005 by Center for Nonviolent Communication
Website: www.cnvc.org | Email: cnvc@cnvc.org | Phone: +1.505.244.4041

Feelings Inventory[2]

The following are words we use when we want to express a combination of emotional states and physical sensations. This list is neither exhaustive nor definitive. It is meant as a starting place to support anyone who wishes to engage in a process of deepening self-discovery and to facilitate greater understanding and connection between people.

There are two parts to this list: feelings we may have when our needs are being met and feelings we may have when our needs are not being met.

Satisfied Feelings List:

AFFECTIONATE
compassionate
friendly
loving
open hearted
sympathetic
tender
warm

ENGAGED
absorbed
alert
curious
engrossed
enchanted
entranced
fascinated
interested
intrigued
involved
spellbound
stimulated

HOPEFUL
expectant
encouraged
optimistic

CONFIDENT
empowered
open
proud
safe
secure

EXCITED
amazed
animated
ardent
aroused
astonished
dazzled
eager
energetic
enthusiastic
giddy
invigorated
lively
passionate
surprised
vibrant

GRATEFUL
appreciative
moved
thankful
touched

INSPIRED
amazed
awed
wonder

JOYFUL
amused
delighted
glad
happy
jubilant
pleased
tickled

EXHILARATED
blissful
ecstatic
elated
enthralled
exuberant
radiant
rapturous
thrilled

PEACEFUL
calm
clear headed
comfortable
centered
content
equanimous
fulfilled
mellow
quiet
relaxed
relieved
satisfied
serene
still
tranquil
trusting

REFRESHED
enlivened
rejuvenated
renewed
rested
restored
revived

---

[2] Feelings Inventory from Nonviolent Communication © 2005 by Center for Nonviolent Communication
Website: www.cnvc.org | Email: cnvc@cnvc.org | Phone: +1.505.244.4041

Unsatisfied Feelings List:

AFRAID
apprehensive
dread
foreboding
frightened
mistrustful
panicked
petrified
scared
suspicious
terrified
wary
worried

ANNOYED
aggravated
dismayed
disgruntled
displeased
exasperated
frustrated
impatient
irritated
irked

ANGRY
enraged
furious
incensed
indignant
irate
livid
outraged
resentful

AVERSION
animosity
appalled
contempt
disgusted
dislike
hate
horrified
hostile
repulsed

CONFUSED
ambivalent
baffled
bewildered
dazed
hesitant
lost
mystified
perplexed
puzzled
torn

DISCONNECTED
alienated
aloof
apathetic
bored
cold
detached
distant
distracted
indifferent
numb
removed
uninterested
withdrawn

DISQUIET
agitated
alarmed
discombobulated
disconcerted
disturbed
perturbed
rattled
restless
shocked
startled
surprised
troubled
turbulent
turmoil
uncomfortable
uneasy
unnerved
unsettled
upset

EMBARRASSED
ashamed
chagrined
flustered
guilty
mortified
self-conscious

FATIGUE
beat
burnt out
depleted
exhausted
lethargic
listless
sleepy
tired
weary
worn out

PAIN
agony
anguished
bereaved
devastated
grief
heartbroken
hurt
lonely
miserable
regretful
remorseful

SAD
depressed
dejected
despair
despondent
disappointed
discouraged
disheartened
forlorn
gloomy
heavy hearted
hopeless
melancholy
unhappy
wretched

TENSE
anxious
cranky
distressed
distraught
edgy
fidgety
frazzled
irritable
jittery
nervous
overwhelmed
restless
stressed out

VULNERABLE
fragile
guarded
helpless
insecure
leery
reserved
sensitive
shaky

YEARNING
envious
jealous
longing
nostalgic
pining
wistful

What we actually need is an experience of reality, which can be tricky and also is empowering. Affection, autonomy, rest, and humor are states of being -- always available to us if we allow ourselves to have our needs be met. To be able to do that, we must first admit, consciously and/or unconsciously, that we have a need and we want it met. Letting go of the story that having a need is wrong in the first place, creates space to invite in what is possible.

Note: rage is the voice of unmet needs. Many anger issues stem from an inability to identify and accept that a need is present and thus is being ignored. This is often learned by us as children from our caregivers or by trying to emulate "adult behavior" that ignores identifying and addressing personal needs.

I am so glad to honor your needs, celebrate that you have them, and encourage you to own, respect, and care for them!

- ⚀ Needs List Identification on page 152
- ⚁ Clearing Delusion on page 161
- ⚂ Roll Again
    - ⚀ Hugging Yourself on page 298
    - ⚁ Hugging Sitting Down on page 300
    - ⚂ Hugging over Time and Space on page 300
    - ⚃ Hugging with Extremities on page 299
    - ⚄ Hugging Standing Up on page 301
    - ⚅ Group Hugging Exercise on page 302
- ⚃ Still Meditation on page 205
- ⚄ Walking Meditation on page 206
- ⚅ Trust Fall on page 170

No. Stop. Not In My Space.

In yoga, martial arts, live action role playing with foam swords, theater, taking someone else's hands off my body, putting my hands on my body, healing with other people's bodies, I have been taught and learned about the warrior path. The path of the boundary keeper. The path of discerning and ensuring justice. The path of fearlessness and courage. The path of preparedness and training. The path of patience, discernment and action. The path of trust and risk-taking. The path of self knowledge and mastery. The path of heart, vision and wisdom. The path of being both the calm in the storm and the unstoppable force of nature. The path of refining the senses. The path of service. The path of interconnectedness and commitment to the collective.

The warrior's charge is to maintain boundaries at all costs -- with love, without judgment, and with everpresent discernment and clarity. The first task is to show up to what is at hand and witness it in its fullness. The second assignment is to assert and communicate the boundary or line with compassion and respect. The third part of the job is to ensure that the boundary remains intact, even at a cost to oneself in ego or physical form.

It is not the warrior's way to use shaming or bullying tactics, against oneself or others. A warrior cultivates faith in self and in justice, in order to make decisions with integrity and determination.

As a warrior, you cultivate the ability, and the responsibility, to unapologetically say "No. Stop. Not in my space." This is about taking full responsibility for what is happening in your space, and in space for which you have accepted responsibility. This is not about meddling in, or condemning, what happens in other spaces. Baring the heart without aggression is vulnerable and takes courage. Being courageous is being afraid and doing what needs to be done anyway. Being a warrior means knowing your heart, following your heart. Learning to embody and express your full self in your true power means unlearning belligerence and a need for control. This is a card instructing you to take up the charge of your own life, your own boundaries, your calling, and the responsibilities you have accepted, and to stand in yourself as you move through this world.

I call upon the warrior in you.
It's worth it. You are worth it.

⚀ Warrior Pose and Teachings by Grace Perkins on page 371
⚁ "Yes" and "No" "No" variation on page 347
⚂ Rise up, Rise up, Rise up! on page 177
⚃ Warrior Vows on page 292
⚄ Wisdom Circle on page 157
⚅ Communing with your Sacred Warrior Guide on page 222

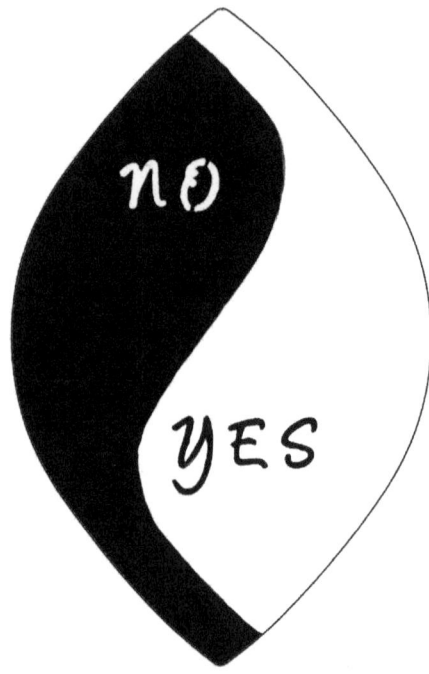

No. Yes.

I give thanks to the Taijitu, the Chinese Yin-Yang symbol, and the Taoist tradition for the images and teachings of Yin and Yang--the image above is inspired by and core Taoist concept that shows nothing is whole without its opposite: light needs shadow, and a Yes always carries a No. This image came to me as a wise way to remind you of the continuum within decision-making, releasing a perspective of separation.

This richly applies to you as you enter into greater consciousness and action. This is because this deep philosophical understanding holds a key to making an empowered choice.

That which appears to be separate and opposite is actually simultaneous, moving into and from itself. Recognizing that the opposite element is present in what you are focusing on allows for nuance, breath, and life force to influence your perspective and experience.

Every No is a Yes for something, and every Yes is a No for something else.

You are faced with a decision. By getting clear about the elements that you want to create, as well as destroy or release, you are owning that which you want to compost and grow. You are taking responsibility for your own power. There is power in knowing what you're saying No to and what you are saying Yes to in every situation.

Things that are polar to each other give birth to one another. The dynamic flow of life is constantly happening, feeding, merging, and reemerging. This movement only appears separate in momentary snapshots. Allow this information about Yes and No to change the way you approach and decide on your next actions. Nothing is as simple as Yes *or* No. Your life decisions are always Yes *and* No.

- ⚀ Yes/No Sorting on page 201
- ⚁ Mirror Meditation on page 241
- ⚂ Unwinding Group Exercise on page 373
- ⚃ "Yes" and "No" on page 347
- ⚄ Inversions on page 345
- ⚅ How to Manifest What You Really Want on page 338

Open Your Eyes

If you want real feedback on your life, look at your life. Your life is not lying or trying to trick you. What you see is the sum of your actions, habits, choices, circumstances, and perspectives. Your life is showing you, with honesty, who you have been.

At times, this can feel like a brutal process.

Here's something to keep in mind as you look around your life: you are always proving yourself right. Let me explain. Our brains are designed to make patterns and fit our perceptions into a reality that we can understand.

We all know someone who, when given a compliment, still finds a way to make whatever's been praised into a reference about how much they are inferior by deflecting in some way. This is an example of proving yourself right. This person is committed to how much they suck and they use every piece of evidence to reinforce this belief. One way to do this is by completely misinterpreting other people's actions and words. Another pathway is to ignore or block out information entirely, in order to maintain the validity of a particular idea.

It is a gift that we are able to construct reality from our observations and experiences. The key to unlocking our perceptive abilities lies in the recognition that what we observe is filtered by our focus and determined by our belief systems.

As you do your best to sort out what's subjective and what's objective, gently bear in mind that any view is inherently a constructed view, no matter how hard you may try to make it "objective." That said, with purposeful intention and attention, we can become more objectively observant. Then we can see our external surroundings and internal landscapes through less skewed lenses. Everyone's lens is subjective. Realizing this, we have an opportunity and responsibility to consciously create the lens we're looking through.

For instance, I choose to believe that no matter what's happening, it's the best case scenario. No matter how goofy or confusing a situation may be, my system is always scanning for evidence that things are always working out. I consciously and consistently foster that belief system, and as such, my mind unconsciously and persistently follows suit as it collects proof to support my case. Since the brain will self select the evidence it needs to prove itself right (and ignore everything else), why not have it choose a kind and loving perspective? What perspective are you reinforcing?

⚀ Observation Bias on page 246
⚁ Naming Foundational Belief Systems on page 152
⚂ Record a Story and Listen to Yourself on page 345
⚃ Still Meditation on page 205
⚄ Alternatives on page 159
⚅ Organic Movement Meditation on page 204

PLAY

It's time to Play. Put down your agendas. Engage in something solely for enjoyment. Do an activity that nourishes you. Play or Li'la, the greek word for the divine essence of play, speak to the raw creative force. In its simplest form, Play is inherently non-competitive, non-sexual, and very sensual.

Being an excellent playmate means meeting your partner where they are, with respect and enjoyment. For example, playing with an object like a half deflated ball requires giving up the need for the ball to be different, such as inflated. The Play is limited and changed but not cancelled by the circumstance. When playing with a person, this means acceptance of them as they are. Their physical limitations, desires, and interests will influence the mutual enjoyment of the activity at hand. So meet them, and allow yourself to be met in an adventure with open ended outcomes, or perhaps no outcomes at all.

Being playful is one of the most essential components to healing and spiritual discovery. The combination of relaxation and letting go of control with focus and engagement is an equation for insight and transformation. Not taking yourself too seriously, while also being attentive to what's at hand, is the state of being that Play teaches us. Play games, Play at life, and be rewarded with authentic joy and growth.

⚀ Contact Movement with Wrists on page 161
⚁ Breathe to Stretch on page 276
⚂ Cosmic Shuffle Dance Party on page 322
⚃ The Funny Face Game on page 163
⚄ Make The Room on page 166
⚅ Fuels of Improv on page 163

Practice

You've probably heard the aphorism, "Practice makes perfect."
Here's my take: Practice makes practiced.
Receiving this card now means it's time to practice.
If you already have practices, lean in and double down. It may be time to study up, work a deeper level, increase attention, and show more dedication to one of your practices.

If you don't have a practice, it's time to start shopping. Examples of practice include meditation, chanting, group ceremony work, dance, art, martial arts, yoga, a sport, your beloved religion, music, and many other forms. When you are practicing, your system is being trained to stay present in your life in order to handle challenges, pleasure, focus, relaxation, and confusion.

If you do not cultivate intentional ways to navigate through your life, you will continue to go about things as you always have. For most people, our default pathways are determined by a combination of familial and cultural imprinting, trauma, and innate strengths and nature. Through Practice, we get to discern these aspects of self from those of others. Thus, we cultivate ways of being that we would like to keep, and let go of those that no longer help us.

If you consider the possibility that how you do anything is how you do everything, you can look at one small task and get unlimited insight. From this perspective, how you Practice matters more that what you choose to do. Shifting your focus from "what" to "how" can liberate and widen your Practice possibilities.

Pathways are reinforced while we practice. This means if we are cruel to ourselves using abrasive body tension and and judgmental corrective voices while doing whatever we have chosen to use as our practice ground, we are in actually practicing being cruel and judgmental. This is where the how becomes essential. When we practice with kindness and a demeanor we would like to take into the world inside of us and give out to others, such as awareness, compassion, patience, a sense of humor, forgiveness and so on we are practicing being that way in our life. So whatever landscape you choose to focus on, do it in the manner you wish to do everything in your life.

I advise that you get support as you Practice. Find a teacher whose "how" is reflective of what you want. Without a good teacher or strong guidance, we can deepen existing *unhelpful* habits if we are not courageous enough to Practice outside of our familiar zones and learn new ways to respond to stimuli. If nothing else, invite your Sacred Council -- spirit guides, Great Spirit, or whatever form of the mystery you can call on to assist you -- to be present and guide you through your Practice.

⚀ ⚁ ⚂ Players' Choice
⚃ ⚄ ⚅ Pick a Random Practice

Question Everything

Confusion is required while learning something new. This card is more of a heads up or a validation than a command. When we are exposed to new information, most of the time we try to put it into our already established filing system about how reality works. For example, people do things and they consistently land in one file to another, then something new comes along. We go to file it away in the cabinet, only to realize that there's no fitting folder. What has occurred has no place in the system.

This sensation of not having a context for something is confusion. For most people, this can be extremely disorienting, frustrating, uncomfortable, anxiety producing, and sometimes painful. If there is no pre-established folder, then the whole system of comprehending reality is brought into question.

This is great news! You're right on track.

This card encourages you to stay with the feeling of things not fitting neatly. If you are lucky and brave, sticking with that feeling will lead you to dump out your entire filing cabinet, thus requiring you to entirely reconstruct how you view and create meaning within your reality. Have confidence that all will reveal itself. Just stay with the process. The more you do this, the more you will understand how subjective your filing cabinet is, and how important it is to remember that subjectivity while relating to this world.

I recommend getting a lot of practice at fundamentally restructuring the ways in which you perceive life. This means noticing when you initially write something off as not applicable, untrue, or contrary to your beliefs. Over time, you will learn to discern between your wisdom and your beliefs. With practice, the experience of deep and real confusion also becomes associated with feelings of excitement, joy, expansion, satisfaction, invigoration, inspiration, and motivation, because you know you are about to see the world in a new and more whole way.

To explore more about formation and propagation of beliefs through perception read the Open Your Eyes teaching (page 80) for more information on the connection between perception and processing.

- ⚀ Still Meditation on page 205
- ⚁ Organic Movement Meditation on page 204
- ⚂ Mind Mapping on page 196
- ⚃ Death and Rebirth Ritual on page 284
- ⚄ Brain Dump on page 186
- ⚅ Inversions on page 345

Radical Acceptance

Acceptance is often associated with positivity, lightheartedness, and optimism. The act of real acceptance -- radical acceptance -- is absolute engagement with reality and the attributes of reality just as they are presenting themselves at this moment. Radical acceptance is not about giving reality a context, one in which everything is rosy. Rather, it's about having the courage to say, "Yes, this is it, at this moment." Radical acceptance is not an agreement to comply, it is the pure acknowledgement of what is. This is the first step to creating change, becoming peace, and trusting love.

The Radical Acceptance teaching begs you to put down all demands on your life long enough to actually see your life. From here, you have great power and, quite often, great relief. By accepting what is, you forfeit the battleground you have created with the past and projections of the future. In this way, the past becomes simply the past, and the future is allowed to be unknown. As a result, your resources become fully available to you now.

When I was diagnosed with Premenstrual Dysphoric Disorder (PMDD), I spent years learning how to care for myself and my symptoms. There were strict rules that I lived by. I used alarms and notes in my calendar to keep me together. One day I was in a group processing circle and I realized that I had been told my whole life that I was "too sensitive." In that moment, it occurred to me that I was not "too sensitive," I was simply

"THAT sensitive."

I had all of the criterion symptoms in 2005 and now no longer qualify for the diagnosis. I still have major hormonal fluctuations throughout my cycle; I just no longer suffer from it. Remember we are all hormonal everyday of our life.

Now I am even more sensitive, *that* sensitive." In a quest to create stability in my life, I saw there was an imbalance that made my sensitivity overwhelming and problematic. By accepting how sensitive I am, I realized I needed to grow my resilience to be present through what I was experiencing. First I learned how to clarify my boundaries. Then I learned how to translate sensations from inside myself into information I can trust, use, and communicate. When I radically and without negation accepted myself as I was, I stopped just tolerating myself, and I began to really heal.

By accepting both our perceived weaknesses and strengths, we garner the ability to see them and ourselves for the beauty that we are.

- ⚀ I Am Willing to Admit on page 340
- ⚁ Soul Unification Healing Meditation on page 258
- ⚂ Mirror Meditation on page 241
- ⚃ YES I AM! YES YOU ARE! on page 173
- ⚄ Self Swaddling on page 358
- ⚅ Prayer Practice on page 353

Reveal to Heal

Shame is a blanket that covers the wound.

Shunahsii Rose shares that shame cannot be processed, it is lifted by community. That community can be human (I like to say humane), plant, spirit, or animal. Remember, for it to be exposure so it can be lifted, you must believe that your witness is capable of witnessing you. If you don't believe that the plant understands and cares, then it's probably not the right witness for you at this time.

Keeping pains or injuries of any kind hidden, cuts off and inhibits healing from occurring. Lifting the blanket, putting a crack in the shell, and offering up what needs to be healed, incites the naturally occurring process of transformation.

In the image on the Reveal To Heal card, the second phase can be seen as either receiving healing, or offering up and allowing healing. Inherently they are the same continuum, though the experiences can feel distinct. When we offer up our burdens to the full expression and expansion of the innate healing potential, we allow what was limited by the confines of shame, secrecy, and control, into said potential.

Staying vulnerable in the present moment allows for revealing and healing to happen in the now. In the case of wounds from the past, it is as though you are reopening a festering wound so that it may finally be cleaned and heal properly. Often, untruths commonly involving misconceptions of our self-worth are part of the spiritual, mental, physical, or emotional infection. This is part of the cause of the shame which hides the wound or experience to begin with. Revealing or opening the wound allows for proper discernment of lies, what needs to be forgiven, what boundaries need to be taken, and what reclamation of self needs to happen.

We are constantly and innately moving ourselves towards an equilibrium, which means it is our very nature to heal imbalance and wounds. Take heart, let this place be known, and healing will occur.

⚀ I Am Willing to Admit on page 340
⚁ Soul Unification Healing Meditation on page 258
⚂ Mirror Meditation on page 241
⚃ Prayer Practice on page 353
⚄ Physical Storytelling on page 169
⚅ Confession Session on page 150

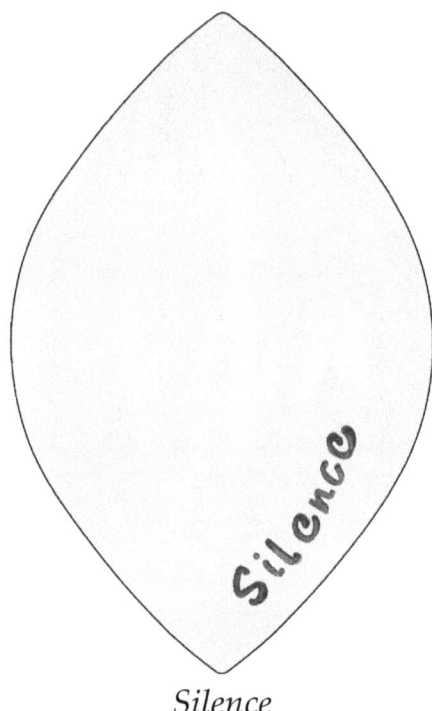

Silence

There is a Silence that holds all sound. It is the echo-chamber that life, birth, death, rebirth, transformation, and stagnation dwell within. The Silence card is a summoning of your ability to listen to and potentially become this restorative and purifying presence. Silence can hold anything without judgment, diminishment, or praise. It is the sound of complete acceptance, divine surrender, profound possibility, and nourishing completion. It can feel terrifying. It can feel blissful. Blessings on each and every experience you have when you touch the endless silence.

The power of Silence lies in its expansive neutrality. It allows and makes sense of all death and all creativity. Now is the time to court Silence. I use the word court, because forced Silence often comes with chains of judgment, whereas surrendering to and allowing in the Silence that exists within you and all around you, is simply an act of deepening awareness -- awareness that brings more and more gifts over time.

⚀ Pro-Active Listening on page 352
⚁ Still Meditation on page 205
⚂ Organic Movement Meditation done to silence on page 204
⚃ Nature Bath on page 346
⚄ Brain Dump on page 186
⚅ Flame Meditation on page 205

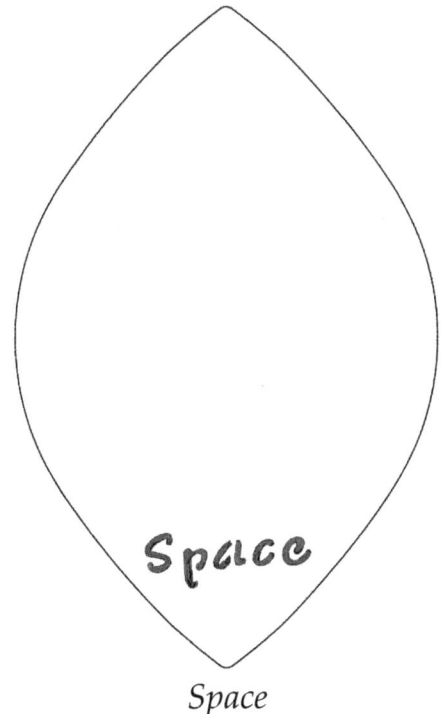

Space

Whether you journey in or out, Space is what you will find. Our entire existence is literally constructed of space. We are held by space. We are made of space. We make space. We are space. It is time to consciously commune with Space.

- ⚀ Organic Movement Meditation on page 204
- ⚁ Still Meditation on page 205
- ⚂ Sensitivity Scanning on page 360
- ⚃ Roll Again
    - ⚀⚁ Healing Hands Circle on page 295
    - ⚂⚃ Healing Hands On Self on page 295
    - ⚄⚅ Healing Hands Shared on page 295
- ⚄ Declutter on page 324
- ⚅ Roll Again
    - ⚀⚁ Bone Breathing Meditation on page 216
    - ⚂⚃ Sing a Song or Play Music on page 281
    - ⚄⚅ Space In Joints Meditation on page 264

Start Where You Are

You are tempted to believe that you need something before your healing can start or your life can change. Perhaps you think you need to be less angry to forgive, that you need more energy before you can build strength, or that you need someone before you can love. We make up equations that say we have to be different from where we are in order to make the life or have the feelings we're longing to experience.

Start exactly where you are -- exhausted, angry, excited, inspired, lost, in love, hopeless, confused, or clear. Make your plan from this place. Your next step is one step away from where you are currently. Acknowledge and discover this starting place. You might be projecting yourself into the future, or holding yourself captive in the past where things may look better or worse.

Return to the now.

Return to your body, the womb, the state that you are currently in. Where are you? Get honest, get real, start here.

- ⚀ Where I Am on page 201
- ⚁ I Am Willing to Admit on page 340
- ⚂ Mirror Meditation on page 241
- ⚃ Prayer Practice on page 353
- ⚄ Soul Unification Healing Meditation on page 258
- ⚅ Organic Movement Meditation on page 204

Stay the Course

KEEP GOING!!!

You are on track. Take a deep breath and breathe in the confidence that you're on the path you need to be on. It is not time to change up direction, reevaluate motives, or alter strategies. It is time to refocus on the commitments that you have already made, trust in the process, remember that you cannot see all of the moving parts, and that you only need to do your part.

You're doing great! It is possible that at this moment it does not feel or look that way. It will serve you to now engage with patience and the risk of trust. Do not back down or give in to voices of self-doubt. To get where you are going you need energy and focus. Be mindful not to waste your inner or outer resources undermining or distracting yourself from what you know needs to be done. Bullying or beating yourself up is an exhausting process, and you need that energy now more than ever. Stamina is what's required.

So dig deep into your faith, remind yourself to breathe slowly, open your heart and mind, make the choice to receive the blessings that are around you, and stay the course.

⚀ Roll Again
  ⚀⚁⚂ Take a Bath on page 361
  ⚃⚄⚅ Bone Breathing Meditation on page 216
⚁ Cosmic Shuffle Dance Party on page 322
⚂ Self Swaddling on page 358
⚃ Stampede of the Elephants on page 178
⚄ Commitment and Course Reflection on page 150
⚅ Roll Again
  ⚀ Healing Hands Circle on page 295
  ⚁ Four Corners of Your Foot on page 310
  ⚂ Healing Hands On Self on page 295
  ⚃ Finger Painting on page 305
  ⚄ Clearing Delusion on page 161
  ⚅ Healing Hands Shared on page 295

Tend Your Altar

Receiving this card is an invitation for you to tend an existing altar or to build one in whatever way you are inspired. In this instance "altar" means to hold a space for sacredness. It may be an actual altar in your home or it may be referencing in the sanctity of your body, a shared place of spiritual practice, or being in nature. So first ask yourself, where are some of your altars? What altar is asking for tending?

An altar is a representation in physical space of spirituality, reflecting your beliefs in the architecture and design of you life. How we use and care for our physical space is a reflection of our values, our priorities, our habits, and often our coping mechanisms.

I want to name the benefit of designating a physical space to hold and reflect an investment in your holistic or spiritual well-being. It is not a metaphor to make space for your spiritual self in this way, it is a practical and concretizing choice. Perhaps you already have an intentional altar. You may also have unintentional altars -- spaces where you put things that inspire, comfort, and remind you of who you want to be, or maybe there's already a place where you have pictures of your loved ones. By my understanding, these spaces are already altars.

Altar tending is a good practice to cultivate if you are interested in doing soul journey work. When you tend an altar, you a paying attention to both the physical and spirit worlds, which are translatable skills to journey work. Altar tending is about noticing and paying attention to both the world that is tangible and the subtle or ethereal parts of life.

Here are some theories and approaches to working with a working an altar. First, is it a shelf for magical and meaningful things to sit, or is it a workspace? This is question only you can answer. I encourage you to sort out the difference if there is one for you.

Altar tending is about being in relationship with things that are important to you. It is about taking the time, effort, and space to listen, speak, feel, notice, and be present with the important and valuable things in your life.

As you select items to place on your altar, explore the idea that these objects are indeed ancestors. Sometimes these beings will be active and working, and other times they'll be restoring, resting, or quiet. Decide if you want to keep everything out all the time, or only when they are active. This varies person by person and time to time. I encourage you to ask the objects themselves as they, in this ancestral view, alive and sentient. Ask the life force where it would like to be, and how it would like to be used.

Clean your altar space regularly, but not obsessively. Dust, replace candles, and sort incense ashes. Allow the altar to be alive and have opportunities to be and work while you are not sitting there. That means listening before assuming what anything needs. Take time to arrive and take in what's happening. Some objects may not be finished, and if they are still working, leave them be, or respond to their instructions of interaction, and let them reach completion. This may take months or years. Other times, a good clean may feel right to do weekly or even daily.

Clearing objects or the entire altar space is about restoring everything into an open and available state. If you think of the altar as a working space -- holding and filled with prayers and processes -- clearing the objects, beings, and physical area is about relieving them from those responsibilities so they can rest, reset, integrate, or enjoy their unassigned natural states. Clearing makes space for new prayers. There are many ways to clear objects or space, further instructions are offered in the Clear Objects and Tools with Resonance practice (page 321). You can always go back or start with basics by putting everything in storage, doing a deep clean, and placing one candle or a single meaningful object in the center of the space.

If you're new to working with altars intentionally, here is a place to start. Write down your prayers or wishes. Place objects that remind you of faith, your best self, ancestors, or the Divine in a designated space with your written note. The you can meditate, sing a song, or follow the guidance in Prayer Practice (page 353).

- ⚀ Build an Altar on page 319
- ⚁ Deep Clean on page 326
- ⚂ Clear Objects and Tools with Resonance on page 321
- ⚃ Flame Meditation on page 205
- ⚄ Roll Again
    - ⚀ ⚁ Healing Hands Circle on page 295
    - ⚂ ⚃ Healing Hands On Self on page 295
    - ⚄ ⚅ Healing Hands Shared on page 295
- ⚅ Roll Again
    - ⚀ ⚁ ⚂ Restoring Our Inner Temple on page 250
    - ⚃ ⚄ ⚅ Visiting Our Inner Temple on page 268

The Monster Carries a Gem

Your teacher has arrived. It is dangerous, horrifying, and out of your control. This, too, is a sacred experience. It's not easy, and I am not going to tell you that it's all good. I am going to tell you that all is blessed, even when you don't feel that way. You are a warrior for peace and love. Those who wield love, grace, faith, and peace must go through rigorous training on their journey to knowing wholeness. There may be times when your teachers are harsh and painful. This card signifies that you are now in the midst of receiving your gift, lesson, or healing through present or past processing of a monstrous experience.

It is your job to stay with this process until the gem is revealed from beneath the monster's cloak. It is a great act of faith to bless the enemy, give thanks for struggles, and claim your wholeness and freedom. Blessing the monster does not mean voluntarily keeping the monster in your path. Instead, blessing the monster means recognizing and responding with consciousness and attention.

Have fortitude in your prayers and actions. Show up for yourself in the way you need, the way you wish someone else would show up for you now. Get help and support in concrete and solid forms. Make decisions and place boundaries. Find your lessons. Tend your heart, mind, body, and soul. This is not easy, this is holy.

⚀ Monster Is My Teacher on page 168
⚁ Professional Assistance on page 350
⚂ Ironic to Sincere "Thank you" Prayer Practice on page 346
⚃ My Little! on page 167
⚄ Roll Again
    ⚀ ⚁ ⚂ Begging for Help on page 316
    ⚃ ⚄ ⚅ Help Through the Crack on page 337
⚅ Roll Again
    ⚀ ⚁ ⚂ BLESS IT on page 317
    ⚃ ⚄ ⚅ Prayer Practice on page 353

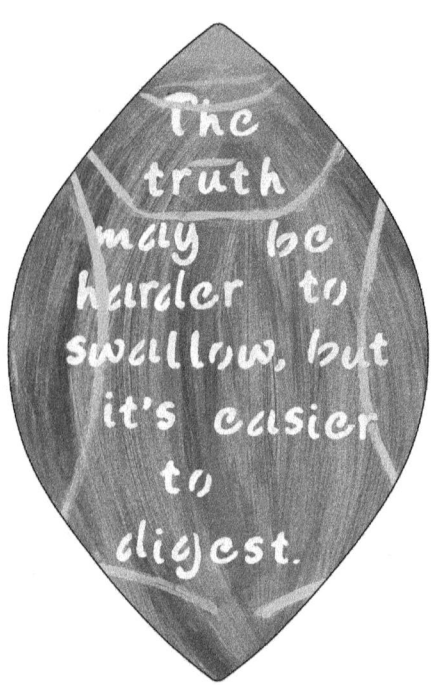

The Truth May Be Harder to Swallow, But it's Easier to Digest

We can spend a lot of time avoiding admitting the truth. To give ourselves credit, this avoidance occurs mostly around things we believe will hurt us. Often there is a sense that once we accept this thing, we have somehow validated it as being okay. Or inversely, there's a fear that if we acknowledge the thing we're avoiding, then we'll be confronted with the responsibility to do something about the issue.

Physically, this type of avoidance can manifest as a lump in the throat, a sore throat, laryngitis, jaw tension, lack of singing, or excessive or unconscious swallowing indicating a need to speak your truth out loud or accept a truth fully. We can have blockage in our throats because of a struggle to share our truth or take it in. We can be swallowing our own lies or unspoken truths or we can be resisting taking in information. That all can show up in the throat.

Lies or half truths or lies by omission, are often told, shared, and believed out of a need to protect. For that reason, lies can often go down pretty smoothly. We are either saying or hearing what we think is wanted or needed.

However, from there we encounter acute or chronic indigestion in the psyche and body, upset stomachs, difficulty assimilating nutrients, and an inability to eliminate, let go, and move forward. This experience can also show up as irritability, hunger for affection and nutrients, and insatiability as we can't transmute or assimilate the existing and present input. There's little substance being ingested, so there is little or nothing to move through.

The truth, however, can be difficult at the onset to take in, hear, or engage. It can be painful, disruptive, and scary. It often carries a sense of challenging the notions of who we are and who someone or something else is. These limited or skewed foundational realities or circumstances are often threatened by honest information.

Fear not, my beloveds, upon swallowing and accepting the truth, the process gets easier the further it goes through the system. When truth first hits the stomach, all bets are off. That's another gate keeper of acceptance or rejection; you may immediately be calmed, or you might experience complete upheaval. Digestion happens in the small intestine. Metaphysically or physically, this is the place where we discern, take in what we need and move the rest on to the next phase. Elimination and the process of only taking in the purest elements happens in the large intestine where our body reabsorbs water. Once you get here, the truth is cleansing your system.

So although notions of self and life are challenged here, upon full acceptance we can allow reality to adjust. This leads to a letting go of what no longer fits and moving forward to a sense of self-reliance that comes from the experience of showing up to what really is.

It may be difficult, and it's worth it. Breathe and show up with courage and kindness to share, hear, remember, accept, and change with the truth.

- ⚀ I Am Willing to Admit on page 340
- ⚁ Hard to Hear on page 151
- ⚂ Admitting a Truth on page 183
- ⚃ Truth Sorting on page 200
- ⚄ Alternate Nostril Breathing on page 274
- ⚅ Break The Chain of Familial Abuse on page 282

There Is Nothing To Fix

As I create spaces that are conducive for healing, I remember that I am not making or doing the healing. With that in mind, one of my healing practice principles is "no fixing" -- there is no fixing allowed because There Is Nothing To Fix.

As a Medicine Caller, massage therapist, Reiki Master, group facilitator, actress and director, cooperative play teacher, and team building leader, I have learned many different ways to facilitate a participant's awakening, empowerment, and connection with their own self. I use many of these same methods for my own healing.

My key approach is: No Fixing.

Our life is what it is. If we want to do it differently, that's a journey of evolving and unfolding, and yet there's no fixing involved. Our lives -- our selves -- are functioning exactly as they are with what they have. In that regard, they are not broken. Perhaps they are unsatisfying or even unjust, and yet they're still not broken.

As a healer, people bring me all sorts of aches, pains, burdens, conditions, and diagnoses. Consistently, I find those things to be expressions of the core person. In essence, the symptoms are deep communications about something that doesn't need to be fixed, but rather something that needs to be heard.

If you want those messages to quiet, sometimes behaviors need to change, but that is a different approach than fixing.

I don't fix other people, I don't fix myself, and I don't look at people like they need fixing! There is no fixing, because There Is Nothing To Fix!

- ⚀ Body Wisdom Approach Practice on page 214
- ⚁ Alternatives on page 159
- ⚂ Fuck It on page 307
- ⚃ Roll Again
    - ⚀ Hugging Yourself on page 298
    - ⚁ Hugging Sitting Down on page 300
    - ⚂ Hugging over Time and Space on page 300
    - ⚃ Hugging with Extremities on page 299
    - ⚄ Hugging Standing Up on page 301
    - ⚅ Group Hugging Exercise on page 302
- ⚄ Mirror Meditation on page 241
- ⚅ Dance of Sustainability on page 224

These Are My Feet

This card is about grounding. Grounding is a term that is used to describe the experience of feeling present and aware within your body, emotions, mind, and spirit. It specifically speaks to your awareness and presence reaching from your head, through your body, to and through your feet.

What I mean by through your feet is an awareness and connection to the literal ground beneath you. This can be simple as feeling the texture of the surface you're standing or sitting on. It can be felt as a cord or tether from the center of your body down into the earth like a tree's root system. Grounding can also be the feeling of your heartbeat being in sync with Mama Earth's heartbeat.

It is time to find your own sense of grounding.

Land. Here. Arrive. Arrive here now.

⚀ These Are My Feet on page 308
⚁ Grounding Cord on page 240
⚂ Four Corners of Your Foot on page 310
⚃ Still Meditation on page 205
⚄ Sing a Song or Play Music on page 281
⚅ Prayer Practice on page 353

Trade Vigilance for Boundaries

Chronic tension and tracking are methods of keeping us safe -- exhausting methods. The ill effects of hyper-vigilance can show up in varied ways. Examples include aggressiveness stemming from lack of self-expression, disappointment in your daily capability to function, and the disorienting state of not knowing yourself. In the body, gripping muscles limits circulation, inhibiting both the release of toxins and the receiving of nutrients. The mental gymnastics of anticipation, manipulation, and mitigation required to keep yourself safe is unfortunate. The cost is high and includes the loss of real intimacy in relationships.

Boundaries mean establishing what you need and want in your life, body, and space. It is often difficult to start establishing boundaries in old relationships and communities. The people who are used to you being a certain way share a mutual habit of relating. Changing a habit takes diligence and repetition.

Our habituated vigilance, which includes tension in the body, general and specific anxieties, and the things that we hyperactivity track are the starting point for discerning what we are trying to protect. Once these things are known, then conscious and intentional boundaries can be imagined. Then you can establish what you want and need from a distance and make the boundaries there, instead of reactively responding after the fact when things have gone way too far. Instead of suffering through life, you will relax. Thus, knowing yourself, expressing yourself, and resting

will become satisfying instead of scary endeavors.
Sound dreamy? It is possible.

⚀ Body Wisdom Approach Practice on page 214
⚁ Desire Admittance on page 190
And ⚂ Unwinding Group Exercise on page 373
⚃ Hyper Vigilance Sorting on page 200
⚄ Professional Assistance on page 350
⚅ Roll Again
        ⚀⚁ Healing Hands Circle on page 295
        ⚂⚃ Healing Hands On Self on page 295
        ⚄⚅ Healing Hands Shared on page 295

Trust the Body's Wisdom

The body is an expression of the soul.
The body does not lie.
Sensations in the body are a telephone ringing from the body to the self -- from the unconscious or subconscious attempting to reach the conscious. When the body creates sensations and symptoms, it's a phone call from a specific thing within you. The Body Wisdom Approach is the process through which you listen to those messages.

The body is telling you the truth, it is telling you the story of the life you have lived and the trajectory on which you are going. Your body's pain and discomfort are direct requests. Pain is a signal to change behavior, as well as a signal that something hurts. Numbness is a message of disconnection.

In general, there is consistency of meaning behind certain sensations and places in the body. The same symptoms are often communicating similar things to different people. That said, it's also true that on a person-to-person basis, the signs and meanings vary of symptoms vary because each body has a perfectly unique system of communication designed for and by that being.

When ideas about right and wrong are released from our consciousness, we can listen to the raw and wise, unbiased messages of the body. In doing so, we get to access something that knows, holds answers, and goes beyond prejudice, generations of trauma, and cultural indoctrination.

Your body's wisdom loves you, so much so that it will be unrelenting until you heed its calls. It will not hide the truth from you for convenience, likability, or pride.

Your body's desires and pleasures are indicators of that which is creative and life-giving in you. This is your life-force, guiding you towards your gifts and purpose through your wants, needs, and desires. Trust connected pleasure and desire. This is different than disassociated, anesthetic, escapism feel goods. Those still ought to be paid attention to, because they likely hold many keys for you about your unmet needs.

Most of us struggle to know what we want, and what we truly believe. Your feelings are a trustworthy map of self-knowing. Sometimes just by knowing a belief consciously, we realize that it's not true. In a moment's perceptive change, the pain or symptom shifts.

This card is also the womb wisdom card. You are invited to explore and come into sacred relating with menstruation. Across the globe traditions have made physical spaces for those menstruating and communing with the divine womb essence. Inside this space, those menstruating and those communing with the powers of creative generative flow enter into a vision and mediating and restorative space. These sacred bleeding temples are called many things such as a moonlodge and red tent temple, and can and are built in many ways. From the simplest changing of bed sheets to red sheets, to dug in the ground ceremony temples, to tented red fabric with cushions to lounge on. The intention od each of these space and in each tradition in their own way and wisdom is to honor the body and sacred ceremony that is this renewing time. We all, across sex and gender, have womb energy. The literal blood from our wombs carries life-force, potency, and potentially. When we learn how to trust our blood and creative center, we learn how to treasure our humanness, celebrate our divinity, and honor and love the simultaneous experience of both.

Trust your body. It knows your deepest secrets and loves you all the more for this awareness.

⚀ Charting You on page 188
⚁ Body Wisdom Approach Practice on page 214
⚂ Organic Movement Meditation on page 204
⚃ Unwinding Group Exercise on page 373
⚄ Roll Again
      ⚀ ⚁ ⚂ Simple Moontime Practice on page 257
      ⚃ ⚄ ⚅ Pelvic Bowl Meditation on page 246
⚅ Roll Again
      ⚀ ⚁ ⚂ Build an Altar on page 319
      ⚃ ⚄ ⚅ Healing Hands On Self on page 295

Trust Truly

It doesn't have to look and feel clean and neat to mean it is in alignment. This is the time to trust the process, trust in yourself, and trust in your faith. Show up to what's happening with eyes open, put judgments to the side, and cultivate a willingness to be changed by strong currents and immense sensations.

Bring your focus to the body's experience and truly feel what is occurring. Name your feelings, describe the environment, observe the circumstances, notice the body's sensations and the stories in your mind.

Cultivate a practice of being *in* your body. This means physically feeling your body in time space. Breathe into the diaphragms of your lungs and your pelvic floor. Soften the roof of your mouth by relaxing the jaw and allowing the soft palate raise, and round, making a dome. Give yourself permission to be just as you are now, to fully arrive. Grant yourself permission to be different and to change. Feel the present in detail while also bridging and reminding yourself of safety of your breath and lean into a benevolent force that unconditionally love you. This level of trust in your body's wisdom and your whole being's ability to fully heal can be applied both in the present moment -- allowing an experience to be fully processed in the here and now -- and in recovering from past experiences. This kind of deep processing allows for vibrancy and full expression of self.

You must embrace the ugly, painful, messy, loud, erotic, and insightful parts of the healing process. When we fully trust the wails of our grief, the screams of our rage, the hiding and festering under our shame, the awkward and ungraceful movement of our joy and ecstasy, and any other parts that we are tempted to deem "not spiritual" or "negative," we allow the space needed to let those elements of our lives be experienced and processed fully.

Emotion is its own form of intelligence. It is a digestive system unto itself, assimilating the nourishing content of what we experience and releasing what we no longer need. To function properly it must move through its full sequence. Learning to express emotions requires allowing sensations to come and go organically. Discover what it means for you to fully express with authentic enthusiasm. How can you allow full expression? Become attuned to when the feeling is legitimately complete. Notice where you are tempted to repeat a story and start the feelings over from the beginning. How can you relax, let go, and move on when the moment and emotion has passed? The full sequence of deep feeling includes the moment or moments after emoting. In this spaciousness, insight and wisdom can be known, appreciated, internalized, and integrated, and these experiences all become available in the ways we need. After a feeling is digested, there is new information to be shared. It takes spaciousness to allow the translation of that information to travel from the emotional body into the cognitive and action-oriented aspects of our selves. This is a process that is obscure before experiencing it, and yet when given time space, your natural process will reveal itself. Translating emotional wisdom into applicable knowledge is a natural process that happens within human bodies.

The result of fully processed emotions and resolved trauma is health and integrated wellbeing. When we cease to hang on to an old story as the defining truth of who we are, and we acknowledge the memory to as an experience that impacted us, we are returned to the present moment in mind and body. While trusting such intense (and sometimes culturally unacceptable) expressions as weeping, screaming, moaning, erotic and sexual expression, shutting down, zoning out, or numbing, the trick is to interrupt and let go of the stories attached to why you are experiencing a particular thing. Judging that your feelings are right or wrong is a conditioned process that needs to be disrupted. Instead, shift to accepting feelings as they are, and allowing movement to happen within the feeling space. Release any attachments to whether or not the feeling is justified, and make space for it be only what it is: a temporary expression of emotions and sensations. Feelings don't tell you the truth about a situation, they tell you how you *feel* about what you are perceiving, projecting, and imagining about a situation.

Unresolved trauma leaves us scanning our environments for anything that resembles our injurious past. When we integrate our past we can apply wisdom and discernment gained from a challenging or painful event while also being present enough to clearly see what is a reminder of a past danger and what is uniquely happening in the now. This means you have access to the intuition that will serve you in this moment. By processing the past you are freed from the mire of your fears. Here, your ability to stay present and be more attuned to your needs and inner wisdom is strengthened. You trust yourself now more than ever before.

Now that we have covered trusting one's self and the trusting the process of healing, let's look at another common question when considering "trust." How do I know if something can be trusted? The thing is, trust is not about trusting something outside of yourself. It is about believing in your own ability to navigate the unexpected. An element at play here is learning to trust that people will be who they are, and that things are what they are. A frequent problem we run into is that we trust people and things to be as we want them to be, or think they should be. When they are what they are instead of what we expect them to be, then our "trust" is broken. Upon deeper reflection, often the disappointment and distrust stems from us not knowing better than to have expected anything different. That in turn stems from ignoring what we may have known or had inklings about the person or thing. This is a call to trust what you know and base your expectations and boundaries on reality as opposed to your wants and should-ing of people and circumstances.

There is a lot happening. It isn't always going to look or feel picture perfect. Trust it anyway. Trust it all the way. Go ahead and truly, truly trust.

⚀ Self Swaddling on page 358
⚁ Wisdom Circle on page 157
⚂ Grief Ritual on page 285
⚃ Unwinding Group Exercise on page 373
⚄ Roll Again
    ⚀ ⚁ Trust Fall on page 170
    ⚂ ⚃ Confession Session on page 150
⚅ Roll Again
    ⚀ ⚁ Healing Hands Circle on page 295
    ⚂ ⚃ Healing Hands On Self on page 295
    ⚄ ⚅ Healing Hands Shared on page 295

Truth Is Relative

When you pull this card it may be time to examine what opinions you have turned into truths. It's time to take a look at what you mean by truth and what meaning you make from it. To start, I'll define and distinguish the following concepts and how I will write them to clarify what is what as we go:

The TRUTH: Finite, definitive, undeniable, constant trueness.
Truth: The experience of truth, the personal knowing of finite definitive, undeniable, constant trueness.
truth: the observable, objective elements to an experience or event.
Story: the meaning we create out of those elements and how they tie together.

Get curious about what's happening, instead of what's "true."
What stories and meanings have you found in your life that you're putting onto other people's realities?
I personally take great comfort in knowing that it is not my job to determine THE TRUTH.
Over the course of my life my capital "T" personal Truths have evolved and changed many times. If you hold a truth hostage, you sometimes miss an opportunity to find an evolved personal Truth and also a deeper and more nuanced Truth.

There is an adage, a saying that goes, "The more I learn the less I know." This is because the Truths we construct are limited by the perspectives that we hold. The more we learn, the larger our context for understanding becomes, and that changes our viewpoints. This often leads to an altering or shifting of what was, what is, and what could be.

Put down the notion that someone has The TRUTH. Lay down attempts to figure out who is *right* and who is *wrong*. Who knows what is true and real? Who is delusional? Pick up an interest in understanding the context for each person's or community's experience that has led them to their view, story, and Truth.

If you can't turn off the system of right/wrong, set the gauge to "everyone is right about their own view." Know that Truth is dependent on who's looking and what they are seeing. Now's a time for you to look at and focus on communication. Who knows the whole deal of reality? *No one*, and if they do, how well can they explain it to someone who does not know? Who would believe this person?

Take a deep breath and stop looking for THE TRUTH. Find the treasure and value in embracing the story as the human you are.

This card can also speak to the frustrating experience of someone else telling you that their truth ought to be yours. Check in to see if someone (perhaps yourself) is trying to tell you that your experience of mysterious truth is wrong. This card is to confirm that your unique and divine experience of love is not to be defined by anything or anyone outside of yourself.

- ⚀ Truth Sorting on page 200
- ⚁ I Am Willing to Admit (I Believe variation) on page 340
- ⚂ Still Meditation on page 205
- ⚃ Organic Movement Meditation on page 204
- ⚄ Go Ahead - Get Heady Convo on page 331
- ⚅ Roll Again
    - ⚀⚁ Wisdom Circle on page 157
    - ⚂⚃ Admitting a Truth on page 183
    - ⚄⚅ Observing on page 198

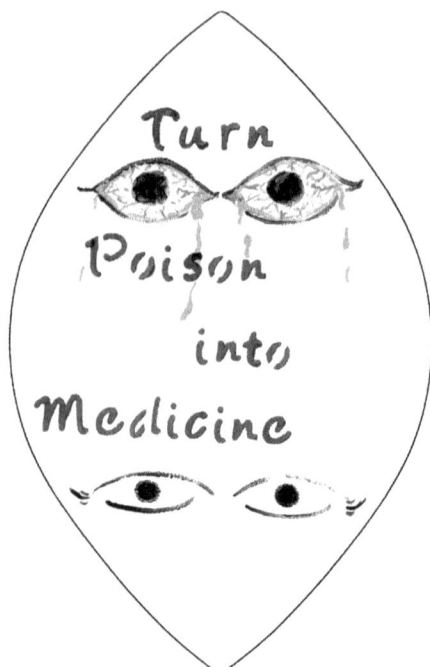

Turn Poison Into Medicine

The process of alchemy is one of turning lead into gold. In this process, more lead means more gold. The alchemy of our lives is in turning the poison of trauma, struggle, blame, and pain into the medicine of wisdom, empathy, compassion, and clarified, empowered action. It is not always a simple equation. Remember, the poison can be anything, and the medicine is embodied, new or renewed, knowing and living.

Transformation comes as a result of determination to be more whole and observant as you live, no matter the circumstances you go through. This cannot be done by simply thinking happy thoughts, looking on the bright side, or by just trying to be a nice person. This requires the courage to go to the very depths; to not stop until you come out on the other side with gratitude for having been inherently and fundamentally changed, by way of the journey itself.

Not everything heals with time. There is a common shared belief that after a trauma we are either "okay" or broken. "Okay" in this case has a general association of what doesn't kill you makes you stronger, but so often there are real debilitating lasting impacts on our ability to function in some way. Many people don't get the additional support they need if they find a way to cope with the experience that makes their needs less visible or invisible to themselves or others. So people are left overly guarded or excessively tired and worn by coping mechanisms.

There is another option, and this is the option of growth, transmutation, and true metamorphosis this is where the truth of what doesn't kill you makes you stronger comes into being. This process of difficultly into rebirth is alchemy.

Alchemy is the process of being completely different and entirely changed. This process changes you into more of yourself.

You can be defined or taken down by the hardships of your life, and some people are. It is also possible to use these experience as a training ground to learn how to rise and alchemize. When you see these situations as initiations into deeper consciousness and soulful evolution, they become thresholds to cross.

No one else can do this to you or for you. You get to learn new skills to become adept at this process. Learn them, use them, and turn what was once your poison into your medicine.

⚀ Alternatives on page 159
⚁ Monster Is My Teacher on page 168
⚂ Self Swaddling on page 358
⚃ Roll Again:
    ⚀ ⚁ Healing Hands Circle on page 295
    ⚂ ⚃ Healing Hands On Self on page 295
    ⚄ ⚅ Healing Hands Shared on page 295
⚄ Despair & Radiance on page 226
⚅ Professional Assistance on page 350

Under Stress More Communication Not Less

If you've pulled this card, it is time for you to start listening and talking.

When things start to get complicated, and we feel even remotely responsible, it's common to launch into a figure-it-out-fix-it-get-it-done mode. Most of us attempt to do that in isolation with the desire to perfect whatever's going on so we can appear good, trustworthy, responsible, lovable, or strong. This can bring out our more manipulative and controlling habits. If not only in singular circumstances, over time this pattern undermines our desires and relationships.

In response to the unpleasant results and expenses of not living by these principles, I developed these following two vows for communication. I live by these tenants as best as I can, always learning and growing into how to do this more:

Under stress, more communication, not less.

Honest communication, at all costs, with compassion for everyone involved, at all times.

If you care about helping other people, working with this practice can be especially difficult. When stress and problems hit the fan, it's instinctual for many caretakers to try to resolve the issue before communicating about what's going on. This card is indicating an opposite course of action. Upon first sight and acknowledgment that there are issues, it's time to start communicating.

In action, this means being vulnerable and bold by doing all of the following:

- Take a breath and get clear.
- Then share what you do know and where you have clarity.
- Next, share what you don't know and what you're confused about.
- Ask direct questions about circumstance and other people's experiences.
    - Listen with care and empathy to their answers without interrupting or explaining your part or anyone else's until the person's sharing is completely finished
- After they are complete, you may share additional or clarifying information, without the agenda of proving why their feelings are wrong -- even though we've all done that before :-)
- If there is missing information, fill them in. Just remember that the perspective they just shared is valid and important.
- Be committed to seeing that there are multiple answers or options to the circumstance at hand, and that everyone has the agency to make choices about their own actions and experiences.

It takes time and effort to cultivate the art of articulate, empathetic, compassionate, and honest communication. That starts with how we speak to our own selves and navigate our most intimate relationships.

Life Hack: When someone else is stressed here is a gift that will serve for decades. Do not ask *if* they need help, *if* they want help, or *if* you can help. Simply ask this simple and direct question, "What can I do to help?"

⚀ Alternatives on page 159
⚁ More Communication on page 197
⚂ Still Meditation on page 205
⚃ Brain Dump on page 186
⚄ Roll Again
    ⚀ ⚁ ⚂ Gibberish Convo on page 162
    ⚃ ⚄ ⚅ Desire Admittance on page 190
⚅ Roll Again
    ⚀ ⚁ ⚂ Group Process Format on page 332
    ⚃ ⚄ ⚅ Needs List Identification on page 152

Use Your Breath As Your Ally

Breath is life force. It is the optimal expression of change. Your breath is your partner. Get into the habit of leaning into this support.

Healing and transformation are a natural occurrence. It is our nature, in body and soul, to move towards an optimal way of being. That movement is the process of change -- change that is already organically trying to happen. We can contribute to change by allowing rather than efforting or forcing. Yes, sometimes we need to take an action to help healing and transformation occur, and yet, most often we just need to allow what is already happening to happen. In many cases it's our resistance to change that slows down the healing, not our inaction. When we come up against an edge, the only thing we really need to do is breathe.

Learn how to use your inhale, exhale, and the hold on either end as your strength. We often hedge the power present in the face of possible shifting, be it physical, spiritual, or emotional. At that point where we have the potential to really step into the moment at hand, we often constrict and hold our breath, restricting the movement of life force through our bodies and beings.

The breath is great for breathing in powerful medicine. Use your breath to give yourself the courage to show up. This is where your breath becomes your ally.

When we breathe in we accept life force.

When we breathe out we let life force flow.

This card is the invitation to utilize breath as a greater force to be called on to bring you through any threshold.

- ⚀ Alternate Nostril Breathing on page 274
- ⚁ Audible Exhale on page 275
- ⚂ Breath of Fire on page 276
- ⚃ Breathe to Stretch on page 276
- ⚄ Cooling Breath on page 276
- ⚅ Mindful Breathing on page 277

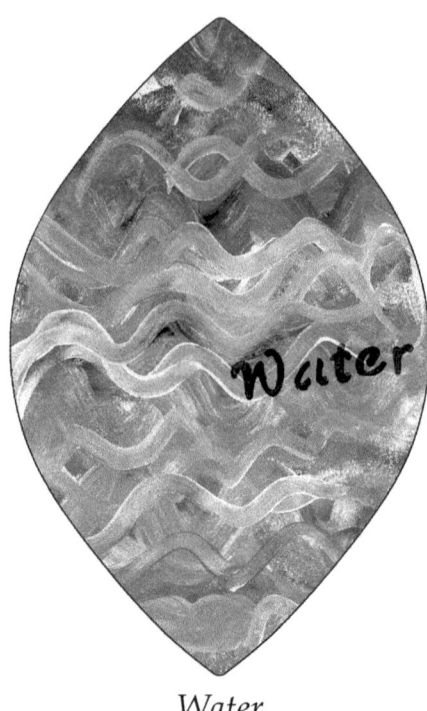

Water

Water. Emotions. Metaphors. Purification. Life. Current. Birth. Fluid movement. Continuous movement. Intuition. Dreams. Flow. Communication to and from the unconscious. Flexible enough to take any shape. Strong enough to break rock. Only needs a crack to get in or out. Dynamic: can be a solid, liquid, or gas.

Water is your teacher and healer right now. Water is always the giver of life. Our physical bodies are mostly made of water. Water tends your body by providing the flow of life for every major organ and system of your physical form. Living or moving water is always a blessing. It is cleansing for our spirit and assists the soul in returning to the center of our being.

Water will help you integrate and unify the wisdom of your dreams and your rational, reasonable self. Its ability to be hard as rock or completely porous means it can teach you how and when to be resilient and unmovable and when to surrender without compromising your integrity. Water is life, and this beloved element wants to help. It is time to either cultivate and begin your relationship with water, or return to this trusted source for wisdom and healing.

⚀ Take a Bath on page 361
⚁ Go Swimming in Living Water on page 332
⚂ Water Healing Ceremony on page 292
⚃ Make an Offering on page 279
⚄ Journaling (Dream Journaling variation) on page 191
⚅ Communing with Elementals (Water) on page 220

We Are Creatures of Habit

We are designed for efficiency. Meaning that we are wired to recognize and initiate patterns. This design can be our downfall as much as it can be our pathway to freedom. The first thing to do here is to acknowledge that you have habits that work towards the life you want and habits that undermine your true desires. Then you can soften enough to observe yourself with compassion, forgiveness, and curiosity.

Here's some good news: we can design and build new habits. We can change the shape of our brain, physical form, and our subtle energetic systems. Through repetition and consistency, we can build new tracks. You can create habits of listening deeply, breathing fully, speaking your truth, connecting with your wisdom, savoring joy, and taking (creating) actions that are in alignment. We can capitalize on our habituating natures.

- ⚀ 40 Day Practice on page 310
- ⚀ Roll Again
    - ⚀⚀⚁ Learn Something New on page 344
    - ⚁⚂⚃ Habit Identification on page 194
- ⚁ Cosmic Shuffle Dance Party on page 322
- ⚂ Habits for Feeling Your Feelings on page 335
- ⚃ Habits for Completing Goals on page 335
- ⚄ Brain Equations on page 187

When We Learn to Mother/Father/Parent as Children We Mother/Father/Parent Like Children

Youthful obsession and lack of grown folk has resulted in many situations that we get to interact with both inside and outside of ourselves. One of those things is the need for people to learn how to Adult.

Directly related is the phenomenon of children parenting their parents. This dynamic can occur through indirect emotional caregiving where the child tries to not need anything. This is also seen when a child has to be the decision maker about when and how things happen like bedtime, eating, what's the schedule, going home and staying out. I am not talking about listening to children's input or needs, I am talking about when the kid is the one who is determining what will happen, directly or indirectly.

When a child is responsible for the wellbeing or general needs of others, they create habits of control for directing life from a limited viewpoint with limited information. Because children do not actually have the means to be the responsible party, they have to come up with creative and often less than ideal solutions. Common strategies are manipulation, people pleasing, tantrums, aggression, bullying, belittling their own needs, anticipating the needs of others, and mitigating conflict and pain in themselves and for other people.

The habits and skills we develop as children are what we use as adults unless we develop alternative methods. While many of the skills developed are useful tools that have resulted in superpowers for people, they are not constructive as habituated ways of being. These are the same patterns we use to navigate within ourselves, as well as with relating to others, be they romantic, business, parental, familial, or social.

When faced with needing to parent a parent as a kid, children tend to navigate the experience in overly simplified ways resulting in juvenile coping mechanisms, like being overly controlling or overly accepting and passive. If new ways of being are not learned, a child who grew up like this will become a grown up who still operates in these immature ways.

These deficits include having no boundaries or sense of self. This can also show up as a willingness to be completely passive in situations where actions are needed, or micro managing things that do not need to be.

Another aspect we are untangling in this process is the cultural pressure to make children and their happiness the focal point for a parent's happiness. Being the primary source of joy for another person is a lot, and is in fact an impossible act to ask a anyone, let alone a kid, to provide.

A well adult can recognize the benefits of boundaries that are clearly defined and also allow for spaciousness, self expression and autonomy. Grown folk know that at a certain point they are not responsible for someone else's happiness or well being. Adulting understands that a clear boundary has an end point, and at some point someone's choices are appropriately beyond your reach. That boundaries for another is limited to caregiving for the innocent or vulnerable. Adulting also understands that different people and circumstance may need changing and dynamic boundaries to be appropriate. Adulting also applies the understanding that there are places and circumstances when strict boundaries, instead of porous ones, are optimal. The ability to navigate and choose what kind of space your are providing for another person through boundaries is an adult discernment skill.

When setting boundaries with other independant being those are based on personal limits and are a personal responsibility to maintain. It is not up to another person to make sure you, as an adult are communicating and upholding your needs in regards to your own limits. That your limits do not need to be justified or pleasing to anyone else, and that it is up to you to navigate those limits with respect and care for yourself and others involved.

This is a collective relearning we are doing. Be brave and kind as you recognize these places of coping and places where you and your loved ones get to grow. This not easy to rewrite as it engages the base programming of our childhood safety and survival. When engaging and changing these habits, hold your tenderness and questions affectionately, because it is vulnerable to ask your survival and relationship training to shift. So gentle gentle as you look around to see where any of these things may be obviously or subtly as work.

⚀ Boundary Patterns Modeled on page 186
⚁ My Little! on page 167
⚂ Fear/Little Meditation on page 237
⚃ Little Check-In on page 323
⚄ Still Meditation on page 205
⚅ Roll Again:
        ⚀ ⚁ ⚂ Organic Movement Meditation on page 204
        ⚃ ⚄ ⚅ Unwinding Group Exercise on page 373

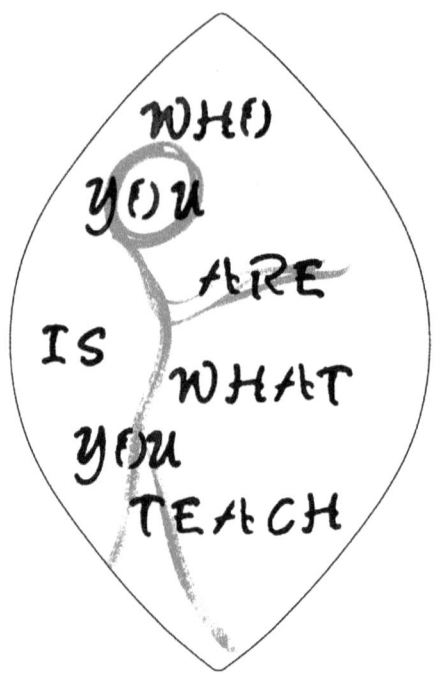

Who You Are Is What You Teach

People often ask me what kind of yoga they should practice. My answer is mostly about teachers. Think of your favorite teacher -- of anything, any subject matter -- and think about what you learned from them. What lasting knowledge did they impart to you? More often than not, peoples' answers are about a sense of "being."

There are exceptions. Exceptional teachers of particular subjects may impart to you a lasting knowledge. Even then, most of the time, the subject is merged with larger life lessons. These come through the nuances -- their sense of humor, honesty, depth of knowledge, commitment to the work, compassion, how articulate and well researched they are -- things that speak more to behavior than information.

Knowing that when you sit with a teacher they will also be teaching you who they are can be incredibly useful. What you practice intentionally is supposed to translate into the rest of your real life. If the majority of what you practice is how you will live, look for teachers who teach in a way that you would want to emulate in your own life with your nearest and dearest.

I look for teachers who have a sense of humor in the midst of challenge; people who call forth an emotional sensitivity and spaciousness. Specifically, I look for someone who's comfortable in the presence of strong emotions, both their own and other people's. I like to see evidence of lived experience with the practice and a commitment to the subject they teach. Be it yoga, therapy, coaching, art, mentorship, and other important teaching relationship. Have the courage and patience to shop around.

As a teacher, you have a profound opportunity to share space with people in an attentive and focused way. Mirror neurons (which emulate behavior and neural activity without conscious engagement) are just one of the ways that we imprint ourselves onto the people we teach while teaching, no matter the subject matter.

The most lasting impact you have on other people could be unrelated to your intended subject. Once you know this, you can capitalize on your strengths and gifts. Integrate the values and personal attributes you'd like to consciously pass on into the topics and structures you are currently teaching.

- ⚀ Processing Feedback on page 153
- ⚁ Professional Assistance on page 350
- ⚂ Design That Match Your Intent on page 190
- ⚃ Soul Unification Healing Meditation on page 258
- ⚄ Boundary Patterns Modeled on page 186
- ⚅ Financial Transparency on page 330

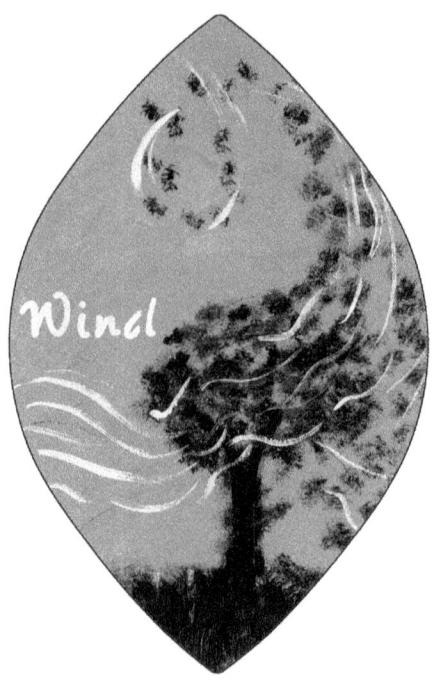

Wind

Air. Mental activity. Creativity. Flexibility. Dynamic change. Complex pattern recognition. The ability to range from subtle to bombastic. Voice and song. Talkativeness. Change. Wild movement. Expression. Playfulness. Responsiveness. Kindness. Breath. Life-Force.

The associations of the wind and air elements are varied. It is time for you to either build a relationship with the element of wind or engage with the relationship you already have. If nothing else, the wind element tells you this: be mindful of you, your breath is your life and power. To live your own life is to express yourself. Change and movement are synonymous with being alive.

- ⚀ Wind Ceremony on page 293
- ⚁ Sing a Song or Play Music on page 281
- ⚂ Wind Prayer on page 373
- ⚃ Roll Again
    - ⚀ Alternate Nostril Breathing on page 274
    - ⚁ Audible Exhale on page 275
    - ⚂ Breath of Fire on page 276
    - ⚃ Breathe to Stretch on page 276
    - ⚄ Cooling Breath on page 276
    - ⚅ Mindful Breathing on page 277
- ⚄ Communing with Elementals (Wind) on page 220
- ⚅ Go Ahead - Get Heady Convo on page 331

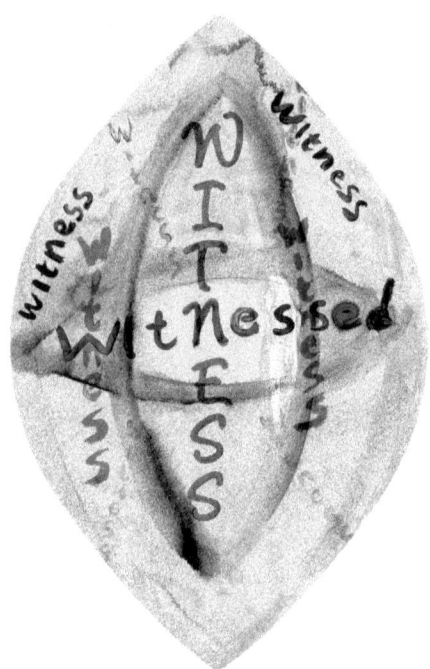

Witness, Witnessed

Being seen, known, heard, and understood is an unparalleled experience for anyone to have. Being with any singular aspect is often transformative. Having them all together at once usually inspires bliss. To witness is to truly be with what is and to hold it with honor. The quality of a witness amplifies the healing potential in any circumstance. Witnessing is the essential element to healing all shame.

Bearing witness and being witnessed are skills. It is time for you to use these skills if you have them, or begin to learn them now for use later. Witnessing is the act of sitting with someone or something and, no matter how you feel about it personally, holding the position of being a loving observer. There are many ways to ensure this stance. Your main focus is to pay attention. Use all of your senses, do your best to soak in the details, and be attentive to nuance. Your job is to be divine at noticing and loving in your presence. This means really taking in what's happening and holding that as more important than your opinion or judgements.

The partner to witnessing is being witnessed. This is a practice of consent and vulnerability. It is not passive to be seen, heard, known, or understood. To allow ourselves to be witnessed requires an engagement of courage and surrender, which is the release of control and, at its core, volunteer exposure. There is power in choosing to be seen and witnessed. All you need is to make the conscious choice and then continue to breathe deeply. Often we must recommit to the choice of being exposed and being seen, breath by breath, moment by moment.

Your witnessing requires self-awareness, self-compassion, and mindfulness because you are responsible to your own well-being so that you may authentically stay present with what's at hand. Here are a few examples to explain the importance of this self-care element of witnessing.

- You have to pee so you are distracted and cannot pay attention. Check in with yourself and then communicate, "Excuse me. I want to be really focused for you. I'm distracted by needing to go to the bathroom. I'm going to do that and come right back. Thank you."
- Someone is sharing an abuse story that is very sad and hard to hear. You can take a deep breath, put your own hand on your own heart, and hold yourself so that you can hold space for them.
- As you're witnessing you feel a dehydration headache coming on. Make choices that allow you to get water and have as much time and space as the feeling needs to move through you.
- You notice that you're having a hard time listening and start to feel disconnected from your body. Share that you are not able to stay present right now. Say that you want the other person to have the focus and attention they need and you are not capable of providing that at this time. Then exit the space or conversation and take care of your own needs to come back into your body.

Both witnessing and being witnessed are arts and needs that many of us are not aware that we have. To be witnessed or to witness in loving observation without having an opinion or judgement is profound. We can develop this reality within ourselves, with others, in nature, and in the midst of any lived experience.

⚀ Eye Gazing on page 228
⚁ Despair & Radiance on page 226
⚂ Unwinding Group Exercise on page 373
⚃ Wisdom Circle on page 157
⚄ Pro-Active Listening on page 352
⚅ Roll Again:
⚀ ⚁ ⚂ Organic Movement Meditation (With Audience) on page 204
⚃ ⚄ ⚅ Still Meditation on page 205

You Are On Time

You.
Are.
On.
Time.
You are not too late. You are not too early. You have not missed your chance. You have not messed up beyond repair. You are on time. There is enough time.

In the journey of awakening, you cannot know what you know until you know. On this journey, it is natural and common to feel upon new awareness that you "should" have known this already. The ache, guilt, shame, frustration, and regret connected to the sense of being late is painful.

Receiving this card means you are not late, nor are you early. There is no wrongness in your place or state of being. You are perfect wherever you are because... that is where you are. The ifs and buts of how off you may be are caused by forgetting that you are a lovable little mystery inside of a gargantuan mystery.

You may be feeling late and behind schedule. You may suffer from a sense of always being behind, especially with important experiences. Even more distressingly, you may feel like you're late to your own life, purpose, or power.

You are not a fuck up. You did not miss your chance.

YOU ARE DOING GREAT!

Feeling bad about not being there sooner doesn't help you get where you want to go. Neither does beating yourself up because you feel guilty about feeling guilty. Feel all the feelings you have and allow the notion that you are still on time even with all of those feelings. Your feelings and the perfection of your timing are not contrary, they are connected. You don't have to understand something for it to be true.

It may be time to reflect on successes you have created. What actions have you taken? How have you changed that brings you closer to being who you want to be? What are you now aware of that has been keeping you back? Are you ready to acknowledge that with love and support so you can move forward? Are you willing to stop trying to shame yourself into changing?

When you pull this card it is likely that you are telling yourself that you are late and bad for it. That's called shaming. That is not as productive as many of us have been led to believe or mentored into doing. Shame is not constructive for personal growth. It is a damaging tactic that undermines our creative problem solving, genuine intimate connections, and our ability to stay present in our bodies. Let's give up shame -- many of us were given this tool as a way to "better ourselves" or show affection and care. This is a good time to recognize that shaming and self bullying are not needed. There are better ways.

What if you chose to believe that, up until this moment, everything, including yourself, has been conspiring on your behalf? What if you let go of wondering where you should be or how you should be different? What happens when you fully take in that you are on time? Do you soften? Do you feel relief? Do you feel possibility and capability opening up inside and outside of you? Do you feel a pang of how it just can't be true? That you have fucked up so terribly? That you've missed your chance?

Bring a hand and a breath to your heart, and let this statement be considered as possible: "I am on time." I encourage you to work with this affirmation if it helps you to open up or show kindness to yourself or another person.

You are on time. Breathe in. Breathe out. You are loved. You are love.

Love is always on time.

⚀ Roll Again:
> ⚀⚁ Healing Hands Circle on page 295
> ⚂⚃ Healing Hands On Self on page 295
> ⚄⚅ Healing Hands Shared on page 295

⚁ Constructive Feedback on page 321

⚂ Roll Again:
> ⚀⚁⚂ Cosmic Shuffle Dance Party (Celebration Style) on page 322
> ⚃⚄⚅ High Fives! on page 162

⚃ I Am On Time on page 307

⚄ Following the Thread on page 329

⚅ Roll Again:
> ⚀⚁⚂ Freeze on page 165
> ⚃⚄⚅ Brain Dump on page 186

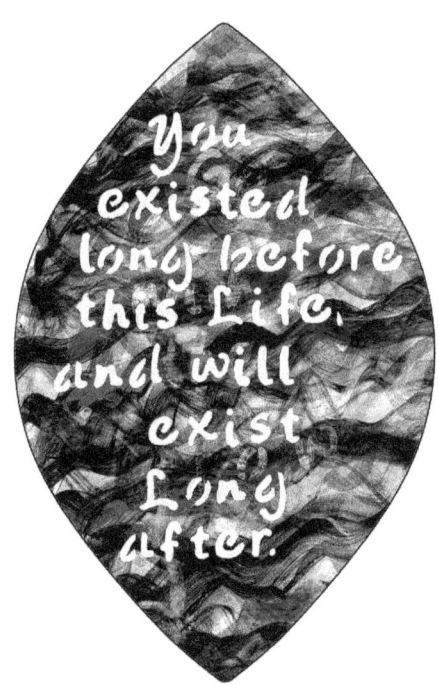

You Existed Long Before This Life, and Will Exist Long After

Whether you know your existence is some profound spiritual mystery or only the concrete proven reality, you have a "you" in this life, and yet what you are made up of is something that began before your current form. The molecular and atomic structures that construct your physical existence started long before you, and will continue to exist long after you. From the soulful perspective, the essence that is uniquely you is by nature infinite, reaching far beyond the limits of the space/time continuum.

This aspect of you is called many things. We create a variety of names for something which is by nature limitless: Soul, Spirit, Love, Satnam, Vibrational Signature, Self, Godself, I Am, Limitless Being, Timeless Entity, more and more. I believe that this is because (same as our numerous names for big Divinity) the action of naming is both powerful and, by nature, simultaneously limiting. The limiting can be both useful and inaccurate.

Breathe into the perspective that you have journeyed from out of the cosmic soup into this limited and sacred form, into this sacred life. We are here on an epic journey of unifying self with Self. I call this process Soul Unification -- unifying our limited self with our limitless Self. The path is the product. No matter its configuration it is sacred. Allow for the peace and possibility that you are more than this life. Relax and see how deeply you can be held by a loving mystery.

Remember what you already know.

⚀ Soul Unification Healing Meditation on page 258
⚁ Stardust on page 179
⚂ Sat Nam on page 308
⚃ Wisdom Circle on page 157
⚄ Birth the World on page 317
⚅ Roll Again
    ⚀ ⚂ Still Meditation on page 205
    ⚂ ⚃ Mirror Meditation on page 241
    ⚄ ⚅ Organic Movement Meditation on page 204

You Make You Orgasm

The only person who has ever made you orgasm is yourself. It's your body, your energy, your ecstasy, and your pleasure. You are the gatekeeper of these experiences. That means two things. One is that no one else is responsible for your pleasure, and two, you are responsible for your pleasure.

It is up to you to know yourself emotionally, physically, mentally, and spiritually.

This awareness is part of ending subtle and overt habits of codependence.

For satisfaction and health, you must own *your* sexuality because it is *your* power. When we give other people control over ourselves in any capacity it is because we have forfeited. Receiving this card is a call back to reality for you to get clear real and honest about who has the reins over your power. It is always your power. You can't give that away. You can question who is acting as director.

Your sexuality is part of your medicine, your healing and wholing self. You want to maximize your healing so you are now being called to get to know your creative and generative self better. Sexuality, orgasms, and ecstasy are not limited to genitalia. Your desires and creative forces are essential components in the creation of your life and manifestation of your dreams.

Own it.

- ⚀ Responsibility Charting on page 198
- ⚁ What I Want In Sexy Time on page 201
- ⚂ Cosmic Shuffle Dance Party (Sensual and Sexual) on page 322
- ⚃ Two Minutes of Silence Then Share on page 156
- ⚄ Self Swaddling on page 358
- ⚅ Tour of the Pelvic Bowl on page 362

Your, My, Our, The Healing

Your healing. My healing. Our healing. The healing.

Embrace the perspective of interconnectedness and oneness. It is time for you to recognize that the healing you experience is yours, and is not *just* yours. Any healing you allow to take place in your being is inherently an act of service. The same is true for someone else's healing.

When you are in a medicine circle and the focus is on another person, you are receiving healing for their process. When you are the focus, your healing and transformation is a gift to all.

This is also true in the collective. When someone, anyone, anywhere, is healing, this reverberates through the entire web of consciousness. Right now, somewhere someone is healing something in themselves and that is rippling through us all. That is because there is an inherent thread that we are all sharing. The healing is not just theirs, or yours, or even just ours, it is in essence the miracle and moment of The Healing, a nature and core vibration of what healing is. The Healing is not personal in its existence, although it is deeply personal in its experience.

All healing is The Healing. Your healing is yours personally to undertake, and no one else's. You must do and allow The Healing in a way that only you can. And also at the same time space, your healing is also my healing. As your healing happens, I have my own personal response and experience of healing in myself. Concurrently, The Healing is also ours, you and I connected, our suffering and healing shared together because on at least one plane of existence it is a unified moment in which no separation occurs.

All vibrational experiences exist in this perspective, and in that way it is true for everything that can be known.

My suffering is your suffering is our suffering is *The* Suffering.

My grief is your grief and is our grief. All because it is the experience of *The* Grief.

Your anger is also my anger, our shared anger because we are feeling *The* Anger.

And so it goes for our joy which is my joy and your joy for it is the presence of *The* Joy.

My gratitude. Your gratitude. Our gratitude. The Gratitude.

These experiences pass through, visit, and are birthed through us.

For this moment allow this perspective to feed you: Your = My = Our = The. It's just what is.

⚀ Roll Again
　　⚀ ⚁ Still Meditation on page 205
　　⚂ ⚃ Healing Hands On Self on page 295
　　⚄ ⚅ Healing Hands Shared on page 295
⚁ Healing Hands Circle on page 295
⚂ Birth the World on page 317
⚃ Soul Unification Healing Meditation on page 258
⚄ Visiting Our Inner Temple on page 268
⚅ We Are In This Together on page 180

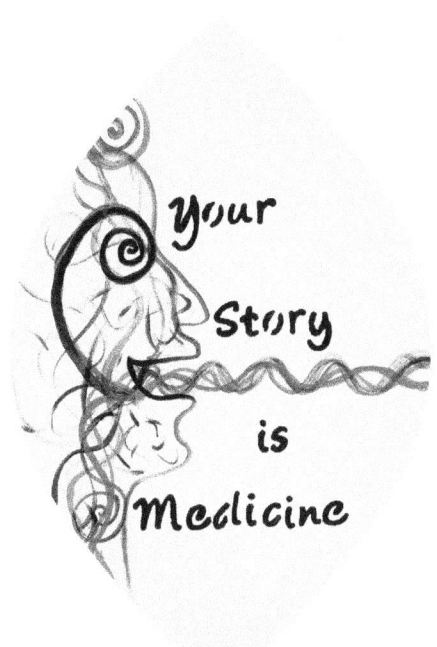

Your Story Is Medicine

As much as your journey is yours alone, it is also equally shared. The lessons that we, the individuals, learn along the way, are the lessons that We, the collective, are learning along the way as well. The suffering that we experience is also shared suffering -- The Suffering. The joy that we move through as individuals is also collective -- The Joy.

When we find ourselves in feelings of isolation, walled off from other people in our experience, lessons that seem uniquely our own can feel to be almost inconsequential or a nuisance to share with others. This is not the case.

When we sit in the profound honesty of our story, our own personal journey becomes exquisite. Your struggles, your questions, and the actions you take to reconcile your feelings and thoughts become a mirror for other people to see themselves in. When we share our story, that which we thought to be only ours becomes reflected, validated, and affirmed.

Time and time again, I have sat in circles and spaces where people have had the courage to vulnerably share their story -- exposing their shortcomings, like anger or personal weakness, and their strengths, like brilliance, resilience, and inspiring love. Let me be clear, these people thought they were just sharing their story, even to the point where they felt it to be burdensome to those with whom they shared. Over and over the people listening felt connection, kinship, empathy, and the peace that comes from no longer feeling alone.

The balm is in the wound. Often while sharing about something that has felt to be a burden within ourselves, circumstance, or experience with radical vulnerability and deep listening to ourselves, we discover new wisdom within the very thing that felt like a weight. It is important, within the space of sharing and wholeness, that we unravel the toxicity of our stories, and unlock the liberating capacity contained therein.

If you already carry the responsibility of knowing your story as medicine, this card serves as a reminder to strengthen the container around what you share. Name it as powerful, own it as medicine. The moment before you share a powerful story like that, say something to the effect of, "May the medicine of this story be strengthened by sharing it and may all those who hear it be served." Give your story the space to embody and allow for the full impact of sharing.

- ⚀ Personal Medicine Story on page 152
- ⚁ Despair & Radiance on page 226
- ⚂ Physical Storytelling on page 169
- ⚃ Heard Medicine Story on page 152
- ⚄ Wisdom Circle on page 157
- ⚅ Record a Story and Listen to Yourself on page 345

Part Two

Practices

Round Robins

INSTRUCTIONS

What to Do as a Group

Round Robin is done by going around the circle sharing. The person who picked the card goes first. Each person shares their response to the prompt or participation in the exercise. Get all the way around the circle and the person who picked the card gets a second chance to go again if they want. If you are concerned about time use a timer and give everyone equal time.

Take a moment before going around the circle for people to silently check in with themselves or take a note about thoughts before the sharing starts. Then focus on actively listening and let go of preparing what will be said. Sharing what comes to you in the moment of your turn is often when some magic happens for people, so do you best to just go with the flow and give up over thinking. Listen and do not talk over one another. Be mindful that each person has uninterrupted space to share. When your time comes, speak about your own experience and not about what other people have already said or done.

What to Do with Yourself

When you are doing this practice on your own, do the prompt as a journaling exercise or say your answers out loud. If you write down your responses, re-read what you've written aloud to yourself. Bonus choice: invite spiritual witness (you can read more about that in the Witness, Witnessed teaching on page 132).

ALIGNMENT

You can review the Instructions for Round Robins on page 149 and then respond to the following prompt.

I know I'm misaligned in...
   I know I can shift one thing by...

CONGRATS YOU SURVIVED

You can review the Instructions for Round Robins on page 149 and then respond to the following prompt.

There is this thing I do in my life that I hate that I do. It is...
   The worst part about it is...
   I can now see that I first started doing this as a way to protect me from...
   Instead, I wish I would...

CONFESSION SESSION

You can review the Instructions for Round Robins on page 149 and then respond to the following prompt.

This is a time to make a confession. Something that you either haven't told people or avoid talking about in general. The main way to move through shame is with exposure. You must share what is covered by the blanket of shame to be able to get clear access to what's underneath so you can move forward. Go ahead... confession session.

COMMITMENT AND COURSE REFLECTION

You can review the Instructions for Round Robins on page 149 and then respond to the following prompt.

Remember and name the commitments you've made.
   Do you have commitments that are silent? (un-communicated or assumed expectations)
   Are you on course with keeping them?
   Do you want to change any of your out loud or silent agreements?

ETHER

You can review the Instructions for Round Robins on page 149 and then respond to the following prompt.

Ask Ether the question, "What are you?" Silently contemplate Ether's answer for three minutes and then share what you've received. There are no wrong answers!

RECEIVING AND EXPRESSING BURNOUT/SUSTAIN

You can review the Instructions for Round Robins on page 149 and then respond to the following prompt.

Write down one thing that you have a hard time receiving or letting in, and one thing you have a hard time expressing, giving, or letting go. Then answer these questions:
　The thing I have a hard time receiving or letting in is...
　The thing I have a hard time expressing, giving, or letting go is...
　The fear of change that is keeping my full, unobstructed flow from happening is...
　I realize...
　I am going to...

HARD TO HEAR

You can review the Instructions for Round Robins on page 149and then respond to the following prompt.

Each person starts by asking the group, "Are you willing to tell me something that you question my ability to really hear?" Everyone gets a chance to offer an answer. No one is obligated to share. If deciding to participate, honesty is the most potent part of this practice.

HEALING IN A MOMENT REFLECTION

You can review the Instructions for Round Robins on page 149 and then respond to the following prompt.

Recall and share these two things:
　First, an epiphany, profound realization, or healing that you have experienced.
　Second, an opportunity when you let a moment pass that you knew was special. Why and what have you learned since then?

HEARD MEDICINE STORY

You can review the Instructions for Round Robins on page 149 and then respond to the following prompt.

Share a story that you carry with you for wisdom or strength. This can be a myth, personal tale, a family parable, religious teaching, something you heard on the radio, or a story from any other source that you treasure as valuable.

PERSONAL MEDICINE STORY

You can review the Instructions for Round Robins on page 149 and then respond to the following prompt.

Tell a story of growth. Start with a problem, struggle, or what seemed like a doomed moment. Share the journey that you took through the experience, including what you learned and how you were changed by the process.

NAMING FOUNDATIONAL BELIEF SYSTEMS

You can review the Instructions for Round Robins on page 149 and then respond to the following prompt.

I still function from the foundational belief system that...
   Comment on whether you think you still believe this.

NEEDS LIST IDENTIFICATION

You can review the Instructions for Round Robins on page 149 and then respond to the following prompt.

Review the Need≠Wrong Need=Need teaching on page 71 and then read through the Nonviolent Communication™ Needs Inventory list. Identify and share at least one need you already knew you had and at least one need you didn't realize you had until reviewing the list.
   Look over the Feelings Inventory List and identify a feeling for when that need is being met in your life, and a feeling for when it is not.

OWNERSHIP PROMPT

You can review the Instructions for Round Robins on page 149 and then respond to the following prompt.

I see now how I contributed to...
 I can space to forgive myself and the other people involved by...

PROCESSING FEEDBACK

You can review the Instructions for Round Robins on page 149 and then share in response to the following prompt.

Read this teaching on processing feedback and then reflect on three experiences you have had in which you have these responses or imagine you could.

Processing feedback is an essential part of empowered learning.
 It's not what is said in the feedback that is most important, it is how you respond to what is shared. Learn how to take what is offered and run it through your own truth-distilling system.
 Here are some examples of approaches to understanding your response to feedback being given.

1. If you get really defensive and feel like the feedback is inherently offensive and "totally out of line" I encourage you to take it in and sit with the experience. It's likely that there is something incredibly valuable in the feedback and what's coming up in response. What's getting to you might not be exactly what was said, but it obviously touched something, so go find out what that something is. This is feedback to sit with and possibly explore with people who you know and will be honest.
2. If you are nonplussed, neither here-nor-there about the feedback, then let it go, for now. If it is simple enough to implement, give it a go and see how it works. Perhaps at a later time you may find more or less value in it.
3. If your response is a very clear, sometimes quiet, and definitive, "No, that's not it," then trust that. Remember not to take anything personally ever, even super-sweet make-you-feel-so-shiny feedback.
4. If the feedback lights up every cell in your being screaming, "I'VE BEEN SEEN! I AM KNOWN! YES! THAT'S TOTALLY TRUE!" Well then, hug that close, follow and tend that information, and carry it to your depths.
5. If there is bottomless pit of, "Give me more feedback more, more, more, more, more..." I encourage you to consider that you are

unable to hear the message for which you're looking. Notice you are looking outside yourself for answers, so it's time to go inside and listen to see what is there, and what may be stopping you from hearing your answers.

Remember to take time to let feedback sink in, using the steps above and other reflective and digestive practices.

SEASONAL WISDOM

You can review the Instructions for Round Robins on page 149 and then share in response to the following prompt.

Read this teaching on the seasons and then reflect on the season you are in.

These seasonal teachings are inspired and refers to shared teachings and my lived experience of four season temperate climate in the northern hemisphere. The teachings have translated well all over the globe, even though the look and feel of the seasons change. So adjust the plants growth descriptions to your local seasonal cycles, and explore to see if the long night, long day serves you. Ask the land you stand on for a more local or specific insight. If you're not sure how you feel, or what's going on, just look at the trees.

Every season has its way of inviting us to slow down, to rest, to integrate. Every season has its way to wake us up, lead us into work, and inspire us.

Spring: Sprouting to Blossom

This is the season of longer days and shorter nights.
    Spring moves from inside to outside, rising pushing energy for new growth and work.
    Decisiveness, shouting, cultivation inside and outside, soften, thaw, emerge, grow, resilience, action, new work. Make a strong container of permission of self for your change, and rest by slowing down to notice the subtle sensual pleasures, smell the brave flowers and soft thawing dirt.
    The gift of the season is it is the fastest period of growth in the journey throughout the year. Ride the current and watch everything change. Fast. The challenge is to not lose your mind while it happens.
    The rising energy ignites and encourages sexual appetite for creative flow. Tend your sexual being with gentleness and attentiveness, channel your powerful energy intentionally.
    A medicine for this time is to create a container that is big enough for the

energy moving, but close enough that you feel supported and held in this vulnerable and massively moving time. What this looks like practically is quiet time for yourself even as the days warm and people come out. Organizing structures to support the new growth, forgiveness and compassion with the havoc feeling, and really slowing down to take in the subtle and nourishing beauty of spring inside you, outside in nature, and in the people who are growing and changing as well. Enjoying your sensuality will help you stay present in this high vibrating time.

Summer: Blossom to Fruiting

This is the season of long days.

Summer summons you go outside and work. Be spent with fervor and rest often as you go!

Giving, singing, sexual and creative expression. Express! Share! Expand!

The Gift of summer is GO GO GO energy surrounding you and the pull for community and connection, the challenge is to take the extra breaths you need to make sure when you rest, you rest, and to communicate in the fast pace of the season. Satisfying community experience requires quality communication.

A medicine for this time is long days with community that involves a variety of playful, focused, collaborative, witnessing connections. Thorough communication about logistics so that the time together is play filled, expressive and exploratory. Exploring is wonderful, and for it to be satisfying for many people at once, voicing our needs and asking questions is important to make sure all are being taken care of well.

Autumn: Harvest to Preparation

This is the season of shorter day and longer nights.

Autumn energy invites us to bring the outside energies inside.

The gift of the season is harvest! All the dreams and wishes you planted in the spring have come to full growth, do the work of harvest . The challenge of the season is this is the season of acknowledging, grief and gratitude. It requires sorting, follow through, and diligent work. This gift an challenge of the season at once is the access to ancestors and the thin space between the material and subtle realms.

A medicine for the season is to sort your harvest to see what is to be kept for winter or in general moving forward. Implement and show up in the physical and material world. Work, savor, feast, and rest. Make strong decisions about what is to be used now, at the peak of the harvest overflow, what needs to be prepared so you will have it when resources are low, and what needs to be put to the compost and let go of entirely.

This is an essential time to be willing to let things go that no longer serve you.

In addition, lean into your lineage and ancestors to help give perspective and wisdom, they are speaking to you - *listen*.

Winter: Fallow to Vision

This is the season of long nights.

Go inside, surrender and let the mystery do the work. Rest outside.

Silence, healing, praying, visions and dream of what you wish to create, clearing, bone truth, simplicity, trusting the long night.

The gift of the season is depth and medicine of nothingness, emptiness, spaciousness, quiet, and rest. The challenge of the season is the heaviness, death, fear, obsolescence, and isolation. The bold action of this season is no, slow, or limited action.

Common practices for nourishing in the winter is to be quiet and go deep, to share ceremonies of light, and gentle festive gatherings of art, storytelling, truth telling, sharing and listening. Slow down, and allow the gatherings to be reflective and truly heart, body, and soul warming events.

Give up the show of go, go, go and winter becomes a sanctuary of growth of deep love.

Seasonal Cusps

This is the time when one season is wrapping up and the other is beginning. It is the time of changing systems and rhythms of life.

The gift and challenge of this time is change and all the things that come with change: excitement, grief, fear, impatience, inspiration, visions, overwhelm. Death and endings of the body, mind, and/or heart. New arrivals of information, resource, agreements of the material and soul. All these things need space to allow full movement.

TWO MINUTES OF SILENCE THEN SHARE

You can review the Instructions for Round Robins on page 149 and then respond to the following prompt.

Take two minutes for silent meditation (see the Still Meditation practice on page 205). Then go around the group and share aloud one at a time. If practicing on your own, journal or speak aloud to yourself after the meditation.

WISDOM CIRCLE

You can review the Instructions for Round Robins on page 149 and then respond to the following prompt.

Take a timed three minutes to breathe in and out of you heart, womb, or wise self or all three.

Go around the circle, allowing each person to share from the deepest part of themselves.

Before you speak, ask yourself, "What needs to be shared right now?"

Only one person speaks at a time.

When it is your time to speak, speak about your own experience. This is not an advice circle.

In-between each person's share, everyone takes three breaths -- one breath to honor what was shared, one breath to come into the present, and one breath to prepare for the next share.

If practicing on your own, journal or speak aloud to yourself after the three minutes of conscious breath.

Games

INSTRUCTIONS

The following exercises are based on the concept and practice of cooperative play, role playing and improvisational theater. This is the art and play of taking on different roles than the ones we usually experience. Role playing can also explore altering one of our existing roles in an exploration of possibility. Here are some things to keep in mind:

1. Play with your body and posture. Exaggerate the physical elements that you are playing with. For example, if you're exploring confidence, let your body be really big. If you're exploring the weight of grief, let the body be really heavy. This embodiment practice will help fuel and guide language that may be helpful in finding something new in the situation.
2. Don't overthink things. Just say the first thing that comes to your head and do the first things you are inclined to do and then go from there. You can't break the game.
3. No one else has to get it right either. This practice is meant to widen perspectives, not to replicate or rehearse how exactly anything was or should be.
4. Trust yourself and trust your scene partners. Let the magic of nonjudgmental play take over, and see where you're taken.
5. Go with the flow.
6. When doing a long form scene-based game, I encourage you to trust the playfulness and magic of letting go of control. If the person who pulled the card needs a re-do, wait until the round completes. This allows everyone to relax and go with the flow without needing to get anything right. Ask to do the role play again with different or additional instructions.

7. Some games we do by ourselves, others with partners, others in a group all together. Some will take a few minutes or even just a few seconds and others will go for over a half hour. It's all good medicine.
8. If you need to pause the scene, say, "Reality Check."[3] Everyone should freeze and repeat, "Reality Check." The person who called it then explains what's coming up. All play is suspended until this person determines it's been resolved. This agreement allows dialogue, such as, "That hurts," or "Stop," to be playable and safe.

ALTERNATIVES

You can review the Instructions for Games on page 158 and then do the following role play.[4]

What to Do as a Group

Finding alternatives to our ingrained patterns can seem to be the most difficult part of transformations. "How could I do it differently?" is a common question. There are two things to bear in mind. First, heal and transform from your core, and you will find yourself just doing things differently. Secondly, find alternatives and then enact them and you will change yourself from the outside in. With both of these suggestions, shaming or blaming yourself does not allow for actual healing, just more patterns of "not getting caught" or "trying to be good." The exploration is for you, in all your beauty, rawness, and wholeness to be here, expressed in a way that honors yourself, the planet, and those you love.

This exercise is intended to help create options for the person who pulled the card to have access to or start the process of embodying alternative ways to be. The more raw and specific you are with the starting point, the more options you have for deeper healing to emerge.

Take a few breaths. Let a pattern, or a coping mechanism you'd like to do differently come to the surface. Then think of a specific example from your real life where this behavior has occurred. Share the details of this scenario: Who is there? What are they like? Describe some defining

---

[3] "Reality Check" is a term I first learned from Howard Moody and Brian Allison as part of their Adventure Game Theater program. Similar and evolved experiences are offered for adults and teens across the country through summer camp and programming by The Wayfinder Experience, LLC.

[4] This exercise is inspired by a number of different theater processing tools I have used. Namely, I draw here from the Theater of the Oppressed model by Augusto Boal, and the recommended model of sharing at the end comes from that practice as well.

characteristics of the people or circumstance. When did it happen? Where were you? How did it play out?

From the group present, enlist the people you need to play the other parts in the scene. You will replay this skit a number of times. The first time, play out what you have been doing. Play the pattern as you see and feel it, in all its glory and dysfunction.

Next, someone else who has an idea about what you could do differently, will take your place and the skit will start over from the beginning. Do this at least twice, and ideally do it over and over again. Each time, have someone else play you and offer an alternative way to navigate this experience. The alternatives offered don't have to be "better" options. They could even be the worst case scenario choices (or what we think those to be), because there may be gems to receive in those rounds too.

After a range of options have been offered, re-enter the space as yourself and play out your own alternative. You can redo the scene a few times to try out multiple versions. Then give yourself permission to possibly take one or a variation of one into the rest of your life.

Sharing after the role play part of this practice is important. First, people who witnessed but did not participate share what they saw and learned. Then people who acted out can share. Finally, you share last, having the final word in that vulnerable and empowering space.

What to Do with Yourself

Follow the instructions above, imagining the role play by writing or narrating the scenarios as stories you are telling.

ASCENDING OFF AND ON

You can review the Instructions for Games on page 158 and then do the following role play.

You can review the teaching of the Ascend onto the Planet Card on page 9.

The person who pulled the card is going to act out two scenes. You can enlist other people, if they are there, to act things out too. If you are not pulled in, your job is to witness.

First, in an exaggerated way, depict what ascending *off* the planet can look and sound like.

Secondly, when that is complete, act out what ascending *onto* the planet can look and sound like.

CLEARING DELUSION

You can review the Instructions for Games on page 158 and then do the following exercise.

Everyone stands in their own space.

Place your feet wide, double hips distance apart and bend your knees in a high squat.

With your pelvic floor open, take a breath and imagine your grounding cord going deep into the earth. (For more guidance on your grounding cord you can do the Grounding Cord practice on page 240.)

Raise your arms above your head, straight over your shoulders, with your palms open and facing each other. Choose to use this motion and breath to clear all delusions and obstructions from your body, mind and spirit.

Take a big inhale in and as you exhale bring your elbows down to your sides with a gently snap, closing your fists, making a loud "HUH" from your gut, and slightly bending your knees. On the inhale, reset to your starting position.

Repeat the motion 10 times.

CONTACT MOVEMENT WITH WRISTS

You can review the Instructions for Games on page 158 and then do the following exercise.

What to Do as a Group

Get into partners.

Sit across from each other, bent elbows distance apart, so you can cross wrists with each other. It doesn't matter how your wrists are touching at the start, just that they are.

Begin with one person leading gentle movement, maintaining contact of the wrists. You can move your wrists up and down, side to side, in circles, or in twists, any way that you want.

Then switch so the other person is leading gentle movement, maintaining contact of the wrists.

Notice how you can move that keeps your partner in sync and what you can do a leader that leaves them behind, practice being a quality leader and follower.

Then try to let go of either person leading. Both of you are leading. Both of you are following. See you you can close track and find a flow.cExplore and play. See what is possible.

Advanced practice: extend this movement up the arms, journeying onto the shoulders or back, rising to your feet, allowing your whole body to do this organic, simple exploration of maintaining contact while in movement.

What to Do with Yourself

Physically sit or stand with your arms out while imagining you have a partner there in front of you. Follow the instructions above with your partner.

Wild times: if you'd like you can invite a spirit guide, angel, or a beloved ancestor to come and be your partner and play the game.

GIBBERISH CONVO

You can review the Instructions for Games on page 158 and then do the following game.

Have a heartfelt gibberish conversation with yourself or in pairs.

Gibberish is a made up language, constructed of sounds, linked together. At times, it may sound similar to other languages you have heard or know about. It is not about pretending to speak a language you don't know or making fun of others languages. The intent is to bypass the rational linguistic part of the thinking process, and allow the voice to express and tell a story without known words.

First, everyone makes all the gibberish sounds they can for 30 seconds.

When in a group get into parters, when prating individually play both parts.

Now you are to have a complete conversation in gibberish. Go back and forth sharing about something that is important to you and then listening to the other persons sharing and responding.Do it all in this made up language. Playfully, heart-fully, just without known words. Share and listen. Listen and share.

After a few minutes of really getting into it, finish the conversation.

HIGH FIVES!

You can review the Instructions for Games on page 158 and then do the following exercise.

Everybody gives each other High Fives or High Ten
   This is meant to be joyful, silly, and simple.
   The trick to a rocking a high five or high ten is to look at the other person's elbow

Embellish with "YES!" or other hip and/or silly terms of excitement and congratulations

THE FUNNY FACE GAME

You can review the Instructions for Games on page 158 and then do the following game.

What to Do as a Group

1. Sit in a circle.
2. One person starts, makes a funny face.
3. Turn to the person on the left, the person on the left mirrors and trie to match the face.
4. Then both turn slowly presenting the face to the rest of the circle, bringing their faces back to each other and then releasing them.
5. Then the person who just received the face, makes a new face, and shares it with the person to the left and presents to the circle. So on and so forth.

What to Do with Yourself

Bring this game to the next social gathering you are part of, you can say, "hey everyone, I would like to play a silly game, would you join me?"

Now practice by making at least 5 different silly faces. Holding each face for a breath or so.

FUELS OF IMPROV

You can review the Instructions for Games on page 158 and then review the following teaching.

Improv is short for improvisational theater. Which is simply when you play make-believe, make up a scene and act it out without a script. Life's an improv game every day. Play it that way using tips and tricks for good improvisational theater and it will improve your way through life.

Fuels of Improv

1. Say "Yes, And..."
    - Accept and build
    - Validate and expand and/or deepen
    - The heart of this fuel is that you first accept the offer that

has been made, make an effort, to accept and validate, acknowledge, with action and word what has been shared with you. This can be by agreeing but it can also be through empathy. THEN follow that with another offer, "Yes, AND" this is also part of the picture. Building upon what has been shared by expanding and deepening the offer by adding details or backing up they story presented.

2. Make your partner look good
   - When we make our partners look good, we in turn make a stronger scene, making our own selves look better. We do this by sighting opportunities to lift up a great offer, idea, or action. We can also do this when we see our partner floundering by jumping in and taking the pressure off them, or by focusing in and making their struggle valid and supported by spacious allowance to have it be revealed and resolved slowly and authentically by them.
   - Make strong offers. Establish what you see, what you want, where you are and your relationship to the objets, character around you or in your story. Avoid asking questions, unless they are establishing character relationship, location, and objective.

3. Go with the flow
   - Say the first thing that comes to mind, trust your intuition and instincts knowing that what they are giving you is valuable information. Take your time and be spacious and slow down in your mind, so that your actions are conscious choices. Do this by not trying too hard. You don't need to try to be unique, by trusting and following your own impulses, your material will be interesting and there will be plenty to work with.

4. Violence Ends the scene
   - In theater, conflict or the threat of conflict, is much more interesting than the violence itself. Violence and death is it's own scene. If you move to violence it is much harder to return to the scene without violence. So take the time and space to play the scene out before moving towards outward aggression.

5. Play the status of the scene
   - In theater status is a way of describing relationship dynamics. Everything has a relationship. Things we treat with respect have higher status than things we treat like trash. People, places, and objects all have status relationships with each other and you. Lean into that and make strong choices to support the communication of that

status position.

FREEZE

You can review the Instructions for Games on page 158 and then do the following game.

What to Do with Yourself

Schedule a game night with a few friends and have everyone bring one game they like to play. You offer this one. In addition, to making these plans if you would like roll again for an additional practice for this moment.

What to Do as a Group

Two people get up in the front.
 THE START:
 Move around and around making funny shapes with your body and faces and then someone from the audience yells "freeze."
 The two people USING the positions of their body start a scene. They are different people. They can be anything-trees, animals, elders at a bus stop, people building the ancient temples.
 GAME:
 Give people a chance to build a scene, establish a location, relationship, and activity or goal about 2 minutes.
 Then go around in the circle twice so everyone gets a chance to get the feel and then a chance to play in the game with a greater sense of flow. You can set a timer to keep the flow going, so the scenes change every 2-3 minutes. When the timer goes everyone shouts "FREEZE".
 The people in the scene freeze.
 The new scene partner goes up tags the person whole is in the position you want to take on, or if the position is not a determining factor tag and take the spot for the person who has been in the longest.
 The new scene partner takes on the physical position of the person they tagged out and now START a NEW scene.
 As the new scene person aim to offer a relationship, where they are and what they are doing as best and as fast as they can
 If you want to keep playing after two round around the circle you can After going around the circle anyone can yell freeze and then they are the person to go tag someone out and start a new scene.
 , someone from the audience yells "FREEZE!"
 The people in the scene freeze.

The person who yelled freeze goes up tags one of the people out and takes their physical position, they now START a NEW scene.

The new scene person ought to offer a relationship, where they are and what they are doing.

Continues on and on.

Review Fuels of Improv (page 163) for more on making freeze the most fun or insightful ever

MAKE THE ROOM

You can review the Instructions for Games on page 158 and then do the following game.

What to Do with Yourself

Schedule a game night with a few friends and have everyone bring one game they like to play. You offer this one. In addition to making these plans, if you would like, roll again for an additional practice for this moment.

What to Do as a Group

Silent Exercise:
Person #1 enters a space and establishes the placement and kind of door goes inside and mimes an object in the room, then exits the room through the same door

Person #2 enters the space through the door uses person #1 object in the room, uses/creates/establishes and ADDITIONAL NEW object in the room and exits through the same door

Person #3 enters the room through the door uses #1 and #2 person's objects and establishes ONE NEW additional object

This continues until every person has entered the space and used all the objects.

Once the room is established two people at a time, enter the room and interact with the space and the items there.

Work to maintain consistency of spacing. USE the door. Turn off the sink , etc.

MY LITTLE!

You can review the Instructions for Games on page 158 and then do the following role play.

Here are guidelines for doing this role play with two or more people to be done in partners, below are guidelines for doing this as an individual practice. This is a practice I use regularly with a doll as a way to tend my Little and to cultivate and practice my Adulting. I encourage whether in group or practicing individually to find a doll or Little to play with like this on your own time, repeatedly.

What to Do as a Group

You are going to play "Your Little" and will pick someone else to be "You" -- role playing you to the best of their ability. The scene will start with your Little feeling discontent or upset. The scene starts with The Other Person Playing You saying, "Hey, Little [Your Name], I'm [Your Name]. Do you know who I am? I am here because I care. How are you feeling?"

Respond as Your Little. Let the scene unfold from there.

The "You" played by someone else needs to have infinite patience and curiosity, and also needs to be authentic and sincere. Do more listening and asking than telling. When Little has questions to ask, answer honestly and fully to your knowing. If the person role playing You needs to ask for clarifying questions to the source, that's fine. Do what needs to be done to be helped through the scene.

If you'd like to describe the situation to two other people and watch the scene instead of playing your Little yourself, that is welcome too. If you'd like to act out a memory from Your Little, sometimes this will occur inside the conversation in the unfolding scene. In this case, you may want additional people from the group to role play as well, or the first person can play multiple roles.

After this first scene is complete, switch. Now someone else plays Your Little and you get to talk to and share with them.

What to Do with Yourself

Be yourself and find a doll or object to embody Your Little. Act out the entire scene being both voices, speaking out loud. Start with the question, "Hey, Little [Your Name], I'm [Your Name]. Do you know who I am? I am here because I care. How are you feeling?" Let the interaction unfold from there.

MONSTER IS MY TEACHER

You can review the Instructions for Games on page 158 and then do the following role play.

Here are guidelines for doing this role play with two or more people, followed by guidelines for individual practice.

What to Do as a Group

Finding the lesson in the midst of a mess -- the diamond in the rough, the key in the mud -- is often radical and risky business. We must step outside our ideas of moral right and wrong, notions about what is respectful, nice, kind, and loving.

The person who pulled the card, pick a person or people to be your "Monster" even if the Monster you want to work with is not an actual human because it is a circumstance or inanimate object. Give the Monster a voice and body. Name the Monster and describe it in detail for the person playing the part of this thing. Share all you know about what the Monster is doing and why. Then let it go and let magic take over. The Monster is going to make a scene. Open with something like this dialogue:

MONSTER: Hey [Your Name], you are a _____ (or) I'm going too _____ (or) I'm glad I _____ *[this is where the monster unabashedly claims its problem making]*

YOU: Hey *[Name of Monster]*! I've got something to say to you...

And then launch into a proper rampage. Tell the Monster all the reasons why it's ruining your day, high, faith, life, the life of those you love, etc. Say why the Monster sucks, what you want it to do instead, and all the wrong and terrible things it does. You can also tell the Monster why you need, love, or are actually obsessed with them. Whatever there is to share, you can use Confession Session style which is share something that you either haven't told people or avoid talking about in general, to really lay into the Monster with your grievances.

Let the Monster respond and keep with the role play, back and forth. In this exercise I want everyone to understand that there is no gag rule. Things may have to get a little crass or uncomfortable to find the sweet, tender truth. In that, everyone must be committed to stay with it until there is a vulnerable tender caring gift revealed. If there is still raging anger, blaming, or shaming (which may rise in the process and is actually welcome here) then the work is simply not complete.

Keep going until there is a crack where something new is revealed, felt, and seen. The monster carries a gem. Keep going till you find it or feel like you've had your fill for the night. It's not the Monster's job to explain or show how it is carrying a gem. The Monster's job is to be a Monster. You're the one who finds the gem. That being said, trust an evolution for the Monster if it occurs, just don't look for it or make that the goal.

When you feel complete you say, "That's it. I got it." Or "I am complete."

Everyone take 5 deep breaths.

Then the person or people playing the monster say, "Thank you for letting me play your monster. I am finished with this role. I am *[insert your name]*. Thank you *[insert person who pulled card name]*."

The person who pulled the card says, "Thank you *[insert names of people who played the monster]* for your service. Thank you."

Settle in for a collective debrief. Sharing after the play part of this practice is important and here's the order I recommend. First, people who witnessed but did not participate share what they saw and learned. Then people who acted out the monster share. Finally, the person who pulled the card shares last, having the final word in that vulnerable and empowering space.

Drink water, take deep breaths and if the group needs something to clear the space more, you can clear the space by things in the Clear Objects and Tools with Resonance or by doing a dance party, or still meditation.

What to Do with Yourself

Follow the instructions form above, only you will be playing both the monster and yourself. You can do this by stepping to one side for one and one side for the other. Or by grabbing a piece of costuming that you take on or off. You can do it in the mirror. The more you can *play with it* the more you are going to be able to access a variety of perspective. Even this will get easier and be more fruitful with practice.

PHYSICAL STORYTELLING

You can review the Instructions for Games on page 158 and then do the following role play.

You can do this individual practice or in a variety of ways in a group.
  For the group, roll again:
    ⚀⚁ Solo with everyone witnessing
    ⚂⚃ Everyone does it one at a time being witnessed
    ⚄⚅ Everyone does it simultaneously.

Pick a personal story you want to share.
  Select a song you want to work with, have another player pick a song, or use Cosmic Shuffle (page 322) for song selection.
  Using your body like a mime or storyteller, do an interpretive dance of

your tale. Avoid using your words. First depict the doomed or pinnacle moment. Then dance your turn around, breakthroughs, insightful moments, or process. Next act out how you emerged. Finally, role play who you emerged as on the other side.

One of the most fun parts about interpretive dance is feeling like a fool (at least in moments), so go big. Another joy is getting to play out your responses to things around you. So when relevant, really imagine things like a wall of fire and ocean waves. For example, you can be the ocean and you also can just be by the ocean. Let things and yourself get bendy and silly.

After you are done everyone take a moment to share what they saw and felt.

TRUST FALL

You can review the Instructions for Games on page 158 and then do the following exercise.

What to Do with Yourself

Schedule a game night with a few friends and have everyone bring one game they like to play. You offer this one. In addition, to making these plans if you would like roll again for an additional practice for this moment.

What to Do as a Group

This exercise is incremental. The goal is success and to strengthen trust. It is a cooperative exercise, not a challenge of how far one person can fall. This is a physically trusting game that carries potential for actual harm to the body if the participants are not aware and present in the process.

Partner Trust Fall

Get with a partner
 Faller: Stand with arms crossed, back straight and engaged, like a board, feet together.
 Catcher: Stand in a lunge position, feet about shoulder width apart, bent knees and ankles, agile and responsive in your legs so you are prepared for receiving weight, with your weight centered in your body.
  *female body weight is often in the hips, and male bodies often in their upper body and chest.

The most frequent accidents happen in two ways

1. When one person begins without everyone being ready. Or someone getting distracted near the end. So the sequence of consent and beginning is essential, and then focus must also be maintained through completion.
2. When people do not hold the body position. If:
   - ... the faller bends at the hips it is more difficult to catch and support them
   - ... the catcher grabs or grips the faller instead of keeping their hands and arms in supportive meeting positions, locks their knees, or keeps feet too close together

Closing your eyes as the Faller is optional. I encourage you to try it out.

1. Faller and Catcher make eye contact, verbally agree to do this exercise.
2. The Faller stands in front of the Catcher.
3. Faller becomes stiff and crosses arms, takes a few deep breaths.
4. Catcher gets in receiving stance, takes a few breaths.
5. First when the Catcher is ready they say, "I am prepared for you to fall."
6. When the Faller is ready they say, "I am ready to fall."
7. THEN the Catcher will confirm, "Fall away."
8. THEN the Faller, keeping feet together, falls backwards, maintaining a straight spine. Catcher receives the Faller at about half a foot, 5-6 inches and then places the faller back on their feet steady, waiting for them to fully take back all of their weight.
9. Repeat steps #6-#9 increasing the distance each round by a few inches, not more than half a foot each time.
10. Check in and then switch positions.

Group Trust Fall

1. Need at least 6 people to do this, 5 in circle, and 1 in the center.
2. Stand in a circle with Faller in the center.
3. All the Catchers get into receiving stance.
4. Catchers must confirm first with a group that they are ready before inviting the Faller to fall.
5. Making eye contact with each other, and then asking,
6. "Catchers are we ready to Catch?"
7. Unison response of "Yes" Followed by unison statement "We are ready for you to fall."
8. When the Faller is ready they say, "I am ready to fall."

9. THEN the Catchers in unison confirm, "Fall away."
10. THEN the Faller, keeping feet together, falls backwards or forwards (maintaining a straight spine) allowing their weight to be caught and passed around the circle by the Catchers.

WORD ASSOCIATION

You can review the Instructions for Games on page 158 and then do the following game.

Word association is about uncensored mind wanderings, sometimes it's insightful, sometimes silly, sometimes mundane. The experience of how it sounds or feels is not the point, it is the side effect of allowing the mind to unwind through association.

Start with one word.

Then follow each word with the word that word made you think of. (If you the mind goes blank and nothing pops up go with with either "blank" or "nothing.")

The words do not need to have any rational or observable connection.

Avoid sentences, though small phrases sometimes happen, you are interrupting the habit of turning a thought piece into a complete thought.

It is okay to repeat the word you just heard, said or wrote until a new word comes to the surface.

Written Word Association

Using your journal or a blank piece of paper
   Set a timer for 3 minutes.
   Start with a word and keeping writing words until timer stops.

Verbal Word Association

What to Do with Yourself

Set a timer for 3 minutes.
   Start with a word and say consecutive words aloud until timer stops.

What to Do as a Group

Set a time for 3 minutes.
   One person says a word, then going around the circle the next person says the first word that comes to their mind, go around the circle until the timer stops.

Notice if you are associating words with what was last said by the person next to you or by someone else's word that stuck with you. Notice there is information in all of it. Can you decide where your focus is? Stay present with the mind. There is NO wrong word.

YES I AM! YES YOU ARE!

You can review the Instructions for Games on page 158 and then do the following exercise.

What to Do as a Group

The Caller is the person who pulled the card. The group will respond in accordance with the script. There are both instructions for what to say as well as what to do physically. This is most potent with played with abandon, so just go with the first that comes up for your body. I recommend doing a quick run through reviewing everyones parts in the sequence and then playing it through a second time full out.

What to Do with Yourself

Play both the Caller and Group parts in the exercise.

The person who pulled the card is the "Caller".
   The caller starts by declaring something about themselves:

Caller: "Yes, I'm......"
   Group: "Yes, you are......!"
   Everyone in the group strikes a pose that expresses full acceptance of that.

Then everyone shouts "What are you gonna do about it?"
   Caller: "I'm gonna own it!"
   Group: "What's that gonna be like?"
   Caller answers: ".......!" and then strikes a pose owning it.

Caller and Group: "That's some radically healing shit!"

Example

Caller: "Yes, I'm that sensitive"
   Group: "Yes, you are that sensitive!"
   Strikes poses of superman or of curling up on the floor or defensive

posture, could be anything.

Group: "What are you gonna do about it?"
   Caller: "Own it!"
Group: "What's that gonna look like?"
   Caller: "I'm gonna weep in public, laugh out loud when I feel good, I'm gonna take showers in the dark, I'm gonna get better with boundaries, I'm gonna trust my sensitivity!"
   Strikes a pose depicting what their owning looks like, example: hair flip.

Caller and Group: "That's some radically healing shit!"

Medicine Songs

INSTRUCTIONS

Each of the following practices shares lyrics to a Medicine Song. Each of these medicine songs has been recorded for your learning and listening. You can access these songs as part of the App, there are a call and response style, and songs you can listen to. You can stream them here or anywhere you listen to podcasts: sophiawiseone.com/i-love-my-life-podcast/

You can access the recordings on most streaming and music distribution platforms:
Artist: Sophia Wise One
Album Name: *Call & Response + Sing Along Medicine Songs From I Love My Life Card Game and Oracle Deck* <- (That was the original name of this body of work)
And at **sophiawiseone.com/member-access/**

You are invited to sing along with the recordings, make up your own melody, listen to the recording and take in the melody and vibrations receptively. Or pick another song that comes to you and sing that for your medicine song practice.

Medicine songs are the sound of healing in motion. The song is not about the "voice quality" of the singer. I invite you to sing your heart out without concern for getting anything perfect or sounding "good." Singing comes from a different place in our being, brain, and body than speaking. Breathe deeply and explore your inner music. Allow the vibrations that come from you, as well as what you hear, to move through your body and see what happens.

You can read more about singing as an offering by reading the practice Sing a Song or Play Music on page 281.

All the songs, unless otherwise noted, are written by Sophia Wise One.

I AM WHOLE JUST AS I AM

You can review the Instructions for Medicine Songs on page 175 and then sing these songs.

I am solid as the oak
   I am free as the wind
   I am healing as the oceans
   I am whole just as I am

GODDESS CHANTS

You can review the Instructions for Medicine Songs on page 175 and then sing these songs.

Do you know any Goddess chants? Sing the one you know. Search online for these titles and make your own up.

The first three chants have appeared around more fire circles than I can count. I don't know who brought them to us first. I honor and welcome credit information that will be added later editions and noted in the App.
   The fourth, came through me.

<u>We All Come From the Goddess</u>
       We all come from the Goddess and to her we shall return like a drop of rain flowing to the ocean

<u>Earth My Body</u>
       Earth my body, water my blood, air my breath, and fire my spirit

<u>The Earth, The Air, The Fire, The Water</u>
>The earth, the air, the fire, the water return return return return

<u>Moon Goddess' skirt</u>
>You are being rocked in the hem of the moon goddess skirt
>As she sings, as she sings
>Rest, rest
>You are loved, you are Love

RISE UP, RISE UP, RISE UP!

You can review the Instructions for Medicine Songs on page 175 and then sing these songs.

This is a summoning song, and you are invited to listen to it and be called forth by me. You are also invited to change the lines that start with "I am" and insert what ever you want as the name you choose to claim. You are also invited to sing and identify with the Divine Aspect of Wisdom named Sophia and with being a child of the wind, and claim that for yourself. There is no wrong way for you to welcome this beckoning march into your space.

I am Sophia Wise One Daughter of the Wind
>I am calling you (2x)

Rise up rise up rise up
>Rise up and take your place (2x)

We have been waiting (3x)
>The time is now

I am Sophia Wise One Daughter of the Wind
>I am calling you (2x)

Rise up rise up rise up
>Rise up and take your place (2x)

We've been preparing (3x)
>The time is now

I am Sophia Wise One Daughter of the Wind
>I am calling you (2x)

Rise up rise up rise up
    Rise up and take your place (2x)

We are united (3x)
    The time is now

STAMPEDE OF THE ELEPHANTS

You can review the Instructions for Medicine Songs on page 175 and then sing these songs.

Do you hear that? Ganapataye Nama. (3x)
    It's the stampede of the elephants Nama

Om Gam Ganapataye Nama (3x)
    It's the stampede of the elephants Nama

Move out! Ganapataye Nama. (3x)
    It's the stampede of the elephants Nama

Om Gam Ganapataye Nama (x4)
    It's the stampede of the elephants Nama

No more! Ganapataye Nama. (3x)
    Obstacles in our way! NAMA!

Om Gam Ganapataye Nama (x4)

STARDUST

You can review the Instructions for Medicine Songs on page 175 and then sing this song.

You see, I'm made of stardust
    Made of song and light
    You see I'm made of stardust
    Immortal as the night

As long as I live here
    As long as my song lives here
    As long as my song lives here
    I belong to the Earth

You see you are made of stardust
    Made of song and light
    You see you are made of stardust
    Immortal as the night

As long as you live here
    As long as your song lives here
    As long as your song lives here
    You belong to the Earth

You see we're made of stardust
    Made of song and light
    You see we're made of stardust
    Immortal as the night

As long as we live here
    As long as our songs live here
    As long as our songs live here
    We belong to the Earth
    We belong to the Earth
    We belong to the Earth

PEACE NOW

You can review the Instructions for Medicine Songs on page 175 and then sing this song.

Peace now peace
    Peace now peace
    I find safety in trust now
    Peace now peace
    I find worthiness in existing now
    Peace now peace
    I find love in faith now
    Peace now peace
    I stand with all who stand with me now
    Peace now peace
    We honor all that came before now
    Peace now peace
    We choose freedom now
    Peace now peace
    Peace now peace
    We choose peace now

WE ARE IN THIS TOGETHER

You can review the Instructions for Medicine Songs on page 175 and then sing this song.

We are not separate from the clothes we wear
    We are not separate when we breathe this air
    Or from the ground we walk upon
    Or from the heat that keeps us warm

We are in this together (4x)

We are not separate from the ocean's waves
    Or from the Earth's deep dark caves
    Or from the heartbeat of the drum
    Or from the pulsing in anyone

We are in this together (4x)

We are not separate from the beauty here
    We are not separate from from the things we fear
    Or from the seeds that grow our food
    Or from the strength that brings us through

We are in this together (4x)

We are not separate from the ceremonies
    Or from the people and their dreams
    We are not separate from the child's laugh
    Or from the cow as she lays her calf

We are in this together (4x)

We are not separate from the speaking trees
    We are not separate from the songs they sing
    We are not separate from the bell's ringing
    We are the weaving of everything

We are in this together (4x)

Writing Prompts

INSTRUCTIONS

Writing our stories or listening to our buried wisdom is a skill that takes practice and involves risk. We must first reveal what we are carrying to be able to discern what is truly wisdom and what is conditioning and lies we are repeating inside our own mind. Give yourself permission to get it down, take a look and get to know yourself, forgive yourself, change, heal, and be inspired, confronted, comforted, and loved by the voices and stories in your mind.

It's important to actually write down your responses to the prompts so you get a clear understanding of what stories or thoughts are in your mind. Many of us think that we don't have particular beliefs. However, when we write it down or say it out loud, we often realize that we've been telling ourselves things that we do not agree with. Sometimes, we don't even realize what we are saying these things to ourselves at all. Perhaps we're actually telling ourselves a great insight and we glaze right over it until we say or write it down.

- Things to keep in mind when working in this way:
- Write down whatever crosses your mind and give up censoring yourself.
- You never have to read aloud or share what you've written, a nd you are always allowed to share what you have discovered when you want to.
- You don't have to keep anything and you can always burn or shred the writing.
- There are no wrong answers.
- The value of these prompts is exposure, so your honesty is the thing that will determine the usefulness of these exercises.

You are invited to write multiple answers for one prompt. For example, if the prompt is, "I love..." you can write, "I love olives. I love dancing. I love waking up feeling rested. I love a hot shower. I love seeing an old friend. I love spring rain." If you don't have an answer, write that. For instance, "I love... I can't think or feel love about anything right now." Repeat each prompt until you think you are empty. When you think you are done, wait a minute or a few breaths to see if anything else comes up before moving to the next prompt. When responding, be sure to write down questions that come up in your inner dialogue, especially if they are coming up as rhetorical such as, "Who do you think you are?" And then, answer all your questions.

What to Do as a Group

Make sure everyone has something to write on and with, if people are present who can't or don't want to write, invite doodling while others write and then sharing from their heart when you each share.

One person reads allowed the prompts. Read each prompt a few times and give people a moment to write their response down. The person reading also writes down their own responses as well. Repeat this process with each prompt.

When the writing is complete go around the circle and share as much of you're writing as you desire. I encourage sharing. Be present and kind while you listen to each other and yourself.

What to Do with Yourself

Make sure you have something to write on and with and then complete each of the prompts. When you are finished writing, invite in sacred witnessing and read your own responses out loud and listen to yourself.

Bonus option: Record yourself reading the completed prompts and then listen to them, rewinding the recording if you zone out and miss something that was said. Really take the time to hear what you are saying. This is a powerful way to do this practice. This way I get to express, be witnessed and witness.

You can also call a trustworthy friend then read aloud your share with them.

ADMITTING A TRUTH

You can review the Instructions for Writing Prompts on page 182 and then use the following prompt.

- A truth that I am having a hard time swallowing is...
- A lie I am having a hard time digesting are...

- A truth that I am having asharing is...
- A lie that I am speaking is...
- A truth I had a hard time swallowing that I was able to digest was...
- To more forward with courage, I need...
- From here, I will...

HEALING SYSTEMIC CONDITIONING

You can review the Instructions for Writing Prompts on page 182 and then use the following prompt.

This subject can be painful be it the first time looking or the 100th. These writing prompts is to assist in healing and identifying where there is a need for healing in systemic and ancestral privilege and poverty.

Be gentle with yourself and each other as this is a tool for cracking a shell, tending a wound, and honoring a vulnerable power. There is a lot of collective shame about these things and it is through having honest and shame free places to discuss and heal that we begin to uncover the places we are perpetuating harm to ourselves and each other. This is how we turn the tide of isolation. Be courageous, be kind, and be loving.

There are amazing resources to gain deeper context and understanding in all these areas, and I highly recommend you search them out. There will be some recommendations inside the App on the Additional Resources page online at **sophiawiseone.com/member-access/**.

Writing Prompts:

- Moral judgements and depictions of poverty
- Moral judgements and depictions of privilege
- Name links between slavery and poverty, privilege and money\
- How has privilege been present in my life or in the lives of those around me?
- How has poverty been present in my life or in the lives of those around me?
- How educated am I about the history and intentional design of the United States and other colonies to maintain poverty for some and financial freedom for others?
- How do you see yourself in relationship to poverty, wealth, systemic pressures?
- What does the phrase "slave mentality" bring to mind to you?
- Do you exhibit any of those aspects?

- How comfortable am I with this conversation?
- Did you talk about this growing up in your house? School? Religion? Anywhere?
- What emotions are coming up for me around this subject?
- What is privilege?
- What access and allowances vary for people who have different kinds of money, different abilities, race, mental health, gender identity, class, sexual orientation, body type, education, or other things? Do you know? Were you aware?
- What are obvious ways you think the world should function differently?
- What would that look like? Who would it benefit? What do you believe would be a better way of life or culture?

After you've shared your answers aloud, you invited each to say this (or a variation that feels right) aloud:

"I honor and recognize that I have had systematic lies passed down to me through the culture I was born into and my ancestry.

I claim the truths of my heritage and release the conditioning that does not serve me and the collective as a whole.

I am here.

I am the birthplace of a *[insert an affirming word of the world you want to contribute to]* culture."

BECOMING

You can review the Instructions for Writing Prompts on page 182 and then use the following prompt.

- I want...
- I'm capable of being...
- I am willing to release...so that I may become...

After writing your answers and reading them out loud, say, "I am already whole. I am consciously engaging in the expression of my soul."

BELIEF TRADERS

You can review the Instructions for Writing Prompts on page 182 and then respond to the following prompt.

Everybody writes down a basic foundational belief you are aware that you have on a piece of paper.

Mix them up in the middle of the circle.

Everyone pick one, making sure you don't take your own.

Then write a possible FLIPPED, inverted belief in response to what's on the paper.

Then everyone reads both beliefs out loud.

When doing this practice on your own, make a list of five beliefs and then write down the flipped belief for each one. Read your answers out loud.

BOUNDARY PATTERNS MODELED

You can review the Instructions for Writing Prompts on page 182 and then use the following prompt.

- Passive boundary behavior looks like
- Passive aggressive boundary behavior looks like...
- Behavior that has no boundaries looks like...
- Behaviors of healthy and supportive boundaries are...
- Examples of behavior that I can't classify as passive aggressive, no boundary, or a healthy boundary are...
- Things I listed above that I do include...
- Instead, I'd like to...

BRAIN DUMP

You can review the Instructions for Writing Prompts on page 182 and then use the following prompt.

The mission is to put whatever goes through your mind into written form so as to ease the internal running amuck of the mind. Sometimes the mind gets so filled with things that we can't sort any of them out. Sometimes it's a rotating to-do list. Other times, all I can hear are days-old regrets or relationship snafus I'm dragging my feet on addressing. Other times still, it's so many creative projects and ideas that are swirling with thousands of micro steps to make them happen. There are so many things that we "keep track of" inside our minds that just become clutter.

The Brain Dump practice helps really see what there is to navigate. It's all about the holistic approach here, not just listing the to-dos that need to be done, but also writing down the emotional, spiritual, and creative thoughts that are swirling.

Let's get to it!

Get something to write on and with.

Step 1: Pour out and list everything you are carrying in your mind. ALL THE THINGS.

Step 2: Then rewrite them in an organized fashion to you. I sort them by theme or action. Work calls, personal calls, work emails, personal emails, logistics, money, relationships, feelings, or nothing to do about. Put everything in a place.

Step 3: Prioritize what you want/need to do first.

Step 4: Schedule when you will address the actionable items.

Repeat as necessary

BRAIN EQUATIONS

You can review the Instructions for Writing Prompts on page 182 and then use the following prompt.

Brain Equation is for once you've identified a pattern or equation that your brain makes without you trying and you want to make a new one.

Step 1: Recognize a pattern of belief
Step 2: Break it down
Step 3: Make a New One Rewrite it

Example 1
Step 1: Recognize a pattern of belief
Having a need means I did something wrong. Equation is need=wrong
Step 2: Break it down
Having a need means that there is an unmet need. That doesn't mean I am wrong. It means something needs attention.
Step 3: Make a New One
New equation is Need=Need
New equation is When I am feeling "wrong"= Ask myself if I need something

Example 2
Step 1: Recognize a pattern of belief
When people don't invite me to hang out with them I think it's because they don't like me and don't want to be my friend. Equation is: Feeling left out=I am unloveable.
Step 2: Break it down
When people don't invite me to hang out with them it means they didn't invite me. Any other story about why they did it is a story I am making up, from "because they forgot or they don't like me" to "because it was a thing

they wanted to share with a particular person or group". I can remember that people have preferences and that is something to celebrate and honor in them and in me, and that everyone is lovable and doing their best. If I still feel left out I can recognize that I am having need for a certain kind of connection, community, or maybe belonging, and that is a precious thing!

Step 3: Make a New One

New equation is Not being invited=not being invited

New equation is Feeling Left Out=I need connection, community or belonging

This is an art. Recognizing that there are things that *automatically* mean something else to you is the key step in this process. Slowing our thought down to see there is an assumption takes practices and fine attention, sometimes getting out of our own perspective.

These are compacted beliefs combining judgements and assumptions and making them truth. Break it down, and then rewrite them into things that are useful.

What to Do as a Group

Get into partners and set a timer 3 minutes.

Each person take 3 minutes to discuss your equations.

Set another time for 5 minutes, everyone write out your old equation notes about it, and your new equations. Write your old equation and new equations out to take with you and post it somewhere you will see it, such as on your altar, take a picture and make it the background on your phone, or on the mirror to remind your self of this new finding.

Then everyone gets a chance to share with the whole group your findings.

What to Do with Yourself

Set a timer for 8 minutes to think, write, talk out loud about your equations.

Write your old equation and new equations out to take with you and post it somewhere you will see it, such as on your altar, take a picture and make it the background on your phone, or on the mirror to remind your self of this new finding.

CHARTING YOU

You can review the Instructions for Writing Prompts on page 182 and then use the following prompt.

Chart, calendar, and map your physical and emotional sensations.

However you'd like: spreadsheet, journal, month calendar, or an app.

Everyday morning, midday, and night make a few words commenting on your:

- Body sensations
- Body symptoms
- Emotional feelings
- Repeating thoughts and stories
- Notable habits or actions

What to Do as a Group

Everyone chart yesterday, today, and if you can the day before yesterday.

What to Do with Yourself

Start right now, by charting yesterday and today and the what you can of the day before yesterday.

Notice how easy or challenging it is too recall past days. Remember that when considering how you will complete this next 3 months invitation.

Chart You for three months. Everyday take the moment to make these brief notes.

Review any patterns you see in the 3 months. There will be cycles. See them.

Deeply consider that wisdom.

CLARITY ON OFFERINGS/GIFTS

You can review the Instructions for Writing Prompts on page 182 and then use the following prompt.

- I am being called to give an offering to...
- This is because...
- If I could give anything, I'd love to offer...
- At this time, I'm available and capable of offering...

DEAR LITTLE

You can review the Instructions for Writing Prompts on page 182 and then use the following prompt.

Each of us was once a tiny, perfect, and lovable child and indeed you still carry and are that precious being still. This child is your Little. Here you are to write a letter to your Little so you can connect and know this part of yourself more consciously.

- Introduce yourself. Tell them about who you are and why you're writing.
- Ask how they are, where they've been, and what they've been doing. Ask your Little what they want, love, miss, and need. Ask what else they want you to know.
- Write a letter *from* your Little in response to you, answering all your questions and sharing anything more that comes.
- Write back and forth a few times.

DESIGN THAT MATCH YOUR INTENT

You can review the Instructions for Writing Prompts on page 182 and then use the following prompt.

As guide, it is incredibly effective and arguably essential to have the values of what you are teaching be reflected and represented in the architecture of your class or place where you offer leadership.

Consider the following:

Is the layout of the physical space reflective of your values and the subject matter?

Is the scheduling conducive to experiencing the values you are wishing to instill and share with your students?

Are you talking about experience? If so, how do you share the experience and have you and your students engage from a place of embodied learning or knowledge?

Is the principle of your subject or the behavior you would like to see reflected in your behavior and the design of the space, class, syllabus, materials, and scheduling?

DESIRE ADMITTANCE

You can review the Instructions for Writing Prompts on page 182 and then use the following prompt.

- What I really, truly, honestly, no holding back, want right now in my life is...
- People close to me know about the following desires...
- My deepest desire that I do not share out loud is...

- If that came into being, the problem would be...
- The best part about my desire is...
- When I really listen, the thing at the center of my longing is...
- In my body, I feel the desire...
- I want to honor and bless my desires by...

FORGIVENESS LETTER

You can review the Instructions for Writing Prompts on page 182 and then use the following prompt.

Forgiveness and amends are different. Forgiveness is about releasing the weight of the past and making space for the present and future. Amend is to change, the power of addressing behavior that was damaging or carries significance and how you will make it up in the future by behaving in a different way. How will you live differently moving forward so as to not repeat the damage done to the best of your ability and knowing?

This is a powerful practice to rebuild trust with you. You can also use it in practice with others. Here you start with your own self, your own actions and impacts.

Write letters to yourself.
- The first one will ask for forgiveness by address the behaviors you participated in and the effects it had and share how you committing to doing things differently.
- The second letter will be your reply, share how it feels to be acknowledged? Was anything missed that you would like to have recognized? How do you feel about the amends offered? Acknowledge what has been shared and say anything that needs to be said.
- Write back and forth as needed to complete the communication.

JOURNALING

You can review the Instructions for Writing Prompts on page 182 and then use the following prompt.

Journaling is an exercise in giving your thoughts, stories, insights, desires, and anxieties space to rest; a place for your mind to lay down what it's been carrying. Journaling is also an opportunity to safely explore things that may seem risky to talk about out loud and with other people. It is a place to write half sentences, answer rhetorical questions, recount memories, and take note of how you feel about your day or the things you filled it with.

*Dream Journaling

When you reflect on dreams it is very common to think of every person and sometimes every object as an aspect of yourself. Although psychic visitations do occur, for dream interpretation there is often massive reward in looking at every piece as a piece of yourself. As you share and as you listen keep that in mind. Perhaps even indicate it as you read.

The content of dreams can vary. Dreams can be landscapes of sensation and emotion, highly detailed narratives, flashes of imagery; the possibilities are as limitless as the imagination. Sometimes they carry the same message, other times multiple different messages. So when reflecting on your dream take note of the story and detail, as well as how you felt waking up or how you feel reconnecting.

Stay soft and listen with your subtle senses. Allow the water element to help bring the meaning into focus.

What to Do as a Group

Everyone take a moment and recall a dream you remember. If you can't remember a dream, write out a day dream, fantasy, or vision. Then go around and share.

What to Do with Yourself

This is for keeping a daily dream journal as a practice. Keep writing material near your bed so that as soon as you wake up, you can write down everything you remember from your dreams. Do this FIRST THING! Before you get out of bed or do anything else, write down all that you can recall. Include fragments, images, sensations, and stories. Write down any pieces that you remember in any order.

Keep your journal going. Sometimes dreams have a way of making sense if you reflect to them going backwards through time.

Below are a few simple prompts to support a general reflection journal as well if you would like, in addition to or after your gratitude journal practice.

*Gratitude Journaling

- List at least 5 things that you're grateful for or know you ought to appreciate.
- Make a two columns with these headings:
    - Things I feel gratitude for...
    - Things I know or think I should feel grateful for...

- Put your list of gratitudes into these columns, each under the heading that feels most honest.
- Now list at least 5 things that brought you sensual pleasure today. Things that felt good to the body, mind, spirit, or heart. Experiences and moments of sensation that were enjoyable.

It is valuable to discover your relationship with pleasure, fulfillment, and gratitude. They are linked, and yet many of us have been highly conditioned, if we were lucky enough to be trained in a practice of gratitude at all, to have thankfulness primarily for things outside of us. It is equally important, and perhaps for some a more important step, to cultivate an appreciation for your own pleasure and delight. This also helps you make informed decisions as you get clearer and quicker at noticing joy, pleasure and gratitude when it is happening in your life. Practice makes practiced.

When making lists of gratitude, your honesty is incredibly important. You are encouraged to share what you are called to share, no more and no less. After reflection, you will likely have more gratitude than you did before the exercise. Go ahead and write things "you know you should feel grateful for" even if you aren't feeling warm feelings about them right now. After making the lists and review, you may move things from one column to the other. Being forthright with your gratitude allows it to grow authentically, and to be the nourishing, healing thing it has the potential to be.

What to Do with Yourself

Everyone follow above instructions and write out today's gratitude journal. Then go around and share.

What to Do as a Group

There are a number of different ways to do daily gratitude practice. The recommendation is to do this daily for 90 Days. This long term practice means writing your gratitude journal daily for at least 90 days. Let it be honest every day. Let it be a space to feel into your perspective and your body.

When doing the columns, remember you don't have to have anything in either column necessarily, let the columns be there to give you permission for the times when you may be feeling heavy or numb, that is part of almost everyone's process at times. If you actually feel grateful for all the things, great. If you just know you *should* appreciate these things, then that's also great. Just keep returning to the practice and listing truthfully. Notice how the lists, and you, change over time.

Below are a few simple prompts to support a general reflection journal as well if you would like to explore that in addition to or after your gratitude journal practice.

*Daily Journaling

Here are a few simple prompts to get you started.

At the start of the day ask yourself these questions:

- What's on my heart?
- How do I want to feel today?
- What's ahead of me today?
- What do I need to remember for my wellbeing today?

At the end of the day ask yourself these questions:

- What did I do today?
- How do I feel now? How do I feel about the day?
- Did I do anything I would like to do differently? What are some alternatives?
- What brought me delight, joy, and pleasure today?

HABIT IDENTIFICATION

You can review the Instructions for Writing Prompts on page 182 and then use the following prompt.

List ten habits you have and ten habits you want.

LOVE LETTER

You can review the Instructions for Writing Prompts on page 182 and then use the following prompt.

Write yourself the love letter you always wanted to receive or the one you need to read in this moment. If they're different, perhaps write both letters. Say all of the things you wish would be said to you. Love is about acknowledgement, appreciation, care, noticing, affection, and kindness. Offer those elements to yourself now. Include things that you can really see and appreciate about yourself right now. You can say things like, "I know you have been feeling..." and be totally right. Do it -- whether it's easy or difficult.

What to Do as a Group

Go around and share read your letter to yourself aloud. Then take the letter with you and set a reminder to re-read the letter in a week.

What to Do with Yourself

Read that letter out loud to yourself. Read the letter everyday for a week. Then consider writing yourself a new letter, or writing back a response.
Enjoy.
You are beautiful.

MONEY SORTING

You can review the Instructions for Writing Prompts on page 182 and then use the following prompt.

- If I had limitless money I would...
- If that was really possible, the hardest or scariest thing about doing it would be...
- If that all came true, my biggest problem would be...
- If all that came true, the best part about it all would be...

MIND MAPPING

You can review the Instructions for Writing Prompts on page 182 and then use the following prompt.

Mind Mapping is a way to dump your ideas and thought on a subject to be able to see how they are relating. It is a non-linear way to explore putting down ideas to look at them and work with them.

Take a moment to pick one subject that you've got on your mind. It could be a project, a relationship issue, a fantasy, a storyline, a work, a philosophy, anything your brain is working on. Pick a name for the center theme.

- Ideally get a huge piece of paper, but any size will do
- Write the "center theme" in the middle of the paper within a circle
- For every other thought or association, make a line to another circle or area, they can keep going out from each other or link back
- Draw lines between circles or zones that are connected in your mind, if they are the connected by a thought, write that thought inside a circle in the middle of the connecting lines

MORE COMMUNICATION

You can review the Instructions for Writing Prompts on page 182 and then use the following prompt.

- The thing I am not saying is...
- I am concerned about the outcome of...
- The information I am missing but I have not asked for is...
- What I know but haven't shared is...
- My ideas about what ought to happen are...
- To have the best outcome I think...

NAMING THE GIFTS OF YOUR LINEAGE

You can review the Instructions for Writing Prompts on page 182 and then use the following prompt.

We all have inheritances from our lineages. We have blood lineages and spirit lineages. Our blood lineage is the genetic imprints that are passed on, this goes beyond just physical appearance and can include behaviors, character traits, or talents to a name a few. We also receive through our spiritual lineages, these can come by way of spiritual initiations into a teaching line, this can come through being adopted and being linked into a family line, and this can happen by way of our own souls carried through experience. For instance, a clear memory of past life and your spiritual practices or family traditions.

Make a chart of those lineage lines from as many or as few as you feel inclined from your blood, legal, and spiritual paths. Following is an example of my chart to show you one option.

Then for each line you name identify at least one skills, talents, positive attributes, physical, mental, emotional, spiritual, and material things that have been passed on to you through your lineages.

Then for each line you name identify at least one to three wounds that has been passed on to you through your lineages.

After sharing with the group or reviewing with yourself I recommend placing this chart on your altar with an offering of gratitude or blessing it. You can get more information on these by reading the teaching for the Make An Offering Card on page 67 and the BLESS IT Practice on page 317.

NAMING AND LOVING COPING PATTERNS

You can review the Instructions for Writing Prompts on page 182 and then use the following prompt.

- What coping pattern do you do and hate?
- The worst part about it is...
- I first started doing this as a way to protect me from / when / if...

OBSERVING

You can review the Instructions for Writing Prompts on page 182 and then use the following prompt.

Think of a particular instance, a moment and experience in time in which you have strong options about what someone else actions meant.
The make four columns with the headings:
- **Observable actions** that happened in the experience (Observational actions are specific things that can be identified without opinion or judgement. Answering the question, as factual as much as possible, of what happened?)
- **Your interpretation** or meaning of those actions
- **Body sensations** experienced during or while thinking the circumstance
- **Emotions experienced** during or while thinking the circumstance
- **What were your needs** during this time, unmet and and met

Reflect on the circumstance and describe what you can about it in each the sections.

See if you can slow down your assumptions about the story enough to identify each of these parts.

If you need more guidance on emotions and needs you can reference the Need≠Wrong Need=Need on page 71 for a list of feelings and needs.

Share and reflect about what happened while doing this exercise.

RESPONSIBILITY CHARTING

You can review theInstructions for Writing Prompts on page 182 and then use the following prompt.

Complete Steps 1 and 2 before reading or doing Step 3.

Step 1: Make two columns.

The first heading is: "Things in my life that work really well and things in my life that are not working or not working well."

The second column: "Who is responsible for what's working or not working in my life."

Step 2: Make a list of items and complete both the two columns

Step 3: Additional insights and reflection questions

After completing the chart, read the following out loud.

Interdependence is when we recognize that we are all in this together, that our actions impact our environment. In contrast, codependency is when we go from knowing we have an effect on people and circumstances to thinking we control, are responsible for, and are to blame or praise for something outside of ourselves, and in the inverse that others control, are responsible for, are to blame or praise for our own selves.

Is there anything that is not working in your life that had to do with your feelings or your life results that you said someone else is responsible for?

Did you list other people's feeling or life results that you said you were responsible for? If so, those can be indicators of codependency and enmeshment.

Review your chart and see where you can identity any of these patterns.

What to Do as a Group

Share with each other and if you want invite feedback on your share to get deeper insight. Group only offer insight if someone asks, and do you best to share what you hear them saying, and what you are seeing or reading. Be mindful not to tell people if there behavior is or is not codependent, unless you are a professional it is not your place to diagnosis this is an exercise to see potential patterns not corner ourselves. Be gentle with yourself and with each other. This is vulnerable stuff.

What to Do with Yourself

After filling out the chart and reading step 2 journal about what comes up looking at this. Allow yourself to ask yourself questions without answers and claim what you know to be true.

THANK YOU NOTE

You can review the Instructions for Writing Prompts on page 182 and then use the

following prompt.

Here's a good basic format for writing a Thank You Note. Be specific about what you are saying thank you for by directly name the gift, which could be an item, event, or considerate action. Then share why that particular thing is valuable, helpful, or has impacted you. Speak to the feeling you experienced from their gift.

Allow your note to be an embodiment of appreciation of what they gave you. Release engaging in habits of exchange. Don't worry about making promises about payback or making it up. If you do have a genuine desire to to extend a gift, offer, or invitation, you of course can add that to your letter. Here are two Thank You Note examples:

"Thank you for the set of napkins, they are refreshing to our table spread. I have actually enjoyed setting the table this week because it looks so beautiful. I think of you and feel grateful for our friendship and how many wonderful meals we have spent together. Thank you for your wonderful taste and long-lasting friendship."

"Thank you for stopping by the other day. I know was not in the highest of spirits, but after you left I realized I felt better, and I wanted to say your presence really helped. I am so grateful for the kindness and understanding you offered to me. Things have been up and down still, and just recalling your short visit has actually lifted my mood. I look forward to being together soon. Thank you again."

TRUTH SORTING

You can review the Instructions for Writing Prompts on page 182 and then use the following prompt.

- Make three columns with these headings: truth, my Truth, THE TRUTH
- Fill out the chart
- Read it out loud without commentary
- Make a new chart with the same three headings
- Then fill out the new chart and see if anything is different

HYPER VIGILANCE SORTING

You can review the Instructions for Writing Prompts on page 182 and then use the following prompt.

- What I really want, but what I think I can't have is...
- I am protecting myself from...

- I wish other people would...
- Something I just don't understand is...
- I need...
- The boundaries I have and will communicate are...

WHERE I AM

You can review the Instructions for Writing Prompts on page 182 and then use the following prompt.

- Where am I?
- What's happening?
- I am...
- What is this really about?

WHAT I WANT IN SEXY TIME

You can review the Instructions for Writing Prompts on page 182 and then use the following prompt.

- Make four columns
- In the first column make a list of the things that turn you on.
- Then in the other three columns write down your answers to these three questions for each turn on:
  - Does a lover do this with you?
  - Have you shared about this turn on with a current lover?
  - Do you explore this turn on with yourself?

YES/NO SORTING

You can review the Instructions for Writing Prompts on page 182 and then use the following prompt.

- Get clear about a situation or decision at hand
  Make two different charts:
  - The title of the first chart is, "If I say YES to [the situation or decision]"
    - Make two columns with these headings:
      - What I am saying No to...
      - What I am saying Yes to...
  - The title of the second chart is, "If I say NO to [the situation or decision]"

- Again, make two columns with these headings:
  - What I am saying No to...
  - What I am saying Yes to...

Fill out the charts
Review

Meditations

INSTRUCTIONS

Meditation is a word that is used to refer to all sorts of different practices that are intended to create a certain state of being. Meditations vary in their effects and in their intentions. Meditation can be done to calm, invigorate, balance, heal, or restore. Meditation is often also done with the purpose of opening and cultivating deeper awareness or personal power, or transcending the mundane. The heart of the meditations offered here is acceptance. They are here to help you to relax the body, and open your presence and being to your own wisdom. This can result in a sleepy soft state, a buzzing energized state, a bored and antsy state, or any number of others. The important thing when practicing is to allow your experience to be what it is. No matter the sensations or thoughts you are having, the act of giving yourself a space and opportunity to listen and discover yourself is known throughout the ages as medicine for the whole being.

Lean into each practice with curiosity and playfulness. Bring your focus and your flexibility.

When doing these practices in a group I encourage you to allow for a few minutes to transition at the completion of the practice, and then make a space for anyone to share. If you concerned about time, set a timer. When people feel complete, which may include no one sharing, move on to the next person's card or to closing the game.

When practicing alone, give yourself a few moments to transition from meditation to the next thing. Do one thing to care for and ground yourself, such as going to the bathroom, drinking water or tea, singing a song, stretching, or saying some closing words for yourself.

Daily or regular meditation practice at first can often generate sense of calm or delight in people. People often have positive associations with their practice and are easily inspired to keep doing it regularly. Then, in a matter of weeks or months, it can become more difficult or less enjoyable. This is common because we are getting closer to the quieter and subtler things that may not always be easy to sit with. When meditation gets hard, my recommendation is to do two things. One is make your body as comfortable as possible by getting support, changing position, or doing gentle stretching before or during. The other is to double the amount of time you are practicing. When it gets tough, it's time for more care, not less. So support and care for your body, make some life choices that are asking you to show up differently, and ideally double that timer.

ORGANIC MOVEMENT MEDITATION

You can review the Instructions for Meditations on page 203 and then do the following meditation.

You can do this practice with music or in silence. Pick a favorite song or let Cosmic Shuffle (instructions on page 322) choose for your. If you'd like to practice in quiet, it can be helpful to set an alarm for five minutes or longer). As a bonus to this practice, you can directly ask your body for guidance and also look to direction from a greater source. See the Call on Spirit and Help card teachings for more information.

Begin in a comfortable position and focus getting still. Close your eyes or keep them in soft focus. From this resting place, notice any subtle movements in your body. Then, slowly allow yourself to move naturally, following your breath. Begin to find the space between exaggerating movements and repressing movements. Explore the subtle and natural unwinding of your body. With the subtle impulses, allow yourself to move through any twitching, momentum, changing position, shaking, or trembling that comes up to take place without restraint.

Sometimes the movement is barely visible. With practice, the Organic Movement Meditation can lead to a complete unwinding. This may move you around the room in a variety of positions, with a range of movements, sensations, noises, and transitions through the surrounding environment. For example, you may start the practice sitting, then laying down, standing up, and moving around the space. This can awaken wildness and provide decompression of tension and inspire involuntary movements in your body.

What to Do as a Group

Everyone does Organic Movement Meditation together simultaneously.

With Audience Variation: The person who pulled the card does the meditation with an audience. To be present witnesses, audience members can sit or stand with open body postures, breathing, and quietly observing. Notice the meditator's movements, stillness, and expressions. Imagine what the person you're observing may be feeling and also allow for any experience that may arise for yourself.

FLAME MEDITATION

Review the Instructions for Meditations on page 203 and then do the following meditation.

This practice is meant to give you a single warming visual focal point to allow yourself to allow everything that is not that one thing drift by, and to open to receive what gifts may be being offered in this simple point of focus. Welcome the insight that could be possible.

- Set a timer for two, twelve, twenty, thirty, or forty-five minutes
- Light a candle placed in a cleared area, if you can't light a candle pick one of the following:
    - An object to look at ideally something that organically moves, like tree branch
    - Look down and watch your own breath moving your belly
    - With your eyes open or closed imagine a flame
- Sit comfortably and begin gentle breathing
- Watching the flame or point of focus, allow your eyes to go in and out of focus, closed or open
- Sit. Breathe. Be. Allow.

STILL MEDITATION

Review the Instructions for Meditations on page 203and then do the following meditation.

Read the Be Still teaching on page 17. Set a timer for two, twelve, twenty, thirty, or forty-five minutes. Find a position that lets your body to be as comfortable as possible. Focus on your breath and ask your body to relax. Breathe.

Most likely, your mind will wander. When it does, bring it back to observing sensations in your form or in your breath. Allow your body to relax, feelings to flow, and thoughts to drift. Bring your focus to the present moment and your own stillness or the slight and subtle movement of your body's breath, heartbeat, and muscles' relaxation.

WALKING MEDITATION

Review the Instructions for Meditations on page 203 and then do the following meditation.

This practice is ideally done with bare feet.

Allow your body to press into the earth with each step (if you are inside take moment to feel for your connection to the earth through your feet).

Enjoy the weight exchange from foot to foot.

Take in your location with deep observation.

Breathe and move with relaxation and attention.

Move slowly or move quickly, just move so that you are connected to your body.

You can walk in a circle, in a line back and forth, or a wander.

Set a timer for two, twelve, twenty, thirty, or forty-five minutes.

Walk.

Guided Practices

INSTRUCTIONS

Notes when doing a guided practice:

The guided practices are written scripts. They are also available as audio recordings available in the App at **sophiawiseone.com/member-access/.** Everything that is said is an offering, an invitation, and an opportunity for you to trust your own wisdom. Trust that your imagination is on your side, and don't worry about whether you are making it up or not. Just listen to it all as part of the journey and the healing you are experiencing. At any point if you start to lose track of what is being said, let your personal experience lead the way, and trust that you can tune back into any part of the guided practice that you need when you need it. If you are having trouble staying with it, just breathe into your body and focus on the guidance being given. Let go of how you think it needs to be, and just do your best.

You can do the guided meditations however you are called; laying down, sitting up, in a posture, standing. You can move around or be deeply still. I recommend making a supported nest, to allow the effort of holding your body to melt away and surrender into deep subtle feelings. Since most of the practices have a journaling time at the completion of the guided portion, grab something to write in and place it near by.

Laughing, crying, farting, burping, twitching, falling asleep, getting bored, visions, sounds, wanting to say something out loud to your self or someone who isn't physically in the room, feeling body sensations, hearing sounds and voices, arousal, deep felt emotions without any specified reason, needing to change positions, getting hot or cold, and much much more are normal reactions and occurrences during healing. I encourage you to allow any and all of that to be welcome in the space with yourself or in a group. Lean in and accept each movement, be it in your body, mind, or spirit, as part of the process.

Note when leading a guided practice in a group:
You can relax as well.

You don't have to say every word perfectly. After years of doing guided practices for people, I can assure you they are either in their own healing zone and don't notice, or they are more focused on receiving the instructions than tracking whether you skipped a line, or said a word weirdly, or repeated what you just said. When in doubt, take a deep breath and remember that you are inviting their deeper wisdom to guide them, and you are not responsible for the healing that may be taking place.

There are often periods of silence between lines of text, you can feel into this. Some of them are written as amounts of time, some of them are written as a number of breaths. Track the breathing of the people practicing, if you can't track their breath use your own. If people need more time, give it another breath, you don't have to follow it exactly, just know the space is there for a reason.

You may find yourself doing the practice alongside the group, and you may find that you can't do both. They are both legitimate ways of holding space. Just also periodically look around to see how everyone is doing, it's a kind thing to do.

There are a variety of ways to do the guided practices:
They are written as scripts so they can be read by one person for the group, as instructions to read and follow when practicing individually, and there are recordings you can access at **sophiawiseone.com/i-love-my-life-library/**.

You are welcome to put on relaxing music in addition to reading a text or listening to a recording.

If practicing with yourself, you can read through the practice once and then do what you remember, or just do it as you read it, you'll have to find out which works better for you.

Allow time for people to transition and then gather and check in to see if anyone needs to time to share after the group practice.

Breathe, adventure, and choose to trust what's possible in this healing moment.

ANCESTORS RE-WEAVING

You can review the Instructions for Guided Practices on page 207 and then do the following guided practice.

Allow your body to relax and take three deep breaths.

[30 seconds]

Give yourself permission to receive everything you need right now.
I give myself permission to experience healing.
I give myself permission to KNOW love.
I give myself permission to change.
I give myself permission to heal.
I give myself permission to BE just as I am.

[30 seconds]

Deepening your breath
Breathing in healing light, breath, sound, love, clear all the bodies.
With each breath, allow yourself to receive everything you need and be nourished
and with each exhale release everything that no longer serves you.

[1 breath]

Tension turns into relaxation.
Stress into clarity.
Tightness into softness.
Resistance into trust.
Gripping into release.

[1 breath]

Lean into the perspective that that which is released is restored.
Like legos or firecrackers, when it is in you it has form.
As soon as you release it, it loses it's form and becomes raw potential, free flowing life force.
So that what was once a burden in you becomes a gift to the cosmos.

[1 breath]

Breathe this light and love, cleansing, healing, restoring, balancing into and through...
... the space around you.
... your skin and hair and nails.
... all your muscles and tissues.
... your digestive organs.
... your blood, cerebral spinal fluid, lymph, all the fluids of your body.
... your heart and all the feeling you have ever had, are having, and will have are held by and cleansed by this light.
... your mind and all the thoughts and the pathways to and from those

thoughts that you have ever had, are having, and will have are held by and washed and blessed by this light.
... your root, generative organs and all the wisdom and deep knowing that you have ever had, are having, and will have held by are honored and sanctified through recognition by this light.

[30 seconds]

Breathing the healing into and from your bones...
... your bone marrow, the place when your blood is made -- where your DNA is reproduced.

[30 seconds]

This loves washes into and through the cells of your whole being.
As you breathe this love, it moves through the space between the electrons.

[30 seconds]

Until the landscape of your being is so filled with light,
that you are inhaling light and exhaling light,
that without effort your whole being is radiating light.

[2 minutes]

Now invite your spiritual council to join you.
Calling on your spirit guides, the Divine, your beloved ancestors.
Calling those who are entirely dedicated to you being the fullest expression of yourself in this lifetime, to come close.
Knowing that any ancestors that need healing will stay outside this circle at a distance to witness and receive the healing that you are doing for your entire lineage.
And those who carry what you need and are able to share with you will come close.

[30 seconds]

Your spirit guides are so respectful, love and trust you so much, that they will only help on the level you actively invite them to.
So decide how deeply and fully you want them to assist.

Thank them for being with you always, whether you have known it or not.
Tell them you are here to connect and establish a conscious relationship with them.

Invite them close.

[30 seconds]

This is a moment of choice:
Tell them right now, where and how you want them to help.
At the edges? In guidance? In the complete arrangement of and assistance in circumstances? In complete cellular reconstruction at the soul core of your being?
It is up to you. Ask them to help you in the way you want them to.
Ask them now.

[4 minutes]

Breathe into your heart.
Focus on your heartbeat and the blood moving through you veins and arteries.
Feel your pulse.
Call to the blood coursing through your body to open the pathway to your ancestral tapestry.

[2 minutes]

The tapestry is the woven threads of each being in your blood lineage, and the weavings of your spiritual lineage.
Your blood carries the wisdom of both.
Allow your blood with every heartbeat to reveal the tapestry in and through you.

[1 minute]

There are places where the threads are worn, torn, gaps, split or cut.
Brutally, sadly, intentionally, accidentally.
Feel the ways in which it is intact and in which ways it is damaged.

[30 seconds]

Call now on Divinity, majesty, mystery, and your spirit guides, your own potency and ask that this tapestry be healed, restored in you.

[2 minutes]

Agree to receive the wisdom, the stories, the wholeness that your tapestry offers you.

[1 minute]

Honor that this tapestry is shared and ask for a blessing upon the threads that are healing and the effect it has on others, that they may be held in perfect love and respect their lives and life force.
Offer yourself as the landscape to have all that has been torn, tattered and lost be restored.

[10 minutes]

Using your breath as your ally,
Give yourself permission to be changed by this healing.
Give yourself permission to feel more whole than you have before in this life.
Offer blessings on your ancestors and all they did to bring you to this moment of existence.
To survive in whatever manner required so as to have their ancestors have a sweeter more whole existence.
That is you.
Here.
Now.
Healing together.
Honor and bless the imperfect human journey that brings you here.
Invite the blessings that beauty be the path forward for you and yours.
You are the answer to your ancestors prayers.

[3 minutes]

Our ancestors walk and heal with us, they give us wisdom.
Yes, and they also learn and heal from our walk.
This is a living relationship,
the ancestors are here too, healing, being healed.
Honor and bless the truth of that mystery.

[2 minutes]

Taking the next few minutes to come to completion with your guides and healing journey.

[5 minutes]

Take this moment to offer a gift of gratitude to your Sacred Council.

[1 minute]

Make space to receive any gifts, messages, or offerings they may have for you.

[1 minute]

Slowly deepening your breath.
Taking 3 deep, cleansing breaths,
releasing all that is ready and willing to be released and restored.
Let it go.

[5 deep breaths]

Now, in whatever way you are inspired, summon back to you from all time and all space,
your Soul, your Truest Self to come home to you here.
Knowing that what returns to you is you in your optimal form.

[2 minutes, or until a big settling breath]

Take 3 gentle breaths integrating on all levels of your being, unifying self with self.
Grounding and rooting in your light lattice with this light lattice of Earth.
Allowing the space that has been made, the self that has expanded and returned,
and the new self to enter this world in a gentle manner.

[30 seconds]

Softly bringing your hands to your body, patting and petting, brushing and greeting your emerged self with loving affection.
Lightly pressing yourself with loving contact,
honoring this sacred self into its sacred vessel of a body.

[2 minutes]

Gently begin moving, rocking, holding, breathing.
Gently. Gently. Gently.
Take the ten minutes to do whatever you need to care for yourself.
Journal, go to the bathroom, eat, rest.

[When practicing in a group]

We will keep this space quiet and ask that if people want to talk to do it
_____ *[name a location]*.
Knowing that as we return with our precious selves,
we will greet each other with tenderness.

BALM OF FORGIVENESS

You can review the Instructions for Guided Practices on page 207 and then do the following guided practice.

Take three deep breaths.
Look inward to your physical, mental, and emotional landscape.
Perhaps it is something you know of or perhaps it is unclear,
either way, ask something that is in need of forgiveness to reveal itself in detail.
Take a breath and really feel, see, know, and become aware of this place in you.

[2 minutes]

Imagine a bottomless bucket of the Balm of Forgiveness.
Coat what has shown itself, allowing a moment for the forgiveness to be absorbed.
Reapply as much as is needed.

[5 minutes]

Take a few deep breaths and come to a close. Knowing you can reapply at any time, any where.

BODY WISDOM APPROACH PRACTICE

You can review the Instructions for Guided Practices on page 207 and then do the following guided practice.

If anyone hasn't done something like this before, say to your body, "Hi, I know that this is new, and I'd like to have a different experience communicating with you. I'm asking, and I'm listening" After you say that, "if there's anything you want me to address, forgive, or apologize for, now is a good time to let me know."

So take moment to get settled and comfortable.
Allow your body to relax and take three deep breaths

Give yourself permission to receive everything you need right now
I give myself permission to experience healing
I give myself permission to KNOW love
I give myself permission to change
I give myself permission to heal
I give myself permission to BE just as I am

Notice how your body is feeling.
With the next five breaths allow all your general tension to melt away.

[30 seconds]

Scan your body for a place of discomfort or go to a place that already has your attention.
Take a few breaths to and from that one place.
Imagine your breath actually going to and from this place.

[30 seconds]

Ask yourself the question, "What do you want to share with me?"
Imagine that question dropping like a coin into a well in that place in the body.
Listen for responses by becoming the water which the coin lands in.
Allow that answer to emerge from the ripples.
The answer may come in physical sensation, auditory message, visualization, sense of knowing, taste or smell.

[3 minutes]

Allow space for another question you have to come clear
and then drop that in once the first ripples have settled.

[3 minutes]

Take this time to listen and ask whatever you want, in whatever way your body is guiding you.

[3 minutes]

Take the next minute to come to a close .
Be sure to thank your body for this time of connection.

BONE BREATHING MEDITATION

You can review the Instructions for Guided Practices on page 207 and then do the following guided practice.

Take a few deep breaths,
And allow yourself to settle,
Dropping any surface body tension, jaw tension, joint tension.

Allow you hands to fall and relax or place them lovingly on your body.

And give yourself permission to receive exactly what you need right now
Give yourself permissions to be just as you are.
Give yourself permission to experience your true self and your peace.

With a few strong inhales and exhales allows yourself to drop deeper into your own body.

Any now begin breathing from your bones.
So that your skeleton is inhaling and filling with the breath of life, with light, with love, with healing vibration.
Inhaling everything that you need,
and as you exhale allow the bones to rinse,
to release, as though you are wringing out a cloth.
You want the breath to bring in fresh breath, fresh light and exhale any and all debris.
Breathing in to your bones, your bones are breathing in and filling.
As you exhale they are releasing any debris.
Debris of other people's agendas, the debris of your own judgements, the debris of ancestor's wounds, anything that no longer serves you.

Relaxing into the perspective that what you release is restored.
So that as this debris is exhaled and leaves you it becomes raw potential loosing it's form so that that which was once a burden in you becomes a gift to the cosmos.

[1 minute]

Inhaling all that you need and exhaling.

With every breath, more of the exhale from your bones is that healing light.

[1 minute]

And as that exhale becomes clear, like water running clear.
Light inhaling and exhaling from your bones,
allow the breath into expand so that you are filling your bones and then your flesh
so that your body begins to breathe,
filling with this literal breath of life.
Everything that you need is filling your being with each inhale
and each exhale, that same breath of life, is carrying away,
releasing any debris from your flesh, your organs, your heart, your mind.

[1 minute]

With every breath you are filling with your own self and releasing all that is not you.

Filling with permission and blessings.
Exhaling permission and blessings, feel as they carry away everything that is debris.

[1 minute]

As the breath comes into your whole body and comes out from your whole body
more and more clear,
allow this to include the space that is off your body, the space is still you,
it is sometimes referred to as your biofield or aura.
So feel the breath as it is filling you,
filling in your bones, filling in your flesh, filling in this energetic space,
this space that is yours, your body, your etheric body.

Breathing in this nourishment into all these levels of yours being.
And with the exhale, release from the center of the bones to the edges of auric space.
You are releasing all that is not serving you.

[2 minutes]

With every breath begin integrating.
Integrating from the center of your bones, through your body, through your body, through your energetic space, you.
Knowing that with every breath, it passes through, it nourishes, and it cleanses all of your being.

Offer yourself the blessing that throughout the day, though the night, whether you are conscious of it or not may every breath be so fully received and may every breath be so deeply cleansing and releasing.

Bring one hand to your heart and one hand to your belly and take three deep breaths honoring this precious being.

[3 deep breaths]

Blessing this life and giving thanks to the mystery that is existence.

CALLING IN SPIRIT

You can review the Instructions for Guided Practices on page 207 and then do the following guided practice.

Opening Prayer

Life Force Who Is All Existence, Great Mystery, Beloved, seen and unseen, heard and unheard, known and unknown, Spirit, Holiness, all that and more,
I/we call and welcome you here.
In celebration and joy I/we give thanks to the mysteries that have brought life and wonder into my/our experience.
Join me/us here and offer your guidance, love, wisdom and kindness to our journey.
Receive my/our actions and words as an offering.
May you be fed by this communing and may I/we be brought closer to our own deepest knowing and experience of true love.
Bless us and help this be an embodiment of creativity and beloved spirit.
Thank you.

Closing Prayer

Life Force Who Is All Existence, Great Mystery, Beloved, seen and unseen, heard and unheard, known and unknown, Spirit, Holiness, all that and more,
I/we give thanks for your presence and blessings here.
Thank you for your guidance, love, wisdom and kindness in our journey here.
We are grateful for this time to be together and offer up all the revelations of our time to be nourishment for the earth and all people who want it.
We give thanks that our healing is The Healing and that it is by the nature of interconnectedness that all that has transpired for us here is shared with

all. Thank you for this comfort of connection in this time of manifested form in which we feel so much separation.
We ask that all our words and actions be blessed and be a blessing.
We truly hope and deeply know you have been fed by our communion in this time and we are grateful to be closer to our own deepest knowing and experience of true love.
Thank you. Thank you. Thank you.

Opening a Circle or Shared Space

We are gathered here in a circle.
Our intentions are to allow for healing which is naturally occurring to occur fully,
to have space and be supported in community and with witnesses.
We give thanks to all that is sacred and to the Earth, our home, and the life that is provided by them.
We invite wisdom, kindness, and love to be our guides and companions in this time together.
Bless us by your presence and expression through each of us in our own unique way.
Let the circle be open.

Closing a Circle or Shared Space

We have gathered here in a circle,
Watched and heard each other share.
Been transformed through our honesty, reflections in one another, and undeniable beauty.
Sacredness and the Earth have held us in this time together.
We are more whole because of it.
Thank you wisdom, kindness, and love for showing up through each of us.
Your presence and expression has lead to and through a journey of weaving a peaceful and healing world together.
May this weaving continue as we walk.
May we walk on a blessed path, and as we walk may we bless our path.
Let the circle be closed.

CALLING THE DIRECTIONS

You can review the Instructions for Guided Practices on page 207 and then do the following guided practice.

I call to the light and precious birth of the East,
Your wisdom and healing is welcome east.
I call to the fire and the passionate peak of the South,
Your wisdom and healing is welcome South.
I call to the integration and maturity of the West,
Your wisdom and healing is welcome West.
I call to the silence and the sacred death of the North,
Your wisdom and healing is welcome North.
I call to the infinite potential of the cosmos,
Your wisdom and healing is welcome Cosmos.
I call to the miraculous and generous life giver of the Earth,
Your wisdom and healing is welcome Earth.
I call to the mystery and Divinity of the light and sacredness within,
Your wisdom and healing is welcome Sacredness within.

COMMUNING WITH ELEMENTALS

You can review the Instructions for Guided Practices on page 207 and then do the following guided practice.

Get comfortable, breathing in and out and settling in your body.
With every inhale, feel yourself expand.
On every exhale, notice the container of your body holding you.

[30 seconds]

Feel the dynamic ways your body gives you space and supports you.
Notice the waves and relax into the way your breath rocks your body.

[30 seconds]

Allow that to slow your mind, soften your body, and allow your spirit to settle in the here and now.

[1 minute]

Call to *[insert the specific element]* Elemental introducing yourself, stating your intention to connect and commune with them.
Offer a gift to the Elemental you are calling.

[30 seconds]

Invite and summon the Elemental to join you here and make itself known to you.
Request the *[insert the specific element]* Elemental to reveal itself to you in a way that will work for you.

[2 minutes]

Ask what you can do for the *[insert the specific element]*.
Tell them you are here to listen and receive their wisdom.
Ask for them to share it with you in a way that you can understand.
Open. Listen. Pay attention.

[6 minutes]

Take the next 2 minutes to come to a closure for now.
Knowing that you can commune with each other at any time.

[2 minutes]

Take this time to offer a gift of thanksgiving and be open to receiving any closing messages from *[insert the specific element]* Elemental.

[1 minute]

Allow your breath to deepen as you slowly and gently bring yourself

through this process.
Reach for your journal and take notes or draw about your experience.
In about 5-10 minutes we will gather and share.

[Set a timer or decide you will wait until people are done and when most people are finished let people know it's time to wrap up.]

COMMUNING WITH YOUR SACRED WARRIOR GUIDE

You can review the Instructions for Guided Practices on page 207 and then do the following guided practice.

Take a moment to get settled in your body. Allowing yourself to release any way you are holding up your own weight.
Begin breathing in healing light,
breath,
sound,
love,
clearing all your many bodies.

With each breath, allow yourself to receive everything you need and be nourished and with each exhale releasing everything that no longer serves you

[30 seconds]

As you breathe in this healing notice
tension turn into relaxation.
Stress into clarity.
Tightness into softness.
Resistance into trust.
Gripping into release.

[30 seconds]

Lean into the concept that that which is released is restored.
Like legos or firecrackers, when it is in you it has form,
As soon as you release it, it loses it's form and becomes raw potential, free flowing life force,
So that what was once a burden in you becomes a gift to the cosmos.

[30 seconds]

Breathe this light and love, cleansing, healing, restoring, balancing into and through...
... the space around you.
... your skin and hair and nails.
... all your muscles and tissues.
... your digestive organs.
... your blood, cerebral spinal fluid, lymph, all the fluids of your body.
... your heart and all the feeling you have ever had, are having, and will have are held by and cleansed by this light.
... your mind and all the thoughts and the pathways to and from those thoughts that you have ever had, are having, and will have are held by and washed and blessed by this light.
... your root, generative organs and all the wisdom and deep knowing that you have ever had, are having, and will have held by are honored and sanctified through recognition by this light.

[30 seconds]

Breathing the healing into and from your bones...
... your bone marrow, the place when your blood is made -- where your DNA is reproduced.

[30 seconds]

This loves washes into and through the cells of your whole being.
As you breathe this love, it moves through the space between the electrons.

[30 seconds]

Until the landscape of your being is so filled with light,
that you are inhaling light and exhaling light,
that without effort your whole being is radiating light.

[2 minutes]

Now invite your Sacred Warrior Guide to join you.
Calling on your Sacred Warrior Guide.
Your Sacred Warrior Guide is so respectful, loves and trusts you so much, that they will only help on the level you actively invite them to.
Offer a gift to your Sacred Warrior Guide.

[1 minute]

Ask your Sacred Warrior Guide to reveal themselves to you in a way you

can comprehend.
Ask what you can do for your Sacred Warrior Guide.

[1 minute]

Tell them you are here to listen and receive their wisdom, and ask for them to share with you in a way that you can understand.
Open. Listen. Pay attention.

[8 minutes]

Take the next 2 minutes to come to a close for now.
Knowing that you can commune with each other at any time.

[2 minutes]

Take this time to offer a gift of thanksgiving and be open to receiving any closing messages from your Sacred Warrior Guide.

[1 minutes]

Allow your breath to deepen as you slowly and gently bring yourself through.
Reach for your journal and take notes or draw about your experience.
In about 5-10 minutes we will gather and share.

[Set a timer or decide you will wait until people are done and when most people are finished let people know it's time to wrap up.]

DANCE OF SUSTAINABILITY

You can review the Instructions for Guided Practices on page 207 and then do the following guided practice.

Put music on or do the movement in silence and allow your dance to emerge.

The "..." are there to allow for the time needed to people do to the movement, maybe 30 seconds, maybe 2 minutes... trust the unfolding of the movement.

Stand up, make sure you have your own space to move in and close your eyes...
Shifting weight between your feet with the beat of the music or half time...
Reach your arms above you head...

Up... and Down...
Left... and Right...
Sweeping from floor, to the ceiling and around again...
Rocking side to side in your hips...
Front to back...
Little circles in your hips...
Getting bigger circles in your hips...
Allow your body to move and turn and twist...
Letting your body lead the way, move into the movement of who you have been, how you have been feeling, and what you've been carrying and how you've been moving through the world...
Discover the movement that shows you being stuck and not letting things go, expressing who and what you are...
Now explore and find the movement of you resisting, not receiving and refusing nourishment, support, discovery, inspiration...
Find the places where there movements and postures are familiar...
Breathe into them...
Let them go ...
Shake your limbs... and head... and hands...
Shake your butt and move like a snake through your spine...
Now - Explore and discover the movement of you fully opening and receiving...
Find the movement of your unleashed expression and letting flow move freely...
Alternate between the two and find the places that feel familiar...
Now allow them to move into one united sequence of motion...
The movement of fully receiving and expressing filling and pouring...
A channel of life force flowing into and then communing with you then flowing from you...
You are touched by Divinity and Divinity is touched by you...
Have an entire song or at least 5 minutes of you dancing this feeling.

DESPAIR & RADIANCE

You can review the Instructions for Guided Practices on page 207 and then do the following guided practice.

[This practice has two parts. The first is done with everyone spread out with as much space for personal movement as possible,, and the second part gather in a circle.]

Everybody stand up and get in their own space.
Ideally space where you can move around.
Close your eyes.
Take a deep breath.

[30 seconds]

Think of yourself in complete despair, when you feel your worst, perhaps so bad you'd never want someone to see you in that space, your tender, aching, pained self.

Breathing in and out.
Allow yourself to make a statue of that state
Physically express that state. Allow your body to tell the story of this part, this place in you.

Breath in, and trust your body.

Make the image.

[30 seconds]

Breathe the way this posture this statue would breathe and allow a phrase to rise to the surface giving voice to the statue.

What are you feeling? What are you saying in this despairing place?

For one minute hold this posture.

[1 minute]

Take a deep breath in and release the posture.

Relax out of the posture.
Stretch and take 3 deep breathes.
Shake it off.
Shake it off, shake it off, shake it off.
Big Breath
Bend your knees, relax your jaw, make a sound. Shake it off.
Let it go.
Take you hands and gently press them lovingly on your chest, holding your heart.
Breathe in.
Breathe out.
Breathe in.
Breathe out.
Think of yourself in your most radiant self, when you feel you most amazing, perhaps so good you'd hesitate to share it with other people, your precious spectacular radiant self.
Imagine it.
Feel it. Think it.
Close your eyes.
Taking a deep breath, choose to be courageous and then more in a statue of this state. Physically express this radiant state. Allow your body to tell the story of this radiant part of you.
This radiant You.

[1 minute]

As you stand, allow your breath to take on the breath of this posture, this state.
Allow a phrase to rise to the surface giving voice to the statue.
What are you saying or feeling in this radiating state.

[30 seconds]

For two minutes hold this posture

[2 minutes]

Take a deep breath in and relax out of the posture.
Integrate and let it go.
Stretch and take 3 powerful breathes

[3 big breaths]

The second part of this practice is sharing.

Come back together in a circle standing.

[If practicing individually you can do this part where you are or in front of a mirror.]
[In a group, read through the instructions all the way through together and then just be ready to cue people in case they need reminders while its happening.]

One person at a time will stand and do this:
You are going to allow yourself to use the wisdom of your body and to trust your body to take you through an evolution. You are going to melt the first posture through unwinding movement until you emerge as you radiant self posture.
Let the movement be continuous.
Stand up and share your first pose and the phrase of the despairing self, hold it, share it, be seen in that.
Then close your eyes, go to your breath, melt inside dissolve the first form, unwind, roll around, flop, trust your body and morph until the radiant self to emerges.
Once you have arrived in your radiant self, share that posture and phrase at least three times. Repeating it, being seen in that embodiment.
Then after relaxing and dropping the postures, be witnessed here.
Everyone else in the group, or if you are doing this in front of a mirror, bows and says, "Thank you."
Everyone takes three breaths.
Now the next person shares.

[After you have completed sharing in the circle take moment to see if anyone has something to say about the experience.]

EYE GAZING

You can review the Instructions for Guided Practices on page 207 and then do the following guided practice.

What to Do with Yourself

Review the exercise and dream of, or invite, who you want to do it with. Right now go and do the Mirror Meditation Practice on page 241.]

What to Do as a Group

Get a partner
Sit across from your partner.

Pretty close, somewhere between not touching and less than a foot apart.
Choose who is "A" and who is "1"

[15 seconds]

"A" Closes your eyes
"1" Look at "A"
Really look at them.
Below are prompts of things for you to look at, do so with neutral observing, do it in a loving, noticing manner.

Notice "A"'s construction:

The shape of their eyes, nose, lips.
The lines on their face.
The textures of their skin.
The presence or lack of presence of hair.
Notice scars or birthmarks.
Take in the shape and structure of their face.

[1 minute]

Now look with empathy.
Does "A" look:

Content?
Relaxed?
Tired?
Angry?
Stressed?
In pain?
Self conscious?
Happy?
Sad?

[1 minute]

Now change the way you are looking to a softer look...
can you see past the structure of their face, can you see them? See their story?

[30 seconds]

"A" I want you to make the choice to really be seen

Did you make the choice before?
Do so now. Choose to allow "1" to really see you.
"1" Make the choice to really see them. Notice what happens here, and then do your best to really see them.

[30 seconds]

"1" Now you close your eyes as well
"A" & "1" sit for 1 minute with eyes closed

[1 minute]

Now switch
"1" keep their eyes closed
"A" open their eyes Looks at "1"
Below are prompts of things for you to look at, do so with neutral observing, do it in a loving, noticing manner.

Notice "1"'s construction:

The shape of their eyes, nose, lips.
The lines on their face.
The textures of their skin.
The presence or lack of presence of hair.
Notice scars or birthmarks.
Take in the shape and structure of their face.

[1 minute]

Now look with empathy.
Does "1" look:

Content?
Relaxed?
Tired?
Angry?
Stressed?
In pain?
Self conscious?
Happy?
Sad?

[1 minute]

Now change the way you are looking to a softer look...
can you see past the structure of their face, can you see them? See their story?

[30 seconds]

"1" I want you to make the choice to really be seen
Did you make the choice before?
Do so now. Choose to allow "A" to really see you.
"1" Make the choice to really see them. Notice what happens here, and then do your best to really see them.

[30 seconds]

"A" Now you close your eyes as well.
"A" and "1" sit with your eyes closed.
Make the choice to be seen with your eyes closed and decide to see the other with your eyes closed.
Notice what you can, are you imagining what you saw before?
Can you feel them across from you?

[30 seconds]

Can you sense a being? What do you sense?

[30 seconds]

Can you feel the environment and space between and around you?

[30 seconds]

Can you feel them sensing you?

[30 seconds]

Can you sense yourself and them at the same time?

[30 seconds]

Can you sense them, you, and the space at the same time?

[30 seconds]

Take 3 deep breaths together

[3 breaths]

Now slowly open your eyes and look to each others eyes

[3 minutes]

"1" in some way make a silent motion honoring and thanking them.
"A" in some way make a silent motion honoring and thanking them.
"1" and "A" take a moment to close with one another in a way that feels good.
When you finish, let's gather in a circle together again and check in.

EXPANDING TO HOLD PAIN

You can review the Instructions for Guided Practices on page 207 and then do the following guided practice.

[This is a guided somatic experience of physically feeling the pain and using breath to expand consciousness and self beyond identifying with pain.]

Standing, sitting, or lying down take 3 deep breaths clearing as much as you can from your whole self.
Get as comfortable as you can in a position so you can relax.
Allow your body to settle just as it is.
Breathing in and out.

Giving yourself permission to feel exactly how you feel right now.
Releasing all expectations of what a meditation is supposed to look like or feel like.
Ask your spirit guides or Sacred Council to join you and support you here.

Breathing into your discomfort.
Inhaling and and exhaling loudly.

[1 breath]

Again.

[1 breath]

Breathing in, holding it for 1, 2, 3, 4.
And now exhaling through your mouth.

Again.

[1 breath]

Letting yourself be, just as you are.
Giving yourself permission to heal and change, and be as you are.
Can you do both? Let yourself be and let yourself change?
Breathe.

[1 minute]

Scanning your body and taking a general inventory of how you are feeling, what feels alive and flowing, what feels stuck, what feels numb and absent... how and where are you?

[1 minute]

Now identify a specific place of pain.
Notice the outline of the space.
Where does the pain begin? Where does it end?
What's the temperature?
Density?
Texture?
Quality?

[3 breaths]

Can you focus on the pain and stay present or do you start to drift away or feel consumed?
Is it never ending or is there an edge?

[3 breaths]

Bring yourself back, breathe into this place, this process.
Ask the pain, "What do you want?"
Listen for what comes up, in sensation, words, images, associations, stories.
It's okay if there is not an answer you can decipher, you're just inviting a conversation, you don't need to force anything...
this is no right way to do this.

[1 minute]

Ask the pain clarifying questions, "What do you mean?" "Do you mean this...?" "What can I do?" "What else can you share with me?"

[2 minute]

The conversation may be helpful, but it is not the end.
Begin breathing into and from this place.
Inhaling directly to this place and exhaling from this place.

[1 breath]

With every inhale, bring in resiliency and patience, inviting spaciousness and permission.
With every exhale, allow yourself to expand and allow your body and your experience to shift.

[30 seconds]

Inhale to the place of pain, holding and honoring it.
Exhale, expand your presence around the pain's edges.

[30 seconds]

Bring your hands somewhere to your body, place them lightly and lovingly on your body and being.
Again, you don't have to feel any different, and yet you are allowed to feel different at any moment.

[1 minute]

Imagine the pain of your body, soul, and/or life in front of you.
Imagine it in a form that has a shape and size. It may look like you, it may look nothing like you.
It is the pain of you.

[30 seconds]

Look at it.
In detail, all around, 360 degrees.
See the outside.
See the inside.
Feel it.

[30 seconds]

Notice the size.

[1 breath]

Notice the size in relationship to yourself.

[30 second]

Now breathe into yourself, and watch, as you breathe, breathe yourself bigger.
Expand your self to get wider, deeper, taller, as big as you need to be to be able to hold the pain inside your presence without the Pain shrinking at all. The pain is exactly that big.
You, on the other hand, are dynamic and infinite, breathe into your center of being and feel the space between your electrons spreading so that you can contain the pain.
Breathe as you integrate, yourself, whole and intact, and your pain as held and supported.

[1 minute]

Relax your jaw, soften the roof of your mouth, breathe into the space of your joints, allow whatever feelings you are experiencing to be here and to move.
Feel.

[3 minutes]

Allow your breath to be your ally.
Change nothing and breathe deeply into this moment, this space as it is.
You have the permission you need to let whatever is ready to change to change.
Your only work is the work of the breath.
Let the breath do the rest of the work.

[3 minutes]

Offer yourself a blessing and open to receive the blessings being offered to you.

[2 minutes]

Take a few integrating breaths, releasing what's to be released, keeping what is to be kept, allowing movement for what's here to be moved.

[45 seconds]

Say thank you or make an offering to your Sacred Council that came to support you.

[1 minute]

Inhale recognition for what is happening as it is.
Exhale permission for you, your infinite self, to be capable of holding the pain.

[30 seconds]

Inhale, loving what is, without having to change it.
Exhale, Honoring the difficulty without having to manage it.

[3 breaths]

Inhaling discernment
Exhaling connection

[3 breaths]

Over the next couple minutes, ask for help and guidance and then just sit with yourself, as spacious as can be, holding the pain without having to change it.
You are not the pain, the pain is not you.
It is an experience you are having.
Hold that precious and painful experience in infinite love and wisdom as best you can.
Breathe.

[3 minutes]

Take a few clearing breaths.
Knowing you can take this practice and feeling with you, you're holding and embracing, spaciously carrying this ache in your life.
You are capable of tending and carrying this ache until it shifts.
It will.
All things change.

[1 breath]

Breathe and allow yourself to gently come through.
Touch your sacred body, making contact with your form and blessing yourself with gentle and supportive affection.
Fully arriving in this place, in this shared now.
Integrating, giving thanks to yourself and those who walk with you.
Take the next 5 minutes to do what you need to do.

FEAR/LITTLE MEDITATION

You can review the Instructions for Guided Practices on page 207 and then do the following guided practice.

If you are younger or don't know how to be a good adult to yourself, call upon the Wise One in yourself to be present to cultivate and teach you how to do this.
Get comfortable, let your body soften and open. If you are sitting up, allow your spine to be tall and relaxed.
Take a breath in granting permission to yourself to get exactly what you need out of this Fear/Little meditation.[5]

[1 breath]

Take a few deep breaths.

[3 breaths]

Imagine yourself in the passenger seat of a car.
You are riding down a road when the driver pulls over.
And pulls out a cigarette and says, "No way, I am not going anywhere."
You realize in this moment that the car is your life and the driver is your fear.

Allow a deep breath

[1 breath]

Get out of the car and walk around to the driver's seat
Do what you must to get this fear out of the driver's seat and you into it

[2 minutes]

---

[5] Inspired by Anastasia Netri's fear meditation for getting fear out of the driver's seat.

Once in the driver's seat, you realize that fear has appeared in the passenger seat, as you turn to face Fear,
You see a small child in the passenger seat looking at you.
It's you-a young, precious you.

[1 breath]

Ask, "Why were you in the driver's seat?"
Listen to their answer.

[30 seconds]

Respond with the level of care you would if addressing the most innocent fearful child you've ever come across.
Be kind and curious.
Ask clarifying questions.
Be honest, no placating, and be sure answer their questions as well.
Ask "How long have you been there?"

[30 seconds]

"Who put you in the driver's seat?"

[30 seconds]

Ask "how did you feel in the driver's seat?"

[30 seconds]

"How do you feel being in the passenger seat?"

[30 seconds]

"How do you feel right now?"

[30 seconds]

"What do you need?"

[30 seconds]

"What would make you want to get back in the driver's seat?"

[30 seconds]

Tell your Little,

"You are not to get in the driver's seat again.
That is not where you belong, I apologize that I missed it earlier and that you were there in the first place.
Ask for my attention, I will do my best to listen and respond.
I stay in the driver's seat and you in the passenger seat."

Explain to your Little you, that you are the grown-up, and that you will do your best by them.
Explain that you know you have missed some opportunities in the past to take care of them, and that moving forward you will do better and better with practice.

[2 minutes]

Share that you are going to do your best, and they can trust you not to leave them behind.
You will not be perfect, and you may not always know the right thing to do, and you know how and when to ask for help, from a wiser version of yourself, from your spirit guides, from whatever you have faith in and where you go for counsel.
Sure them that you and them will get all the help you need.

[1 minute]

Tell your Little that they can look to a greater power than you and put faith in love and Divinity to offer comfort and support if you ever fall short, and that together in faith and commitment to each other you will have a great time together.
That you will not go anywhere and there is nothing they could do that would make you not love them or make you leave them.

[1 minute]

If you need to clean up some behaviors in the past, do it. Acknowledge your shortcomings and the ways you may have hurt yourself in the past without knowing any better. Ask them to share with you where that happened that perhaps you didn't mention?

[2 minutes]

Ask your Little what they want and what they need from you in the next couple days to confirm and show them you really are going to be listening and caring for them.

[1 minutes]

Be honest about whether or not you can do what is asked and make commitments on a realistic timeline. Better to make smaller agreements and keep them, than make well intended ones you won't be able to do.

[1 minute]

Get settled on an agreement.

[1 minute]

Hug them, tell them you love them.
Tell them you will always be there for them in love, if imperfect at times.

Breathe in and out and place your hands on your physical body holding yourself with care and affection.
Breathe and allow yourself to gently come through.
Touch your sacred body, making contact with your form and blessing yourself with gentle and supportive affection.
Fully arriving in this place, in this shared now.
Integrating, giving thanks to yourself and those who walk with you.
Take the next 5 minutes to do what you need to do.

[5 minutes]

GROUNDING CORD

You can review the Instructions for Guided Practices on page 207 and then do the following guided practice.

Sit or stand comfortably.
Imagine a line from high above your head dropping down through your skull dropping down through the center of your being, exiting through the center of you hips, and reaching down deep into the earth.

As you breathe, allow your pelvic floor to soften and relax.
Opening towards the earth.

[3 breaths]

Allow this line to expand to a thick rope or cord, or vibrationally, a chord pouring down to the heart of our mama earth.
With the next three breaths, imagine this chord expanding to be a six to twelve inch channel.
Reaching through your whole being, down into the building or earth beneath you.
Moving through the layers of the planet you are on.
Through the water-table.
Down past the plates of the planet into the heart of our planet.
Feel for the heartbeat.

[3 breaths]

Take a breath and with clarity from your heart send a message of gratitude to the earth down this whole channel, feel it traveling down until it is received.
Feel for anything you may receive in return.

[45 seconds]

Over the next few minutes send your breath and excess stuff down this wide open channel and open to receive life force up from this tap root into the earth.

[5 minutes]

Take a moment to integrate this experience, and breathe into the possibility of connection with yourself and the planet at all times.

[1 minute]

Bring your practice to a close and do what you need to take care of yourself for the next few minutes.

[3 minutes]

MIRROR MEDITATION

You can review the Instructions for Guided Practices on page 207 and then do the following guided practice.

[You can do this with yourself or with everyone all together in front of a mirror, speaking aloud with music on, or silently. I encourage to voice aloud. You can do this practice by looking into your phone camera, although you can't do eye contact that way, so it's different, and then bonus round of self compassion is to film it and then watch it. Find away to be with yourself eye to eye if possible.]

Sit or stand very close to a mirror, just a few inches away.
Make eye contact with yourself.

Then take a moment to really look at yourself.

[30 seconds]

There are prompts of things for you to look at, do so with neutral, loving, noticing as best you can.
Even if you find yourself judging yourself, see if you can see that judgement in your face, how you are expressing it, and notice and watch that as well.
Notice any signs of how you may be feeling.

[30 seconds]

Do you see:

Content?
Relaxation?
Tiredness?
Anger?
Joy?
Stress?
Pain?
Sadness?
Peace?

[1 minute]

Notice your construction:

Your eye color
The shape of your eyes, nose, lips
The quality of your skin
The presence or lack of presence of hair
Notice scars, birthmarks, inherited traits

[1 minute]

Now begin speaking to yourself emphatically
Identifying the emotions you see or imagine the face you are seeing is expressing.

[30 seconds]

Acknowledge the feelings and validate them.
They exist so offer affirming knowing why they would be there.
You have an inside scoop. Let go of the judgement of whether they are worthy reasons, and recognize that the feelings are what they are.
Release the need to explain why you should or could be feeling something different.
Tell yourself what you see, tell yourself how you look, what you are seeing, feeling-wise.
And then respond.

[1 minute]

Ask yourself if that's really what is happening.
Answer.
Ask yourself how you are.
Answer.
Offer supportive words to yourself.

[1 minute]

Respond with honest vulnerability.
Do you believe these kind words, are you afraid or hopeful, nervous or guilty?
Tell yourself the truth. You can admit your opinion here.
Respond with empathic understanding, tell her what she needs and wants to hear from an honest, wise heart.
Allow the conversation to just GO THERE.
If you cry, watch yourself, let yourself. If you laugh or feel shy, see that. Be with yourself.

[Untimed, 10 minutes, or a couple songs]

Keep going until you feel that the wise self and seen self in the mirror know one another.
Perhaps even have merged and there is a sense of unity in yourself.
Are one another.

Bless yourself.
Bow and move on.

NOURISHMENT IDENTIFICATION

You can review the Instructions for Guided Practices on page 207 and then do the following guided practice.

Get yourself settled.
Take a few strong, clearing breaths.

[3 breaths]

Inhale and exhale as you imagine any clutter, be it yours or anyone else's around you being washed away.
Take 3 breaths into your body, allowing yourself to expand and take up your own space, watching as anything that is not you or yours move away like leaves on a river flowing downstream to become sacred compost and nourishment elsewhere.

[3 breaths]

Choosing to rest in the concept that that which is released is restored.
That which is congestion or a burden in you, when released becomes free-flowing potential and becomes a gift to the cosmos.

[30 seconds]

Now gently begin slowing your breath.
Allow your body and mind to settle with each inhale and each exhale in your own space.

[30 seconds]

Take a moment to give yourself permission to connect to subtler parts of yourself that you may not consistently consciously connect to.
Breathing in and out as you open to hear your own wisdom.

[30 seconds]

Ask yourself where you are needing nourishment, and notice any sensations or images that rise.

[30 seconds]

When the area becomes clear,
breath in and out of that area,
noticing without needing to change anything as best you can.
Notice color, density, temperature, images, sensations, associations...

[30 seconds]

Now ask this part of you what it needs to be nourished? Listen to words, images, knowings, sensations...

[2 minutes]

Ask yourself where else you are needing nourishment, and notice anything that rises.

[30 seconds]

Now ask this part of you what it needs to be nourished?

[1 minutes]

Finally ask yourself if there is anywhere else that needs to share how it needs to be nourished, and notice what happens.

[2 minutes]

Take the moment to let your body know what you will do in response to this new found wisdom. Only make commitments you are willing to keep. Better to make smaller agreements and keep them, than make well intended ones you won't be able to do.

[90 seconds]

Thank your body and self for communing with you.
Take a few breaths coming into completion.
Settling and integrating with what you have discovered.

[5 breaths]

Reach for your journal and take notes about our experience.

OBSERVATION BIAS

You can review the Instructions for Guided Practices on page 207 and then do the following guided practice.
[*There is a section of this practice where you are prompted to direct people to look for a thing, that are listed as red and blue in the script you can do this exercise with a focus on any color, shapes of object, or repeated visual aspect in the space.]

This practice is observing and discussion.
I invite you to take a breath.
Everyone look around the room,
take in what's there,
what is seen,
what objects are in the room.

[1 minute]

Everyone close your eyes. Keep your eyes closed and share aloud what you saw.

[1-2 minutes]

Everyone open your eyes and look around for things with *blue* in them.
Everyone closes there eyes.
What is *red* in the room? Where is there *red* in the room?
Go a head and with your eyes closed name things that are *red* in the room?

[1-2 minutes]

Everyone open your eyes and look around.
Notice and start naming things with red in them.

[1-2 minutes]

Now we discuss. Did you think you accurately observed the room?
Did you?
What impact did having a focus have?
Did people notice he same or different things?
Do you see the space differently now that you did before?

PELVIC BOWL MEDITATION

You can review theInstructions for Guided Practices on page 207 and then do the following guided practice.

Set yourself up either sitting, or if possible lay down on your back, elevating your hips on a cushion.

[let people get settled]

Bring you hands to rest gently on your hip bones, hold your root, on lower abdomen, or resting your hands on your pubic bone.

[3 breaths]

Invite your spirit guides or Sacred Council to join you here and invite their assistance.
Deepen your breath and allow your body to settle, entirely giving into gravity.

[1 minute]

Scanning the space around your body, notice if there is anything you sense that is other people's stuff or just stuff that you don't really need to carry around with you.
With 3 deep breaths, release and clear any clutter from this space.

[30 seconds]

Scanning the surface of your body and the general tension of your body, notice if there is anything that is not yours or just things that you don't want to keep carrying.
With 3 deep breaths, release and clear any clutter from your body.

[30 seconds]

Scanning the inside of your body and subtle self, sense if there is anything that is not yours or something that you no longer need to carry.
With 3 deep breaths, release and clear all of the clutter in your body and self.

[30 seconds]

Bring your focus to your root, where you hands are.
Feel into this space and notice what's there that is not yours and what you are ready to release and no longer carry.
With 3 deep breaths, release and clear the clutter from your root.

[1 minute]

Now slow your breath down, find a space you can connect to in your spine.
Breath into that space of focus.
As you inhale, bring that focus up the spine to the base of the skull.
As you exhale, bring the focus down the spine, to the sacrum, and to the base of the spine.

Inhale to the head.

Exhale to the hips.

Once more, inhale to the mind.

And now exhale to the sacrum and stay there.

As you inhale, circle the focus around to the front of your pelvis under your hands.
As you exhale, circle the breath back around to the back body.

Inhale to the front.

Exhale to the back.

Inhale to the front.

Exhale to the back.

Release the control of breath and notice the sensations of the root.

[1 minute]

Bring your awareness to the landscape of your root.
All genders, if you have the organ or not, have a wombspace. It may be inside your root or holding you outside your body.
Breathe into your womb energy.

[1 breath]

Check in on it with curiosity.
Ask, "What do you need?
How are you?

What's happening?"
Listen and feel for answers.

[1 minute]

Using your own loving power and invite the participation of your guides to welcome and offer blessings to yourself and care for the answers you were given.
Allow yourself to receive what is being offered to your being in this moment.

[1 minute]

Feel the generative organs of the ovaries or testicles physically and/or energetically, breathing in, sensing these star bundles of creative energy.

Check in one at a time, left side, right side.
Ask, "What do you need?
How are you?
What's happening?"
Listen and feel for answers.

[2 minutes]

Using your own loving power, and inviting the participation of your guides, welcome and offer blessings to yourself and the answers you were given by your star bundles of creativity.
Allow yourself to receive all you need in this moment.

[1 minute]

Feel for the constellation of your creative root.
The relationship between the front and back of your pelvis, the left and right, the center.
Breathe in and notice.
Ask your Root as a whole, "What do you want me to know right now?"
Listen.

[3 minutes]

Using your own loving power, and inviting the participation of your guides, welcome and offer blessings to yourself and to the insight offered by your root.
Allow yourself to receive all the blessings.

[1 minute]

Taking this moment to thank yourself and to thank your guides and Sacred Council.
Bless yourself, those who held you, and this space.

[2 minute]

Taking the next few minutes to bring this journey to a close and bringing yourself all the way through.

[1-3 minutes]

Using cleansing breaths, gentle affectionate touch on your own body, and slow and deep listening to yourself.
Come through to the here and now fully.
Take a few minutes to write or draw in your journal.

[10 minutes]

RESTORING OUR INNER TEMPLE

You can review the Instructions for Guided Practices on page 207 and then do the following guided practice.

Allow your body to relax and take three deep breaths.

[30 seconds]

Give yourself permission to receive everything you need right now.
I give myself permission to experience healing.
I give myself permission to KNOW love.
I give myself permission to change.
I give myself permission to heal.
I give myself permission to BE just as I am.

Deepening your breath
Breathing in healing light, breath, sound, love, clear all the bodies.
With each breath, allow yourself to receive everything you need and be nourished
and with each exhale release everything that no longer serves you.

[1 breath]

Tension turns into relaxation.
Stress into clarity.
Tightness into softness.
Resistance into trust.
Gripping into release.

[1 breath]

Lean into the perspective that that which is released is restored.
Like legos or firecrackers, when it is in you it has form.
As soon as you release it, it loses it's form and becomes raw potential, free flowing life force.
So that what was once a burden in you becomes a gift to the cosmos.

[1 breath]

Breathe this light and love, cleansing, healing, restoring, balancing into and through...
... the space around you.
... your skin and hair and nails.
... all your muscles and tissues.
... your digestive organs.
... your blood, cerebral spinal fluid, lymph, all the fluids of your body.
... your heart and all the feeling you have ever had, are having, and will have are held by and cleansed by this light.
... your mind and all the thoughts and the pathways to and from those thoughts that you have ever had, are having, and will have are held by and washed and blessed by this light.
... your root, generative organs and all the wisdom and deep knowing that you have ever had, are having, and will have held by are honored and sanctified through recognition by this light.

[30 seconds]

Breathing the healing into and from your bones...
... your bone marrow, the place when your blood is made -- where your DNA is reproduced.

[30 seconds]

This loves washes into and through the cells of your whole being.
As you breathe this love, it moves through the space between the electrons.

[30 seconds]

Until the landscape of your being is so filled with light,
that you are inhaling light and exhaling light,
that without effort your whole being is radiating light.

[2 minutes]

Now invite your spiritual council to join you.
Calling on your spirit guides, the Divine, your beloved ancestors.
Calling those who are entirely dedicated to you being the fullest expression of yourself in this lifetime, to come close.
Knowing that any ancestors that need healing will stay outside this circle at a distance to witness and receive the healing that you are doing for your entire lineage.
And those who carry what you need and are able to share with you will come close.

[30 seconds]

Your spirit guides are so respectful, love and trust you so much, that they will only help on the level you actively invite them to.
So decide how deeply and fully you want them to assist.

Thank them for being with you always, whether you have known it or not.
Tell them you are here to connect and establish a conscious relationship with them.
Invite them close.

[30 seconds]

This is a moment of choice:
Tell them right now, where and how you want them to help.
At the edges? In guidance? In the complete arrangement of and assistance in circumstances? In complete cellular reconstruction at the soul core of your being?
It is up to you. Ask them to help you in the way you want them to.
Ask them now.

[4 minutes]

You are being called by your wombspace (all genders, organs or not, have a wombspace either inside your root or holding you outside your body) this is your generative creative space. The land of your divine creative self where spirit and inspiration move from formless into form.

[3 breaths]

Your wombspace has a door or threshold.
As you approach, honor and take your time, approach with respect.
Is this the first time you have seen or felt this space?
Take in the detail, and when you feel ready, not before, enter.

[2 minutes]

You have entered, wander around and explore.
If this is your first time here, it is likely there are ruins of sacred ritual sites.
Overgrown and untended.
Feel the magic of this place.
Inspect the remains, see what you can see, touch anything you want.

[2 minutes]

Somewhere in here there is a Temple candle.
Find it.
And if it is not lit,
Light it.

[3 minutes]

Call upon your sacred Temple Keeping Kin for help to restore this temple to its finest glory.
It is time to remember the truth and power that is here.

[1 minute]

Upon your invitation for help, a flood of Grandmothers, Grandqueers, Grandfathers or whomever are your sacred Grands, who remember and carry the skills to repair it all, come flowing in.
With loaded tool belts, magic healing powers, and hearts full of love they immediately flood in and get to work.
Singing and tending,
honoring with songs of remembrance.

[3 minutes]

You watch as abandoned gardens are healed and turn into flower-filled

space.
Where altars that were cracked are fixed and restored.
Where paths were overgrown, they are now clear.
Dry creek beds begin flowing with crystal clean water.

[5 minutes]

From a distance you hear your kin calling to each other.
"I found it!"
"It's here"
"Over here"
"This is it"

[1 breath]

Everyone leaves what they are doing and moves towards a wall, overgrown and covered with vines.
One of your kin is pulling back the overgrowth and revealing a message.
The others come and place flowers at the base of this wall.
Sitting, wringing their hands, weeping.
Other 's placing flowers and dancing, singing, full voice.
As you get closer you get this foreign yet familiar feeling.
You walk up and trace the images on your Temple Wall.

[3 breaths]

The kin weeping are saying things like, "We've been without this for soooo long. Too long. Too long."
"How did we last so long with it so silent?"
The Kin singing, laughing and crying, celebrating the emerging wisdom.
"It's still here, it was here all along. It remains! It's here!"

[3 breaths]

The message on the wall is your medicine.
Your story.
Your soul's etched knowing.
That which no one else carries like you.
Your healing journey, and that which you carry and share by your very being.

You get close and trace and remember your signature, unique knowing that your divine sacred essence etched the on the walls of your temple.

As you remember, are celebrated and treasured, the complete restoration of your Inner Temple occurs.

[10 minutes]

Now go the place where you plant your intentions, grow your creations, and cultivate your gifts.

[3 breaths]

Tend this space.
Check-in to see what is there.
Do you want it all?
Decide what you want to keep and what you want to clear, and then do it.

[2 minutes]

Now take a moment to clarify your newest seed to plant.
What do you want?
Breathing in and out, allow your desire to come into focus, fully revealing itself.
Allow it to expand to it's fullest expression.

[1 minute]

Bless the seed with your deepest wisdom, that it may be for the most optimal expression of you, inviting a purifying light to bring it into its most concentrated, radiant, gem form.
Blessing the very heart of this desire, the bead of this prayer.
Ask for your spirit guides and kin to bless it and you as well.

[1 minute]

Now place this seed or gem upon your growing space, whatever it is, in whatever way makes sense in you.
Bless it and watch blessings be poured upon it.

[3 minutes]

Take the next couple minutes walk through and savor this beautiful, restored Inner Temple. Complete your time here for now,
knowing that it is here in you,
all that time,
always available for you to come to tend to and remember,

and to heal in and with.

[2 minutes]

Give thanks to the Grands as they complete their work and bless you and leave the Inner Temple grounds to your soul's trustworthy keeping.

[5 breaths]

Take this moment to offer a gift of gratitude to the Grands and your Sacred Council.

[2 minutes]

Make space to receive any gifts, messages, or offerings they may have for you.

[2 minutes]

Slowly deepening your breath.
Taking 3 deep, cleansing breaths, releasing all that is ready and willing to be released and restored.
Let it go.

[5 deep breaths]

Now, in whatever way you are inspired, summon back to you from all time and all space, your Soul, your Truest Self to come home to you here.
Knowing that what returns to you is you in your optimal form.

[2 minutes, or until a big settling breath]

Take 3 gentle breaths integrating on all levels of your being, unifying self with self,
Inner Temple with body temple. Body Temple with Life Temple.
Grounding and rooting in your light lattice with this light lattice of Earth.
Allowing the space that has been made, the self that has expanded and returned,
and the new self to enter this world in a gentle manner.

[30 seconds]

Softly bringing your hands to your body, patting and petting,
brushing and greeting your emerged self with loving affection.

Lightly pressing yourself with loving contact,
honoring this sacred self into its sacred vessel of a body.

[2 minutes]

Gently begin moving, rocking, holding, breathing.
Gently. Gently. Gently.
Take the ten minutes to do whatever you need to care for yourself.
Journal, go to the bathroom, eat, rest.

[When practicing in a group]

We will keep this space quiet and ask that if people want to talk to do it
_____ *[name a location]*.
Knowing that as we return with our precious selves,
we will greet each other with tenderness.

SIMPLE MOONTIME PRACTICE

You can review the Instructions for Guided Practices on page 207 and then do the following guided practice.

Arrange your body so that you are comfortable.
Place your hands over your lowest abdomen, holding your wombspace.
All genders, if you have the organ or not, have a wombspace energy. It may be inside your root or holding you outside your body. Breathe into your menstruating womb energy.

[1 minute]

Breathe into your body, follow your breath through your nose into your lungs and back out.
Imagine your breath moving down your body into your wombspace breathing to and from there.

[1 minute]

Let go of the breath and allow your whole body to soften.
Tell yourself, "I am here to connect to the wisdom of my blood and menstruum."
Allow your mind and thoughts to soften and slow down.
With every breath, invite your body to be at ease with the relaxing of your muscles.

Let go of holding up your body and allow the earth to be the chest of the Cosmic Mother and gravity to be the arms gently and securely losing you.

[1 minute]

Feel the location where your body is resting, feeling the surface you are on receive you, wrapping around your body as you relax and allow your weight to be held.

[1 minute]

Imagine a sacred river of blood, this is the cosmic mother's sacred menstruum flowing, this river carries every nourishment you could ever need, while also it is so powerful and cleansing that it has the power to dissolve any burden, heal any wound, cleanse anything.

[2 minutes]

Connect and choose to trust this Sacred Red River.
Allow your own Sacred Red River to commune with all it has to offer.
Submerging your body in this Sacred Energetic River, providing anything you need and carrying away anything that not longer serves you.

[10-20 minutes]

Give thanks to your menstruum.
Give thanks to the sacred union that is the shared ritual that wombs have shared for millennia.
Be blessed, feel blessed.
Be a blessing, know you are blessing.
As you are ready, get up slowly and with as much attention to and fulfillment of your body's desires as possible.

SOUL UNIFICATION HEALING MEDITATION

You can review the Instructions for Guided Practices on page 207 and then do the following guided practice.

[This practice take a little less than an hour. If you done this practice before and need a shorter practice in a group or individually, do the **Bone Breathing Meditation** *on page 216 (10-15minute practice) with the intention of releasing all that it not you and filling and unifying with your true self.]*

Take a few breaths settle and arrive.

[30 seconds]

Give yourself permission to receive everything you need right now
I give myself permission to experience healing
I give myself permission to KNOW love
I give myself permission to change
I give myself permission to heal
I give myself permission to BE just as I am

[1 minute]

Deepening your breath
Breathing in healing light, breath, sound, love, clear all the bodies.
With each breath, allow yourself to receive everything you need and be nourished
and with each exhale release everything that no longer serves you.

[1 breath]

Tension turns into relaxation.
Stress into clarity.
Tightness into softness.
Resistance into trust.
Gripping into release.

[1 breath]

Lean into the perspective that that which is released is restored.
Like legos or firecrackers, when it is in you it has form.
As soon as you release it, it loses it's form and becomes raw potential, free flowing life force.
So that what was once a burden in you becomes a gift to the cosmos.

[1 breath]

Breathe this light and love, cleansing, healing, restoring, balancing into and through...
... the space around you.
... your skin and hair and nails.
... all your muscles and tissues.
... your digestive organs.
... your blood, cerebral spinal fluid, lymph, all the fluids of your body.

... your heart and all the feeling you have ever had, are having, and will have are held by and cleansed by this light.
... your mind and all the thoughts and the pathways to and from those thoughts that you have ever had, are having, and will have are held by and washed and blessed by this light.
... your root, generative organs and all the wisdom and deep knowing that you have ever had, are having, and will have held by are honored and sanctified through recognition by this light.

[30 seconds]

Breathing the healing into and from your bones...
... your bone marrow, the place when your blood is made -- where your DNA is reproduced.

[30 seconds]

This loves washes into and through the cells of your whole being.
As you breathe this love, it moves through the space between the electrons.

[30 seconds]

Until the landscape of your being is so filled with light,
that you are inhaling light and exhaling light,
that without effort your whole being is radiating light.

[2 minutes]

Now invite your spiritual council to join you.
Calling on your spirit guides, the Divine, your beloved ancestors.
Calling those who are entirely dedicated to you being the fullest expression of yourself in this lifetime, to come close.
Knowing that any ancestors that need healing will stay outside this circle at a distance to witness and receive the healing that you are doing for your entire lineage.
And those who carry what you need and are able to share with you will come close.

[30 seconds]

Your spirit guides are so respectful, love and trust you so much, that they will only help on the level you actively invite them to.
So decide how deeply and fully you want them to assist.

Thank them for being with you always, whether you have known it or not.
Tell them you are here to connect and establish a conscious relationship with them.
Invite them close.

[30 seconds]

This is a moment of choice:
Tell them right now, where and how you want them to help.
At the edges? In guidance? In the complete arrangement of and assistance in circumstances? In complete cellular reconstruction at the soul core of your being?
It is up to you. Ask them to help you in the way you want them to.
Ask them now.

[4 minutes]

Begin scanning your body for your essential truth, your Soul, your truest self, the self that has been here long before this life and will be here long after.
Locate this place in you.
Breathe into you.

[1 minute]

Here is another moment of choice.
I am inviting you to choose,
to give the authority over your entire life to that place in you...
Do you want your Soul, your holy essence, your truest self to have the authority over your life?
If yes, then declare that right now.

Hand over the entire landscape of your being to your Truest Self.
This means your Truest self is deciding what words you speak, the tone you use.
How you listen and what you hear.
What steps you take and the decisions made.
All aspects of life and being.

[1 minute]

Hand over the chemicals of your brain and the hormones of your body, how your cells and DNA replicate, to the wisdom and discernment of your Truest Self.

[1 minute]

Invite your Self to have the authority over your life and actions...
Where you go, how you feel, what you see,
what you touch, how you digest your food, and
the meaning you find in things.
Your entire life...

[1 minute]

All that you are and all that you are becoming is now under the direction
of your Soul.

[2 minutes]

Now we are going to enlist the power of witness
and the wisdom of your spirit guides, your Sacred Council.
Invite your council to come in and see deeply, and entirely,
all that you are, see you in all your beauty,
your divine essence, allow all that you are and all that you have been to be
seen and known

[1 minute]

Now, invite them to see all that you have been that is not you...

[1 minute]

Choose to be exposed...
Choose to allow them to see all the ways in which you have side stepped
your wisdom,
betrayed your own body or trust,
blamed or shamed,
forgotten your power,
denied that you are lovable.

[2 minutes]

Lift it up, or simply choose to be completely exposed and have them see
you,
witnessing and lifting any shame that may be present,
allow their love and wisdom to see every place and every way you can
bare to have them see you.

Be known as who you have been that you are not, and who you really are...
Allow their loving presence to help discern and heal disconnect...

[1 minute]

Invite them into details and subtleties of it all.

[1 minute]

Choose to expose all that is you, and all that you have been that is not you and allow *all* of it to be loved and healed.

[2 minute]

Invite their guidance, their healing, as the truth of you emerges and expands,
filling the landscape of our being with your Truest Self.
Surrender to your wisdom.

[15 minutes]

Taking the next few minutes to come to completion with your guides and healing journey.

[5 minutes]

Take this moment to offer a gift of gratitude to your Sacred Council.

[2 minutes]

Make space to receive any gifts, messages, or offerings they may have for you.

[2 minutes]

Slowly deepening your breath.
Taking 3 deep, cleansing breaths,
releasing all that is ready and willing to be released and restored.
Let it go.

[5 deep breaths]

Now, in whatever way you are inspired, summon back to you from all time and all space,

your Soul, your Truest Self to come home to you here.
Knowing that what returns to you is you in your optimal form.

[2 minutes, or until a big settling breath]

Take 3 gentle breaths integrating on all levels of your being, unifying self with self.
Grounding and rooting in your light lattice with this light lattice of Earth.
Allowing the space that has been made, the self that has expanded and returned,
and the new self to enter this world in a gentle manner.

[30 seconds]

Softly bringing your hands to your body, patting and petting, brushing and greeting your emerged self with loving affection.
Lightly pressing yourself with loving contact,
honoring this sacred self into its sacred vessel of a body.

[2 minutes]

Gently begin moving, rocking, holding, breathing.
Gently. Gently. Gently.
Take the ten minutes to do whatever you need to care for yourself.
Journal, go to the bathroom, eat, rest.

[When practicing in a group]

We will keep this space quiet and ask that if people want to talk to do it _____ *[name a location]*.
Knowing that as we return with our precious selves,
we will greet each other with tenderness.

SPACE IN JOINTS MEDITATION

You can review the Instructions for Guided Practices on page 207 and then do the following guided practice.

Get yourself in a comfortable relaxing position.

[30 seconds]

Relax the joints of your feet

Breathing into the knuckles of your toes.
The bones of your feet.
Your ankles.

[1 minute]

Softening and relaxing your knees.
Allowing each breath to move completely through your joints.
Flowing through obstruction.

[1 minute]

Following the femurs to your hips.
Making space by relaxing in the hip sockets to where the femur meets the pelvis,
expanding through into the sacrum.
Feel the space at your root soften and expand as tension falls away and your breath and blood fill and flow smoothly.

[1 minute]

Breathing into the bones of the hands.
The knuckles on each finger.
The wrists.
Allowing them to fully relax and allow sensation to increase through the body and breath.

[1 minute]

Allow the entire arm to let go.
Release the grip.
Put down whatever you are carrying.
Increase the space in your elbows so that the bones meet in generous and floating space.

[1 minute]

Breathing into the shoulders.
Space and breath moving into the armpits.
The top of the shoulders.
As the weight and tension melt away and your self fills in.

[1 minute]

Breathing into the hips and sacrum.
Feeling the base of your spine.
As you breathe, allow the breath to spiral up the spine giving space and fluid to each and every vertebrae of your back bone.
Feel the lifting and floating of each rib and the collarbones.

[1 minutes]

Allowing the base of the head to lift and shift with breath.
Relaxing the jaw, and the sutures throughout your skull.
Witnessing breath and fluid move through the entirety of the head and flowing down through the body.

[1 minute]

Taking the next few minutes to feel your body in space.
Breathing.
Pulsing.
Shifting.
Still.
Here.

[4 minutes]

Take a moment to offer yourself a blessing or say thank you for bringing yourself here.

[5 breaths]

Taking a few integrating breaths, relaxing and receiving.
Fully arriving in this place, in this shared now.
Take a minute to bring yourself through to this shared and sacred space.
Slowly opening your eyes and bringing all of that felt and integrated self here.

[1 minute]

STEALING FROM OURSELVES

You can review the Instructions for Guided Practices on page 207 and then do the following guided practice.

Get comfortable.
Begin intentionally breathing in and out.
Settle in your body.

[5 breaths]

With every inhale, feel yourself expand.
On every exhale, notice the container of your body holding you.

[30 seconds]

Feel the dynamic way your body gives you space and supports you simultaneously.
Notice the waves of your breath, your heart pumping blood through your body and feel for even subtler currents moving through you.
Relax into the way your body is being rocked.

[30 seconds]

Allow your mind to slow, your body to soften, and your spirit to arrive and settle in the here and now.

[2 minutes]

Invite your spirit guides or Sacred Council to gather close.
Invoke and ask directly for their assistance in revealing to you
your own patterns and ways of being
in a manner that is useful and that you can comprehend and understand.

[1 minute]

Start with an admitting.
Change the following example so that it is honest and feels true or appropriate to you.:
"It has come to my awareness
that I may be stealing energy, time, money, or resource

from myself due to patterns of subconsciously not getting my needs met or not feeling like I deserve to or being taught to behave this way."

[30 seconds]

"I am asking my consciousness and my guides
to reveal to me the ways in which I do this or have done this.
Help me see and know how this behavior shows up
in actions, thoughts, and bodily experience."
"Help me see alternatives"

[10 minutes]

Good job.
Allow your breath to deepen.
Take 3 deep clearing breaths.

[30 seconds]

Take this time to complete your process and make an offering to your guides and be sure to make space to receive any message or gift from them.

[2 minutes]

Take a few breaths, settling and integrating what you have discovered.
Reach for your journal and take notes about our experience.

VISITING OUR INNER TEMPLE

You can review the Instructions for Guided Practices on page 207 and then do the following guided practice.

Allow your body to relax and take three deep breaths.

[30 seconds]

Give yourself permission to receive everything you need right now.
I give myself permission to experience healing.
I give myself permission to KNOW love.
I give myself permission to change.
I give myself permission to heal.
I give myself permission to BE just as I am.

[30 seconds]

Deepening your breath
Breathing in healing light, breath, sound, love, clear all the bodies.
With each breath, allow yourself to receive everything you need and be nourished
and with each exhale release everything that no longer serves you.

[1 breath]

Tension turns into relaxation.
Stress into clarity.
Tightness into softness.
Resistance into trust.
Gripping into release.

[1 breath]

Lean into the perspective that that which is released is restored.
Like legos or firecrackers, when it is in you it has form.
As soon as you release it, it loses it's form and becomes raw potential, free flowing life force.
So that what was once a burden in you becomes a gift to the cosmos.

[30 seconds]

This love washes into and through the cells of your whole being.
And as you breathe, this light moves through the space between your electrons.

[30 seconds]

Until the landscape of your being is so filled with light,
So filled with the love that you are,
that you are inhaling light and exhaling light,
that without effort your whole being is radiating light.

[2 minute]

Now invite your spiritual council to join you.
Calling on your spirit guides, divinity, your beloved ancestors.
Calling those who are entirely dedicated to you being the fullest expression of yourself in this lifetime to come close to you here.
Invite them close.

Ask them for exactly the amount of support you want.
Welcome their assistance.

[4 minutes]

You are being called by your wombspace (all genders, organs or not, have a wombspace either inside your root or holding you outside your body) this is your generative, creative space. The land of your Divine, creative self move spirit and inspiration into form.
Come to the Inner Temple's threshold.
Enter.

[30 seconds]

Take your time exploring and checking in.
The landscape may be the same or entirely different from the last time you were here,
it's a magical place.
Explore with openness every time.
Notice how you feel.

[30 seconds]

If anything needs tending, tend it.
If it needs clearing, clear it.
If it needs cleaning, clean it.
If it need attention, attend to it.
If it need loving, love it.

[5 minutes]

You have come here for a reason, you do know why.
If you are not conscious of that purpose,
ask your body or ask for a guardian to show you,
and then surrender and trust that what you have come for is taking place.
Allow.
Surrender.

[10 min]

Now go to the place where you plant your intentions,
grow your creations, and cultivate your gifts.
Tend this space.
Checking in to see what is there, how your planted intentions are.

Do you want what's growing or living there?

[1 breath]

This is your space, and only what you want belongs here.
Nothing else.

[1 breath]

Keep what you want and release the rest.

[5 minutes]

You are invited to take the opportunity to set a new creative seed take a moment to clarify it.
What do you want?
Breathing in and out, allow your desire to come into focus, fully revealing itself.
Allow it to expand to it's fullest expression.

[3 minutes]

Bless the seed with your deepest wisdom, that it may be for the most optimal expression of you and honoring the Earth realm as well.
Invite a purifying light to bring it into its most concentrated, radiant, crystalline form.
Bless very heart of this desire, the seed of this prayer.
Ask for your spirit guides to bless it and you as well.

[1 minute]

Now place this seed or gem upon your growing space, whatever it is, in whatever way makes sense in you.
Bless it and watch blessings be poured upon it.

[3 minutes]

Take the next couple minutes walk through and savor this beautiful, restored Inner Temple. Complete your time here for now,
knowing that it is here in you,
all that time,
always available for you to come to tend to and remember,
and to heal in and with.

[2 minutes]

Give thanks to the Grands as they complete their work and bless you and leave the Inner Temple grounds to our soul's trustworthy keeping.

[5 breaths]

Take this moment to offer a gift of gratitude to the Grands and your Sacred Council.

[2 minutes]

Make space to receive any gifts, messages, or offerings they may have for you.

[2 minutes]

Slowly deepening your breath.
Taking 3 deep, cleansing breaths, releasing all that is ready and willing to be released and restored.
Let it go.

[5 deep breaths]

Now, in whatever way you are inspired, summon back to you from all time and all space, your Soul, your Truest Self to come home to you here.
Knowing that what returns to you is you in your optimal form.

[2 minutes, or until a big settling breath]

Take 3 gentle breaths integrating on all levels of your being, unifying self with self.
Grounding and rooting in your light lattice with this light lattice of Earth.
Allowing the space that has been made, the self that has expanded and returned,
and the new self to enter this world in a gentle manner.

[30 seconds]

Softly bringing your hands to your body, patting and petting, brushing and greeting your emerged self with loving affection.
Lightly pressing yourself with loving contact,
honoring this sacred self into its sacred vessel of a body.

[2 minutes]

Gently begin moving, rocking, holding, breathing.
Gently. Gently. Gently.
Take the ten minutes to do whatever you need to care for yourself.
Journal, go to the bathroom, eat, rest.

[When practicing in a group]

We will keep this space quiet and ask that if people want to talk to do it
_____ *[name a location]*.
Knowing that as we return with our precious selves,
we will greet each other with tenderness.

Breath Practices

INSTRUCTIONS

Wisdom practices across the globe and throughout time have used and use conscious breathing as a major tool of self regulation and self mastery. Breath is known to be one of the fastest ways to link your consciousness to the under surface areas of self and body. Because we breathe both unconsciously and consciously it becomes the perfect landscape to play and intentionally connect and explore the conscious, sub and unconscious self.

The practices vary and the research and study in both western science and spiritual endeavors are constantly discovering and remembering ways to care, restore, activate, calm, and invigorate our beings through our breath.

I encourage you to explore and lean into these practice and other breath practices that come your way.

Know this, they are powerful and effective medicines that can make huge impact on your systems, so practice with confidence and care.

ALTERNATE NOSTRIL BREATHING

You can review the Instructions for Breath Practices on page 274 and then do the following breath practice.

I learned this breathing technique through yogic lineage and where it is called Nadi Shodhana Pranayama. There are many ways to do this practice that includes various hand positions, side sequencing, visualizations, and timing. The effects vary depending on the variations used and can be activating or calming. Do research, explore, try different variations yourself, listen to your body as you breathe, trust your teachers, and find out more. The method I offer here is a simple starting point that will support the balance of your system.

- Curl your pointer and middle finger into your hand
- Bring the thumb and ring finger to make a U shape
- Rest the pads of your thumb and ring finger on either side of your nose
- Inhale and exhale fully
- Gently press your thumb against your nose, closing that nostril
- Inhale through the open nostril
- Close both nostrils
- Keep your ring finger side closed
- Release your thumb and exhale through that nostril
- Then inhale through the same nostril
- Close both nostrils
- Release the ring finger and exhale thought that nostril
- Then inhale through the same nostril
- Close both nostrils
- Continue this sequence for two minutes

AUDIBLE EXHALE

You can review the Instructions for Breath Practices on page 274 and then do the following breath practice.

Using your breath and shifting vibrations of sound inside your body to different places can make the healing and movement of stuck things go from seemingly impossible to simply and truly happening. Work with this breathing exercise to see how you can connect with, practice, and explore audible breathing. Feel free to add variations including the location that you're breathing from as well as the quality of sounds you make.

Big breath in. Let it out. Big breath in. Let out a sigh. Big breath in. Huff out the nose.

Big breath in. Let out a louder sigh. Big breath in. Let out a guttural huh.

Big breath in. Let out a groan. Big breath in. Let out a high pitched sigh.

Big breath in. Let it out through gently closed and relaxed lips so they tremble.

Big breath in. Let whatever wants to come out, come out.

Big breath in. Let out whatever feels best.

Do ten more big breaths in with audible exhales however you feel called. Revisit ones that were hard or ones that felt great. Play with relaxing your body or adding movement, let the sounds and the breath and you evolve and change as you breathe.

BREATH OF FIRE

You can review the Instructions for Breath Practices on page 274 and then do the following breath practice.

This yogic pranayama practice has many wise variations. Trust the teachers that share different versions. This is a solid option to work with. Breath of Fire can be done slow or fast. The whole body will slightly rock or bounce with each inhale. The breath is audible as it moves in and out of your body. Practice Breath of Fire for two minutes.

- Sit in a relaxed manner with your back straight
- Inhale and exhale fully
- Breathe in a half breath
- Using your abdominal muscles, exhale by pulsing your belly back to the spine
- Loosen your jaw, keep your mouth closed, and breathe through your nose
- Relax your lungs and breathing effort
- Allow the belly pulling in and then relaxing to move the breath in and out of your body

BREATHE TO STRETCH

You can review the Instructions for Breath Practices on page 274 and then do the following breath practice.

Reach your hands above your head, up towards the sky. Reach forward as far as you can, and then release your arms down, coming into a forward bend. Then, still folded over, back off from your edge. Just hang out, allowing your body to relax in this posture. From here, take five HUGE breaths. Allow your body to lift out of the pose and stretch on the inhale. Soften into the fold on the exhale.

Let your breath move your body. When you engage with your breath, you can allow it to lead you into transformation. Your work is to breathe, the breath does the rest.

COOLING BREATH

You can review the Instructions for Breath Practices on page 274 and then do the following breath practice.

Roll your tongue so that it makes a tunnel, or bring your lips together in an open kiss shape. Breathe in through your nose and the make a slow audible exhale twice as long as your inhale. This breath is like a cool wind blowing out the opening of cavern.

Do this for 2 minutes.

MINDFUL BREATHING

You can review the Instructions for Breath Practices on page 274 and then do the following breath practice.

The heart of mindfulness is to be aware of what you are doing. That is the whole deal. Mindfulness is about bringing consciousness to your feeling, acting, choosing, and being. To have mindfulness is to have awareness. Mindfulness meditation is then a simple practice of sitting and enjoying sitting; breathing and enjoying breathing. It's an opportunity to notice your experience with attention, observation, and awareness.

The practice of mindful breathing is not meant to be a place where you sit and think, though thinking will likely happen. Even though we are not our thoughts, we do think our thoughts. Mindfulness is the witnessing that you are, what you are, and if you are not thinking. It is consciousness in the space around the thought. The same goes for feelings and sensations.

Use the focus of your breath, the sensation of your inhalation and exhalation, and the sensory observation of your body sitting and breathing to bring you back to where you are. Again and again, notice that you are doing whatever you are doing, feeling, thinking, and experiencing. Then notice yourself as you breathe and be aware of what you are doing.

The purpose is not to beat yourself up for not being still, focused, enlightened, or smart enough. The point is to be here on the planet, breathing the air that is here to breathe. Be here and know that you are here. Simple. Profound.

Sit comfortably, allow your eyes to gaze lightly upon a singular place or gently close them. Sit in silence or put on relaxing and music, though know you can do this practice anywhere. It travels very well.

Set a timer for two, twelve, twenty, thirty, or forty-five minutes.

Offerings

INSTRUCTIONS

Offerings are a gratitude and thanksgiving ritual.

You can make offerings before, during, or after an event has occurred. You can make offerings as part of a ritual when you want to express your thankfulness. You can make offerings for something you want, or something that was rough that you want to bless and possibly release. You can make offerings for something when you are compelled to even without a specific conscious understanding of why or what for. You can make offerings at thresholds, crossroads, homes, sacred places, and anywhere in nature.

As you make your offerings in this practice, trust the soft parts of you that experience longing, desire, appreciation, and humbleness.

Allow the three steps of ritual to simplify and support your practice of making an offering. You can review the Instructions on page 282.
1. Open the space
    - You can do this with your breath, speaking aloud, silently in your mind, in song, etc
2. Make the offering
    - Allow a moment to let the impact of the offering being given from you be felt, feel the space it came from, feel or watch for it landing or traveling on its way, free from your hands, because it has now been handed over
    - Name what you are making an offering to
    - Name what you are making the offering
    - Name what you are making the offering for
    - Example, *"I offer to the Earth in gratitude my blood, this sacred menstrum, life force that flows from me, that is of me, that you may feel my devotion. I ask that you receive thankfulness for your life giving food, water, and air, your body that makes my*

> *body. I ask to be shown how to be a birthplace and home of peace, well being, justice, and kindness. Thank you."*
- Follow you inclination and make the offering you feel inspired to, literally pour your offering on to earth, blow your breath to the wind, take flowers to your grandmother, send money to the cause, dance the dance

3. Close
- Allow a moment to let the impact of the offering being given from you be felt, feel the space it came from, feel or watch for it landing or traveling on its way, free from your hands, because it has now been handed over

In a group, check in with each other about closing or transitional comments.

In individual practice, take a moment to create a supported transition for yourself.

For the full teaching on offerings go to the Make An Offering on page 67.

MAKE AN OFFERING

You can review the Instructions for Offerings on page 278 and then do the following practice.

Get clear about your statement of curiosity or prayers at this moment. Read through the list below. Then take three breaths. Ask yourself what offering resonates with your right now. Make an offering now and also know that you can make another offering in the future. If you're inspired to make an offering that's not on this list, you're of course welcome to follow that thread. Here are some offering options and ideas:

Food
    Plants or herbs
    Sing a song or play music
    Menstrual blood or wine or juice
    A commitment or vow
    Stones or crystals
    Ritual
    Your time
    Emotional support
    Spiritual or etheric gift
    Money or valuables

Art
Dance
Labor
Skills
Meditation

MAKE AN OFFERING TO YOURSELF

You can review the Instructions for Offerings on page 278 and then do the following practice.

Read through the list below. Then take three breaths and ask what you'd like to do as an offering to yourself. Allow the answer to come directly from the list or be inspired by an entirely new idea. Here are some offering options and ideas:

- Make yourself your favorite food
- Sing a song or play music to yourself
- Offer Menstrual Blood or wine with prayers of thanksgiving to your own journey and existence
- Make a commitment or vow to yourself
- Gift yourself flowers, plants, or herbs
- Do a ritual for your own wellbeing
- Dance a blessing for yourself
- Meditate

MEDITATION GIFT

You can review the Instructions for Offerings on page 278 and then do the following practice.

Start by stating out loud or in your mind that this meditation is an offering.
　Sit for a few minutes, breathing and connecting with your body.
　Allow yourself to settle.
　Invite your spirit guides and Sacred Council to join you.
　Breathe and feel spaciousness.
　Allow what is to be.
　Notice and release what is happening.
　Set a five minute timer.
　Come into harmony with what is alive and in existence in this time and space.
　Allow your breath to deepen.
　Before you close, open to receive any messages or gifts you are being

offered.

Set a two minute timer.

Bow or take three breaths to close the practice.

SING A SONG OR PLAY MUSIC

You can review the Instructions for Offerings on page 278 and then do the following practice.

Singing or playing a song as an offering is one of the most powerful ways of make an offering

The song doesn't need to original or epic, it doesn't need to be sung beautifully or in key, just played or sung from the heart

Sing a song from your heart, it can be a nursery rhyme, a pop song, a chant, a humming with no words, the options are limitless.

Music has the power heal. Not just metaphorically also literally. So explore sound boldly and expect to find something new.

Allow your body to soften as you breathe and allow a singular tone or sounds to come out your mouth. Let a simple tune known or unknown to you repeat itself over and over. Allow all notions of what *singing* is supposed to be. I believe our voice is another commonly underdeveloped sense. That with practice we sense what sounds and words need to be spoke, sung, hummed.

Allow your singing to be expressing, playful, and dynamic. Use this space as a way to find your voice not just use it. And also, once you are connected - USE IT! Pour forth with abandon.

The song does't need to be original or epic, it doesn't need to be sung beautifully or in key, just sung from the heart or soul or root.

Sing a song from your heart, it can be a made up thing, a nursery rhyme, a pop song, a chant, a humming with no words, the options are limitless.

Music has the power heal. Not just metaphorically, but also literally. So explore sound.

You can use any of the Medicine Songs on page 175 in this book or any sound that you're inspired to do or rises from your being.

SING! Your Soul Wants to Sing!

Rituals

INSTRUCTIONS

To create a ritual, and anyone can, and many of us do, all you need are:

An opening. A purpose. A closing.

As long as you come to a ritual with clarity of purpose and an honest heart, whatever you do in these three sections will serve as powerful ceremony.

All rituals and ceremonies are essentially made up, arising from a human's moment of insight into a larger mystery. The same is true for how I created the rituals I share with you here. They are powerful. They are inspired and informed by my years of experience participating in and leading rituals with myself, my ancestors, and various artistic, religious, and spiritual communities.

Please defer to your own wisdom, your lineages, and your inspiration at any point. Also lean in and trust what is here. These ceremonies can offer the space and support needed to move, transform, and heal profoundly.

The rituals in their full length do take some time. When needed, you can amend a ritual in a way that feels doable to you and the group. Each part is in there for a reason, and yet, a little ritual is better than none, and a completed ritual is a stronger container than an unfinished one. That being said, healing rituals like this have a way of completing themselves in just the right way even (and perhaps especially) when they go differently from how they were planned. So whether it feels too short, too long, too complicated, or too simple, trust the process. Be clear and confident in your purpose and engagement in the ritual and you will receive all the benefits and blessings that are here for you.

BREAK THE CHAIN OF FAMILIAL ABUSE

You can review the Instructions for Rituals on page 282 and then do the following ritual. *If people are nervous about the "scene" element in this ritual you can review the Instructions for Role Plays on page 207 and then do the following role play.*

Do an opening prayer. If you'd like guidance for this, choose from Calling In Spirit (on page 218) or Calling The Directions (on page 220).

Then, stand in a circle and say: "We are here to break the chain of familial abuse, here, now, today. Where abuse once grew and was passed down, ends and is healed in me, and from me, health and wellbeing, soul honoring will grow."

Split into two groups (they do not have to be equal numbers). The person who pulled the card is in Group A groups, then that will share a story exemplifying the abuse line that they carry. The group together makes a tableau or short scene from thirty seconds to two minutes of dialogue or movement. Make it repeatable, because when you present it you will do the scene on a loop. Once the scene is ready, move onto the next phase.

Group A presents a scene on loop, doing the scene at least twice.

Group B watches and when everyone has got a sense of the scene, they signal to each other they are ready and yell "Pause!"

Group B decides on a moment they see the scene they collectively want to change the course of the scene. Once they establish that moment together, Group A runs the scene from the beginning. When the moment comes Group B moves physically into the scene puts their bodies in the midst of the abuse and yell "Stop!"

Groups A and B freeze.

With everyone frozen the person whose story it is says, "I am no longer part of this, I live in another way," and steps outside the frozen image, everyone stays frozen.

When the person is ready, they say, "Thank you for what I have learned. I bless and release you, to live and heal as you will. This is no longer my reality."

Now both groups unfreeze and completely collapse, going limp, and as the spell of release is cast over them, the image falls away with whispering, sounds, or silently whatever wants to come from the groups as they release. If possible collapsing right where they are as if melting until laying on the floor, or draped over furniture.

Take moment of stillness or a breath.

From there everyone rolls away from the image and joins the person on the other side of the room. Silently bowing or offering a hug.

Note: If someone cannot step away from the scene or cannot honestly say it's over, do not force anything. Give the person plenty of time to transition, but if they can't, instead ask for acknowledgment or support is needed to make that possible someday, if after sharing and having a moment ask them again gently, "Is it over for you, are you walking now in this ritual?" If they answer "yes," let them do the whole proclamation from the start and continue the process from there. If they say "No," then have everyone else release the scene except for the person whose story it is. Have that person stay in their position and instead use the Unwinding Group Exercise (page 373).

End with a closing song, dance party, or three minutes of sitting in silence.

DEATH AND REBIRTH RITUAL

You can review the Instructions for Rituals on page 282 and then do the following ritual.

Everyone sits or stands in a circle. Say, "We are here to honor the death and embody the rebirth. We welcome our spirit guides and our teachers in this realm to guide us through this journey." Everyone lays down on their back with arms crossed, eyes open looking at one fixed place, still as can be, eventually allowing eyes to close. Lay here in your death. Take five minutes here.

Then, pour yourself over to the side in a fetal position, imagine yourself as the space before conception. Feel limitless potential and vulnerability. Slowly allow your new self to gather in your tender body. Again, take five minutes here.

Roll over so you are in a bud on your knees. Feel your new self growing inside of you, cultivating and pulsing your life force through your body, bones, cells, and auric space. Keep your body relatively still as you move this self through the tight and safe container of you. Take three minutes.

Put on a song. As you listen, allow this new life force to move through and begin to move your body, emerging, fierce, gentle, and whole. Move to music until you feel done!

You can use the closing prayers from the Calling In Spirit (page 218) or a variation on Calling The Directions (page 220).

FIRE CEREMONY

You can review the Instructions for Rituals on page 282and then do the following ritual.

Collect three offerings for opening, three offerings for closing, a personal prayer, and something you're ready to release to the fire. The opening and closing offerings can include songs, herbs, and other gifts.

Location options for ceremony include an outdoor fire-pit, outdoor metal vessel, indoor fireplace, and a candle inside. This practice can also be done ceremoniously, with intention, at an electric fireplace or electric candle. Be conscious of seasonal dangers, fire hazards, and general safety. As you build the fire, be mindful that letting the fire burn all the way down is recommended, size, structure, and elements will all contribute to the length of time that the fire will burn, and someone will need to be there tending to it.

Open with a prayer. You can use Calling In Spirit (page 218) or Calling The Directions (page 220). Before lighting the fire, call to the Spirit of Fire (if your lineage has a specific name, use it now). Invite and welcome Fire, ask for its wisdom and gentleness with you. Present your gifts either before, during, or directly after lighting the fire. If it's a song, during and after the fire is lit works well. If you've brought burnt offerings, like herbs, you can build and light the fire with the offerings or you can light the fire and start by burning the gifts.

Now it is time to sit with the fire with your own personal prayer in your heart. When you are ready, bring your item to release. Speak to Fire silently, quietly, aloud, or loudly sharing your prayer and asking Fire to receive and transform. Give the item to release.

After everyone has done their prayers and sat to completion, give the closing three offerings. You can use the closing prayers from the Calling In Spirit (page 218) or a variation on Calling The Directions (page 220). Tend the fire until it has burned down, safely extinguishing coals properly if you've used an outdoor fire pit or indoor fireplace.

GRIEF RITUAL

You can review the Instructions for Rituals on page 282 and then do the following ritual.

Avoiding grief can cause a lot unpleasant things in your life that could be alleviated with just a little bit of focus and spacious time spent honoring what's being pushed aside. Grief is not bad, it comes with any change (even "good" change). Grief comes with acknowledgement and it comes with being awake and seeing the state of our world. Grief is heavy and can weigh us down. Under and through grief is our love and the things we most treasure. Honor your grief, find your joy.

There are two rituals offered here. One Grief Ritual for carried grief and a second Grief Ritual that can be used when actively grieving a loss such as a loved one.

Ritual for Carried Grief

If in a group, do the following ritual together. If you're practicing alone, do something to create some softening and make some sacred space. Examples include running a bath, putting on some music your heart loves or cosmic shuffle, and lighting a candle. Make space for yourself. Either way, do some sort of opening prayer. You can use Calling In Spirit (page 218) or Calling The Directions (page 220). It can also work well to open with a song.

Then, do this writing exercise. Repeat each prompt until you feel empty. Give a moment before moving on to the next one, waiting to see if anything comes up before going on. You are blessed and loved and adored. Be honest -- this is your pathway to freedom. Remember, use your breath as your ally.

- I have grief for...
- The heaviness in me is from...
- My body carries my grief and...
- What I need to let go so I can make space for what is to come...
- I am still carrying grief from...
- The grief I carry wants me to know...
- The thing the grief is asking me to do is...
- The pain of my grief...
- My grief has taught me/my grief is teaching me...
- I am afraid to feel the grief because...
- Right now, my soul wants me to know...
- I am willing to remember in this moment...
- I know...
- The moon is saying to me...
- The earth is sharing with me...
- The mystery/universe/god/goddess/holy one wants me to know...
- The thing I left out that I need to say is...
- I love and am grateful for...
- What I am welcoming into my life where the grief used to be is...

Go around, and without response, each person share their written responses to each prompt one prompt at time. Then everyone put their papers together, holding the collection of wisdom and acknowledgement in your hands, close together. Sit in silence for five minutes. Sing one song together. Next, burn, shred, or bury the papers. The point is to release and hand all the weight and wisdom over so it can integrate into wholeness within you. Then, everyone reaffirm what you are welcoming into your life! Sing a closing song or use the closing prayers from the Calling In Spirit (page 218) or a variation on Calling The Directions (page 220). Finally, do a group hug or have a Cosmic Shuffle Dance Party (page 322).

<u>Ritual for the Passing of a Loved One</u>*

The first thing I do is to light a candle and pray for the whole and complete passage of the soul. Some traditions say this takes four days, others say forty days, and still others say one year. Time is an illusion. What I know is that there is a gateway, a threshold that they have to pass through in order to move from their Earth-walk, into oneness. So light the candle and pray for that. Open your heart and honor and say anything left unsaid, or anything you want to say again, and give your blessings for them to fully go.

Tell them you know you'll be closer in this passage than ever, that their crossing is a gift and an honoring of all that their life was. Leave the candle lit safely as long as possible. Sometimes I get electric candles and put them on a mantel or on my altar. Place the candle there until either you intuitively feel it's complete or it burns out. You could also get tea lights and light one everyday (until you start forgetting to or you feel the ritual is complete) then light three and honor the wholeness and completeness of this practice.

Sit and meditate. Ask to hear anything needed to be known. Then free write and let that pour out onto a blank page. Make an offering to the earth in thanksgiving and with your prayers. If you menstruate, the next time you bleed make a blood offering for the person who has passed and their life giving presence to you. Blood offering quick tutorial: collect your blood. If you use something other than a menstrual cup, you can place your other kind of menstrual product in a bucket of cold water and let it soak, and then use the blood water and pour it on the earth while you pray.

You can give the person an intuitive healing session (if you know they would be open to it) everyday until it feels done. If you don't know if they are open... ask, listen, adhere, and trust yourself. Invite them to receive the healing, and then do it without expectations.

And ahhhhh yes, you can also sing sing sing to them.

*Because letting go for a person from a certain relationship agreement, such as transition of romance or right of passage in family, or big work transition all require a deep surrender and. Passage you can use the structure of the ritual for grieving the passage of a soul off the planet to honor the passage and movement of a soul on the planet as well.

HEALING WITH BIG ANCESTORS

You can review the Instructions for Rituals on page 282 and then do the following ritual.

Light a candle or take three deep breaths. Say, "I am here to speak to my big ancestral line. I am here to do healing for them and for myself. Please join me here for this. I'd like to have a dialogue with you. I'm going to share and then I am going to listen. I am willing, I am open, and I am ready to be part of my ancestor's healing. Send me any guidance and information I need to have so that can take place." Then share out loud by using and completing the following prompts.

- I am willing to admit that...
- The thing I am afraid to say is...
- I am grateful for...

Then listen quietly for one to two minutes. Repeat this process a few times. Clear the air, speak honestly. In closing, blow out your candle or end with three intentional breaths.

You can use opening and closing prayers from variations on Calling In Spirit (page 218) or Calling The Directions (page 220).

What to Do as a Group

You can put on some music to hold a sound container since everyone will be speaking at the same time and it can help hold the sound space so its easier to focus on you, it is also powerful to do these things in silence together, so do whatever feel supportive. Everyone claim a spot standing up, sitting, kneeling or facedown where are not facing another person either towards the outside of the circle, in a line in front of an altar or agreed upon direction, or into a fire or natural element. Then do the do the speaking and communicating simultaneously.

There is an additional video for this practice and many other resources as part of the App at **sophiawiseone.com/member-access/**

HEALING WITH RECENT ANCESTORS

You can review the Instructions for Rituals on page 282 and then do the following ritual.

Light a candle or take three intentional deep breaths. Pick a specific, recent ancestor. Call them by name to join you in the present moment, that you are here to have a dialogue. Tell them you are going to share and then you are going to listen. Tell them you are will and you are open. Stand as you're able and make space to have a private and real dialogue. Then have a super uncensored conversation that you start, by just saying it ALL. Say the things you never said, or want to say again, or never knew how to say. Just get it off your chest, don't make it sound like anything it's not. If you're mad be mad and yell. If you're sad, cry and show those tears. If you love them and you want them to know, tell them all the reason why and how that feels. Tell them.

Keep going until you get grateful. Don't rush it, believe in it. Get messy and don't back down until it opens into a new insight naturally and without effort becomes gratitude, generosity, and appreciation for something. Get rid of the toxic top layer until your love underneath is what is pouring out. Have it out. Blessings.

You can use opening and closing prayers from variations on Calling In Spirit (page 218) or Calling The Directions (page 220).

What to Do as a Group

You can put on some music to hold a sound container since everyone will be speaking at the same time and it can help hold the sound space so its easier to focus on you, it is also powerful to do these things in silence together, so do whatever feel supportive. Everyone claim a spot standing up, sitting, kneeling or facedown where are not facing another person either towards the outside of the circle, in a line in front of an altar or agreed upon direction, or into a fire or natural element. Then do the do the speaking and communicating simultaneously.

There is an additional video for this practice you can find under the "Ancestors (No Words) Video Transmission. There are many other resources for you in the App at **sophiawiseone.com/member-access/**.

HEALING THE HUNTED WOUND

You can review the Instructions for Rituals on page 282 and then do the following ritual.

You can open and close with a song, or you can use opening and closing prayers from variations on Calling In Spirit (page 218) or Calling The Directions (page 220).

Then do this writing prompt. *You can review the Instructions for Writing Prompts on page 182 and then use the following prompt.*

- In my body I feel fear, which I have been carrying for generations, it is...
- In my mind I see the ways in which I was or my ancestors were silenced, they were...
- If they knew...
- I was hunted and killed by or my wisdom carrying ancestors were hunted and killed by...
- The lies that I am worthless and untrustworthy...
- I fear that if I share my wisdom and power...
- I still believe that if I reveal my wisdom and power...
- I know the truth is that when I reveal my wisdom and power...
- My ancestors want me to know...
- My Self wants me to know...
- I can remember what carrying the wisdom was like, and it was...
- I am afraid to see myself in my full power because...
- I can see myself in my full power, and it looks like...
- I know I am safe because...

If practicing alone, read the written responses out loud to yourself in a mirror. When practicing with a group, go around and without response, each person will share what they wrote down to each prompt one prompt at a time.

If practicing alone do this next section in front of the mirror doing the postures and speaking the group response.

Next, one person at a time, take a physical posture and shares a verbal statement of the wound. Everyone witnesses for three breaths the presentation of the wounding and then says says, "We honor that these pains and injuries are real, we see you, we love you, we recognize the hurt and wisdom in keeping yourself and these wounds hidden. We make space for wholeness. Show us the wholeness you can now live."

The person takes a new posture, and then shares a statement of a wound healed. Everyone witnesses for three breaths the presentation of the healing and then says, "It is a relief to see you whole. We recognize your wholeness as truth and a gift to the planet. Thank you for sharing your beauty with us. Thank you for claiming your power. Thank you for letting us see you. The world is blessed by your revealing radiance. Thank you."

Sit or stand in a circle, holding hands, silently looking around the circle to one another. Close the ritual with a song or a prayer.

WARRIOR VOWS

You can review the Instructions for Rituals on page 282 and then do the following ritual.

You can use opening and closing prayers from variations on Calling In Spirit (page 218) or Calling The Directions (page 220).

One person read the prompts and whoever is inspired to take each of the Warrior Vows steps forward and says, "I do." Each of the vows is optional and is an invitation for you to claim that which you are inspired to.

- Do you vow to stand for justice?
- Do you vow to use your life force for the betterment of the collective whole?
- Do you vow to honor your life as sacred and valuable, and in doing so, do all you can to honor and respect it?
- Do you vow to not run away from death, and instead to walk towards life and inadvertently, with open eyes, towards death as well?
- Do you vow to look with love and compassion to all people?
- Do you vow to see systems of oppression as well as the people who inflict them as related and separate things and, in doing so, be able to honor the soul of a being who may be perpetuating a system of oppression?
- Do you vow to open your eyes and expand your perspectives to see beyond your limited view to recognize the truth present?
- Do you offer to use your body as a means of love, grace, peace, and sacred honoring in all ways you see fit?

Then the facilitator says to each person one by one, "Please repeat after me. I, [insert name], am a spiritual warrior of love, grace, peace and sacred honoring. I will do and become what I must to be loving and peacemaking in this life." The facilitator continues, "All present, did you see [insert name], take vows to be a spiritual warrior of love, grace, peace, and sacred honoring? If you did, please say, 'Yes, we did.'"

WATER HEALING CEREMONY

You can review the Instructions for Rituals on page 282 and then do the following ritual.

Gather water, a vessel to pour water into, and blessings for the water like herbs, flower petals, crystals, and oils.

Sit in a circle with the empty water vessel in the center, have the blessings for the water on hand. Sing a song and/or use opening prayers from variations on Calling In Spirit (page 218) or Calling The Directions (page 220). Take a few minutes to visualize what all the waters of the world could look like, feel like, and be like.

Pass the filled water container around. Each person takes a turn to share from their heart about what they want for the water. Then each person will pour some of the water into the vessel in the center of the circle and add their blessings.

After everyone has gone around and done their part, take a few minutes to welcome blessings from the the healed water. Then go around the circle a second time and do a wisdom council, sharing from the depths of the wisdom that has risen.

Do a closing song and/or use closing prayers from variations on Calling In Spirit (page 218) or Calling The Directions (page 220).

WIND CEREMONY

You can review the Instructions for Rituals on page 282 and then do the following ritual.

Gather some gifts for the ceremony like flower petals, herbs, organic material, feathers, wings, ribbons, or anything else that calls to you. Do opening prayers and closing prayers from variations on Calling In Spirit (page 218) or Calling The Directions (page 220). If your lineage has a name for the wind, use it in place anywhere the following suggestions say the word Wind.

Call to the Wind. Invite and welcome Wind, ask for its wisdom and gentleness with you. Present your gifts to Wind. Sing a song to Wind. Sit or stand or lie down with your prayer in your heart. When you are ready, speak to Wind silently, quietly, aloud, or loudly sharing your prayer and asking for Wind to receive and carry it. When everyone has done their prayers and sat to completion, offer your gathered gifts. Sing a song to close or use the above listed Calling In Spirit (page 218) or Calling The Directions (page 220) as suggested closing prayers.

Healing Hands

INSTRUCTIONS

Placing the hands with care, attention, loving affection, and non-judgment, combined with the added elements of faith, breath, light, energy, or calling on healing vibrations, is an instinct and a tradition that is found around the world and across cultures. From the rapid instinct to hold a bumped knee, to placing a hand on the back of a friend who is heavy-hearted, we inherently know that there is power in touch.

I am confident that every touch has the potential to be sacred and that every blood line and spiritual lineage has a knowing of healing touch.

I invite you to take three deep breaths, and allow your deepest knowing of how to bring healing to a place or moment through your presence and touch to come to your surface, awaken in your body, and be activated in your presence. You are a powerful and healing being. Breathe into your belly, breathe into your hands, relax your shoulders, and remember you don't have to make a single thing happen. The healing is already miraculously underway. Your touch opens the door to the healing that is knocking. Your presence and attention supports the healing that is always happening under the surface. Your being here in this way helps you expand to your fullest potential.

Follow the instructions for each practice and place your hands lightly. Only touch people where they want to be touched, and if you don't know, ask them out loud. If they are unsure, hover your hands above an area or move to another location. Interpret mixed signals as a "no."

Remember you are supporting something that is already there, give up any notions of making something happen, your spacious and allowing presence will contribute hugely.

Relax your own body and take care of your comfort. Most people can feel, at least subconsciously, if someone is uncomfortable around them, so help them relax by taking care of yourself.

Breathe deeply and allow the age-old practice of being still and kind work its timeless magic.

HEALING HANDS CIRCLE

You can review the Instructions for Healing Hands on page 294 and then do the following practice.

Check in with the recipient and find out if there is anywhere they do not want to be touched, and if there is anywhere they would especially like to have contact. Ask the recipient where they would like a root hand placement: outside of hips, hovering over the hips, on the lower belly, the front of the thighs, or somewhere else specifically. The recipient may lie down face up or face down.

Take a moment to breathe in and out of your hands. Place your hands on the recipient where you are intuitively led, while also honoring anything the recipient shared with you before beginning. Some go to hand placements include the head, heart, feet, hands, belly, and root.

End by everyone hovering your hands about six to twelve inches off of the recipient's body, breathing and honoring their deep wisdom and the honor of holding space for them.

HEALING HANDS ON SELF

You can review the Instructions for Healing Hands on page 294 and then do the following practice.

Take one minute to breathe in and out of your hands. If you're practicing with a group, do two minute increments on each of the following positions on your own body. If you're practicing solo, take four minutes in each spot.

Place your hands lovingly on each of the places: your head, heart, lower belly, root, anywhere your body asks or where you are intuitively led. To close, hover your hands six inches off of your body, inviting yourself to integrate and receive the blessings that are being offered to you. Take a few breaths to center and transition into completion.

HEALING HANDS SHARED

You can review the Instructions for Healing Hands on page 294 and then do the following practice.

Choose an amount of time you're each going to receive Healing Hands.

Check in with each recipient and find out if there is anywhere they do not want to be touched, and if there is anywhere they would especially like to have contact. Ask the recipient where they would like a root hand placement: outside of hips, hovering over the hips, on the lower belly, the front of the thighs, or somewhere else specifically. The recipient may lie down face up or face down.

Take a moment to breathe in and out of your hands before placing them on the first recipient. Some go to hand placements include the head, heart, feet, hands, belly, and root. You can also go where you are intuitively led, while honoring anything they shared with you before beginning. End by everyone hovering your hands about six to twelve inches off of the recipient's body, breathing and honoring their deep wisdom and the honor of holding space for them.

Then switch recipients.

Hugging

INSTRUCTIONS

All hugs have many potential dynamics. Following are a few you can explore as you practice any and all of the hugs.

Some Hugging Dynamics

The Holding, "I'm Hugging You" Dynamic: Giving comfort to the other person, one person is the anchor of support. Here, this person literally takes the weight of the other person, who is invited to receive and fully melt into this support.

The Connection Dynamic: This is the equal meeting point, holding each other, leaning into each other, pressing hearts, bellies, and maybe thighs together. The relaxed surrendered feeling is that of shared weight and gentle rocking. Both people take big sighs.

The We're In This Together Dynamic: This is the shared epic need for support, in which there is a clinging sense from both people, as well as a melting into the squeezing of the other's embrace. It's a combination of the Holding and the Connection Dynamics.

The We Could Stay Here Forever Dynamic: This is when the contact comes in together and then no one wants to leave, the weight trades between both people, the hug turns into holding hands, or arms wrapped around each other, tucked feet, or other relaxed bodily contact.

The Point of Contact Dynamic: These are quick hugs that are often done in passing with an affirmative feel. This dynamic speaks to a brief momentary connection, that successfully offers affection and acknowledgement.

HUGGING YOURSELF

Review the Instructions for Hugging on page 297 and then do the following practice.

Wrap your arms around yourself. You can wrap your arms around your torso, bring your knees up and wrap around them, or any other configuration your inspired to find. Now let your palm and fingers land on your body and then gently squeeze with your arms towards the body and then press from the base of your palms through your fingers. Take five deep breaths and inhale softly squeeze and as you exhale, gently rock.

What to Do as a Group

Everyone hug themselves three times, tell each other how it felt, offer your favorite tips of something you discovered. Everyone give yourself one more hug.

What to Do with Yourself

Hug your self in a few different configurations. After the first few long deep hugs explore with briefer or longer hugs, stronger or more spacious holds. Find the the one feels the most nourishing for this moment and then just hold yourself for a song, or a minute. You can caress your face, pet your shoulder, or pat yourself on the back to increase the variety of self affection you are offering your self.

HUGGING WITH EXTREMITIES

Review the Instructions for Hugging on page 297 and then do the following practice.

The essence of a hug is more than simply the physical hug where you each put arms around each other's torso. This is about sharing that essence of a hug through other kinds of contact. The essence of a hug is shared through the feeling of being lovingly wrapped up. Here you practice the art of wrapping up a being by hugging someone's arm, or legs, holding hands, or any other part of the body or being, kike hugging an organ with your hands on the body and your focus wrapping and focusing on holding somewhere inside the body.

It is no longer just the surface or edge of what you are touching the core of this hug is the sending the heart's love in a kind and engulfing affection to any part of a body from any part of yours. This is communicated through squeezing the shape being hugged *as it is* in the shape it is. Be mindful not to compress the shape in a way that is denying or seemingly trying to change the shape, if it is round let your hand, arm, body take that shape as much as possible and go round around and then offer your affection in pressure dispersed in an equal way. It's a soft wrapping around the place of contact. Be it hand wrapping and holding another hand, or your arms from the floor wrapping around a grandmothers legs in the chair; I am not crushing the legs, I am wrapping them, contouring my arms and hands around her shape, not pushing them into the shape of my arms.

What to Do as a Group

Get in partners or groups of three to practice the hug. Ask your partner(s) if they would like to hug. When you get a yes to hug share with each other what extremity you would like to practice hugging or practice hugging with. Be communicative about what is comfortable, practice asking direct questions giving direct answers to one another. Help each other become experts at sharing a hug.

What to Do with Yourself

Take a moment and imagine you're doing this with another person. Then physically reverse doing it, imagine what you would say and say it out loud. Or find someone to practice with in manifested time.

HUGGING SITTING DOWN

Review the Instructions for Hugging on page 297 and then do the following practice.

If it's going to be a longer hug, take a moment to move so that you are closer and more settled. The art to the sit down hug in a chair often has to do with getting comfortable in a twist. There are a few ways to do this. One option is to shift your hips so that you are either close and in a side-body hug. Here, the connection is in the squeeze and the lean.

Another way to do this is to turn your hips and aim to the get your heart to meet the other person's heart. Since the hips will likely be far away and the belly to belly option is out of the picture, you want to send that feeling of warmth and no rush through your arms and heart, keeping yourself balanced enough so that you can focus on the hug being your means to transmit affection.

What to Do as a Group

Get in partners or groups of three to practice the hug. Ask your partner(s) if they would like to hug. Be communicative about what is comfortable, practice asking direct questions giving direct answers to one another. Help each other become experts at sharing a hug.

What to Do with Yourself

Take a moment and imagine you're doing this with another person. Then physically reverse doing it, imagine what you would say and say it out loud. Or find someone to practice with in manifested time.

HUGGING OVER TIME AND SPACE

Review the Instructions for Hugging on page 297 and then do the following practice.

This is can be done in two different ways. The first option is to physically pick up your arms, visualizing the person, pulling them in, and hugging them in your imagination. Take three or four breaths and listen to your subtle feelings to see when the hug feels complete.

A second option begins inside your body. Feel into your heart, extend the feeling of both leaning in and holding. Reach your heart towards the other person's heart. Hold that feeling, breathing and connecting with the love you are offering and the love you are receiving from the hug back to you.

What to Do as a Group

Get in partners or take turns in partners
    There will be three rounds of hugs
    Ask your partner(s) if they would like to hug.
    Decide who in the pair will be "1" and who will be "A"
    Move away from each other in the space, you can be in the same room or within eye sight just try to make some space between both of you
    First, "1" will sending "A" a distance hug
    Second, "A" wil send "1" a distance hug
    Third, "A" and"1" will hug each other at the same time over distance

What to Do with Yourself

Think of someone who you know and would love to hug
    Then, think or say aloud "I would like to hug you, would you like that?" Listen and feel for a response. If you are unsure of the response think of another person and do the same thing. If you are developing your discernment around distant communication like this and you are unsure, before you send the hug say, "I am offering you this hug for you if you want it, please accept it, and if not, let it go to..." Then you have options, some who I love who wants it, or myself in the future or past, or may it go to the right person at the right time, or what ever you want.
    Now, take three deep breaths and hug this person through time and space.

HUGGING STANDING UP

Review the Instructions for Hugging on page 297 and then do the following practice.

With a hugging partner, reach around their body, tilting your head to one side as you wrap your arms around and place one hand on the back of the heart and one hand on the lower back. These are options for hand placements, not requirements. Bring your belly to their belly. Exhale and rest into the hug, about three deep breaths, which is about twenty seconds. Bonus technique: add a gentle rock or sway that leaves a little weight in both feet while you are hugging. Do a little closing squeeze before pulling away.

What to Do as a Group

Get in partners or groups of three to practice the hug. Ask your partner(s) if they would like to hug. Be communicative about what is comfortable, practice asking direct questions giving direct answers to one another. Help each other become experts at sharing a hug.

What to Do with Yourself

Take a moment and imagine you're doing this with another person. Then physically reverse doing it, imagine what you would say and say it out loud. Or find someone to practice with in manifested time.

GROUP HUGGING EXERCISE

Review the Instructions for Hugging on page 297 and then do the following practice.

Group hugs! These are great! Here are a few tips for group hug good times. Remember that the hug is made of real people. Many enthusiasts will hug and lean hard into the group as a whole, making the weight land on the people in the center. This can lead to the center people feeling crushed and in physical danger. Group hugs need to start with everyone holding their own weight.

The hug is about the network of people and bodies coming together, so make conscious and loving contact with the bodies you are hugging, not the idea of the group. Group hugs area rarely concentric circles, they are a network of sides, bellies, and backs. Alternatively, think of a group hug as a layered hug, and you want to make a hug with four points.

Point one is the body in front of you. Keep your own weight, nuzzle your body in close but not so close that they can't move their feet. Points two and three are the bodies to the left and right of you. Make contact, nuzzle in, and connect by sharing in the sideways hugs. Point four happens with any group huggers coming in behind you. Be clear about receiving their affection and letting them into the hug, while also being a guardian to those you are already hugging in terms of weight sharing and potential crushing.

HAVE FUN! COMMUNITY IS GREAT!

Visual and Crafting Healing Arts

INSTRUCTIONS

When doing crafting and visual arts there are a few things to keep in mind.

1) You are a creative being

Many of us have been shamed or told, by our own aesthetic judgements, by peers, or by teachers and family, that we "aren't good" at art and so we ought not do it, and certainly not show it to any one. That was also true for me, it is the poison of comparison. Making art in any manner is a practice of creative play and expression. It is a gift to yourself, to those with whom you share it, and to the creative spirit itself, and that is it, a gift. So lay down whether you are good or not and just explore and play.

2) You definitely have the right stuff on hand

There is a time and place for tools, and I encourage you to invest or say yes to gifting yourself the objects that will support your exploration, and the essence of all of these things can be done with limitless options. Each of these can be done with a pen and paper, mixed up paints, fingers, and newspaper, or a pile of sticks and leaves. You are granted permission to make up how to do the exercise with what you have. One time we did our "vision board" with a small box of markers and lined paper. We drew stick figures and spirals, words and ideas. We shared them with each other and got placed on an altar and worked with them as though they were the grandest of collages ever made.

You could draw it in the sand and it would still work. So yes, follow instructions and go big, and also go with what you got. The tool you need is always within arm's reach.

3) You know exactly what you need to do

Many of us have been taught that "art" is about creating and fulfilling some assignment, and for these, there is no getting it wrong, so play and let go that there is an expectation to disappoint. I just want you to claim and play with this tool too.

COLLAGING OR VISION BOARDING

You can review the Instructions for Visual and Crafting Healing Arts on page 303 and then do the following breath practice.

To collage: gather magazines, things you can cut up, look through them and cut out any images that stir something in you

Then using glue, tape, and other crafty supplies place the pictures and/or draw pictures and/or words on a poster board, cardboard, or anything really.

See your vision board reveal something to you. Place it near your altar or somewhere special.

<u>Your Temple Inscription</u>
Take the knowing of Your Temple Inscription and then open your eyes to see it reflected back to you as you go through the collage process

NON-DOMINANT HAND DRAWING

You can review the Instructions for Visual and Crafting Healing Arts on page 303 and then do the following breath practice.

Do 12 minutes of freestyle drawing with your non-dominant hand.

PAIN RECOGNITION AND SELF EXPANSION

You can review the Instructions for Visual and Crafting Healing Arts on page 303 and then do the following breath practice.

Make an outline of a human body
Then draw the pain as it is consuming of the whole shape
Then redraw the human form big enough to hold the pain and then draw the pain evolving as it is held

1. Pain Consuming
2. Body outline bigger holding the pain
3. Blessing and healing of the pain inside the spacious body

BONUS* Do a life size outline of your body and do the exercise

FINGER PAINTING

You can review the Instructions for Visual and Crafting Healing Arts on page 303 and then do the following breath practice.

Ideally water based paint a surface to pain on like newspaper, big paper, a journal page, or a kitchen table. Remember you can use anything, just be respectful of the relationship between the things, like if your going to paint on the table use things that won't stained that will wash off, and if your going to use paint use it on something that can keep wants the pain. Most of us have toothpaste and a the bathroom mirror.

What you need is:
- **Substance**
- **Surface**
- **Fingers**

Now PAINT! Paint your feelings! Press your feelings, thoughts, desires, prayers through your hands and let the colors and textures move through you. Make images, make layers and swirls, make anything! Play, explore, create!

Chanting

INSTRUCTIONS

Chanting is when you pick a word, verse or phrase is repeated over and over. Spoken or sung.

The benefit is in activating and awakening the part of you that knows it to be true, acknowledging the parts that know it to be true, celebrating and feeding the parts of you that know it to be true, or resonantly activating the very vibration of this aspect of your being.

Mantra is translated often as "mind release" meant to be a practice that leads you into the space in which you are freed from established pathways of your mind. This allows for new pathways, and deeper awakening.

Mantra is not meant to convince your mind or force a new path. It is meant to release and make space for Spirit and wisdom and deep remembering to occur. Secondly, by repeating something while your mind focuses and wanders, you are creating an alternate path in the mind, creating space for options. IF your mind wanders itself towards negative self talk while chanting you are having two thoughts, not just the singular negative self talk path, this allows for options to be available in the mind and being. There are many, many benefits.

Effective use of an affirmation requires the understanding you can actually undermine building trust with yourself if you use positive mantras or manifesting affirmations that are not true, or that are not how you feel, because you experience yourself as lying to yourself. It is better to acknowledge the painful feelings you feel and then ask to feel differently, and sit in the discomfort, than it is to tell yourself over and over that you feel different than you do. Everyone wants to feel seen and heard, especially by our own selves. So start there. Mantras and chanting are meant to create and resonate and support the many aspects of you in healing ways.

To set, to activate, to awaken, to remind. To forge new paths.

What to Do as a Group

Chant for 2 or 3 or 11 minutes.

What to Do with Yourself

Recommended timing of chanting in solo practice is 2 min, 3 min, 12 min, 20 min, 30min, 45 min, 1 hr or 90 min.

FUCK IT

Review the Instructions for Chanting on page 307 and then chant the following.

"Fuck it"
Breathe deep and release control, acknowledge things are beyond your control and hand it off to hands bigger and more capable than yours, allow it to be what it is, let it go, let it be, lean back, throw your hands up and exhale.

I DO WHAT I CAN WHEN I CAN

Review the Instructions for Chanting on page 307 and then chant the following.

I do what I can when I can.

I AM ON TIME

Review the Instructions for Chanting on page 307 and then chant the following.

"You are on time."
Bring a hand and a breath to your heart, let this statement be considered possible.
"I am on time."
Being both the kind voice telling yourself, "You are on time" and then receiving and accepting this offer "I am on time."

PERMISSION INVOCATION

Review the Instructions for Chanting on page 307 and then chant the following.

I give myself permission to experience healing.
   I give myself permission to KNOW love.
   I give myself permission to change.
   I give myself permission to feel.
   I give myself permission to receive all that I need.
   I give myself permission to BE just as I am.
   I give myself permission to heal.

SAT NAM

Review the Instructions for Chanting on page 307 and then chant the following.

"Sa ta na ma" or "Sat Nam"
   Sa - Birth/Infinite/Cosmic Soup
   Ta - Life/Manifested form
   Na - Death/Transformation
   Ma - Rebirth/resurrection

Sat - Truth or true
   Nam - Name or identity
   Sat Nam - Truest self

The year of the Sat Nam was the commitment of, coming to, and connecting with the truest form of myself. The journeying of discovering my soul, its expression and embodiment. It lasted longer than 1 year. In that time I chanted and meditated with the primordial sounds and allowed them to become my teachers. I encourage you to deepen your research about Sanskrit, and Kundalini Kryias which combine the chants with physical practices brought west initially by Yogi Bhajan. These are practices that are much older and broader than one teacher or one practice. Think of the sounds as your partners or teachers in your path of remembering a deeper wisdom.

THESE ARE MY FEET

Review the Instructions for Chanting on page 307 and then do the following.

"These are my feet" is chanted while stomping the feet.

1. Stand up if able (if not do this sitting down or lovingly pound the bottom of your feet or have someone do that)
2. Begin Slow at first
   - One foot per word "These" One foot

- "Are" other foot
- "My" first foot
- "Feet" other foot

3. Pressing into the surface and feeling your feet feel the impact of the contact with the ground or floor
4. Slowly speed up
5. Pressing your feet with every stomp, allow the words and stomping to accelerate and move at your own pace. Do this for minimum of 2 minutes
6. Allow any laughter or other involuntary sounds to mix into and in-between you making this very literal connection to time and space and your body.

Practices

FOUR CORNERS OF YOUR FOOT

There are four pressure points the four corners of your feet that when pressed help the calming of the body, easing of breath, and settling of overall being... aka pressing them has a grounding effect.

1 - At the ball of your big toe
   2 - At the space between the smallest toe and one in
   3 & 4 - Left and right side of the heel

      Press by gently rubbing in very small circles while you take three deep breaths at each point
      Place full foot on ground and imagine all four points pressing into the ground
   Repeat with other foot
      Stand and take three deep breaths, feeling both feet, all eight points connecting with the surface below your feet.

40 DAY PRACTICE

Pick a practice and do it daily for 40 days. 40 days is commonly referred to as the number of consecutive days it takes to make *space* for a new habit. If you want to make a new habit, do it longer. How long? Until it is habit, which means you do it without thinking of it in various situations. 40 Days will help break you out of the previous mindset that thought something else wasn't even really possible.

   I recommend picking a singular practice and picking the same time of day and scheduling it in. If you miss the scheduled time, be committed to complete the practice before going to bed that night and then return to your schedule the next day. That being said, find your way and it will work best for you.

A FALL-APART-Y

This is a designated time to FALL APART and have a PARTY at the same time. You are having a party for and celebrating falling apart.

The Fall-apart-y is held in a sacred orb of purifying magic. This is a space to grant permission for you to "not be your best self" to have space to process, express, and sort out without needing to censor at all. A space to dive in and express that which you work to keep in check or under wraps for the wellbeing or well perceiving of yourself and others.

It's not a way to live your life, it's an exercise in uncensored expression.

Elements often include:

- Emotional rambling, hopefully some blabbering and blubbering
- Thrashing about on the floor
- Stomping possibly accompanied by crossed arms and refusal to talk
- Very judgmental talk about self or others
- Yelling, shouting, and screaming
- Weeping uncontrollably
- Flopping, going limp
- Ranting about how hopeless everything, or a particular thing, is
- AND MOST IMPORTANTLY:
  - A full unapologetic (or apologetic if that's part of it) letting down of all the "supposed to's" and surrendering to the perfect mess that being a human is, so you can express what's got you spinning or stuck

Pour the purse of yourself out, right here, right now, and shake shake shake. After that you can sort what's trash, what's treasure, and what's useful.

I Love You.

ADULT ROCKING

This is a space for us to be held, surrender, and be loved.

Rocking the body, bouncing muscles, and deep breaths are gentle and physically deep relaxation techniques. Being rocked and bounced are ways of relaxing the entire body and optimizing the healing that is attempting to take place.

Rocking is a chance to call forth unconditional love and create a basket of comfort. Being rocked activates a receiving of support, intimacy, and softening, and is appropriate for all people of any age. The human body is designed to receive and respond to soft affection and sustained physical contact that is safe and relaxing. Rocking is a way to collectively reclaim our desire for this experience.

For many people, comfort has been associated with familiarity, and may or may not be truly supportive or healing. Instead, in some circumstances, comfort can be associated with stagnation or passivity. Rocking a beautiful practice that can be used to build trust in the kind of authentic comfort that allows for deep opening and transformative rest and relaxation. Deep surrender can be essential for organic unwinding of tensions on all levels of a being, and it can support the emergence of what is being held inside. You are entitled to being held and loved. We all are. You are here to be loving and offer that love in limitless ways. Here is another.

There are a few things to keep in mind when you are offering and receiving being held and rocked. The most important thing is that you let it be easy even if it's a little awkward. Stay with it through communication, physical adjustments, and moving around for comfort, and find a rhythm that works so that it may be a sanctuary and a comfortable arrival.

Rocking often feels like a rhythmic bouncing. Much like a rocking chair or swing, use just a gentle impulse and then let the relaxation of the body return it to its previous position, ready for another round of movement. It is a little like bouncing a ball of your own body weight, in that the natural weight of your body does most of the work.

You can do this by yourself or in partners.

What to Do as a Group

As the rocker:

Being the Rocker can often take some effort and at times be slightly less than comfortable. That being said, set yourself up to be supported and feel as comfortable as possible. Be verbal and communicate adjustments you may need to make so as to be able to better support the Rockee. Use props like pillows and blankets, or lean against furniture, to allow yourself to be a steady source of comfort. Be sure to take care of yourself. It is important that the person you are holding can relax and not need to take care of you instead of relaxing.

When you're first trying this out, if it's awkward, try going a little slower, then a little faster. You want the movement to be smooth. Breathe and relax. If it's abrupt, it's often because the Rocker is a little tense. You want to be firm, steady, and responsive enough to let the Rockee be as they are. There will often be rounds of more and more relaxation. Sometimes we need to readjust as the weight increases, or as the shape changes. As the Rockee relaxes, the shape and weight often shifts, so as Rocker may need to readjust as well. As the Rocker, invite them to relax as much as possible even during the shifting. Making direct requests that are specific can limit the time of shifting, so this is a good place to practice being direct and supportive at the same time.

As the Rockee:

Practice saying exactly what you need. Is an elbow poking you, do you want a pillow under you butt, do you feel like you're holding one leg up? Voice this and allow the Rocker the chance to really give you the support your body is looking for. Use you voice, and let yourself relax. Let your weight go. As you relax you may find you need even more adjustments. Allow yourself to remain relaxed while asking and everyone is making these adjustments.

If they ask for adjustments as well, say thank you, and enjoy the trust of knowing that if they need something they will ask or do it, so you do not need to track or pay attention their experience in order to take care of them. You can participate in the shift too, and also experiment with really letting yourself stay as relaxed as possible. You are not a burden just because someone needs to shift in some way to stay there for you. Allow the shifting to be another kind of support. You may feel an impulse to apologize, and I invite you to explore alternatives to that. You can say "thank you", take three deep breaths and focus on the care you are receiving, give voice to your feeling of being burdensome or your habituated desire to apologize, and allow even that to be held here.

Allow yourself to be held.

A note about tissues and face fluids:

If you are being rocked and want a tissue or hanky, you can ask for one. If you are holding someone, make sure they are nearby and on hand. I recommend waiting to give a tissue until someone asks, because often, being handed a tissue can activate a feeling of being told to "clean it up" or "pull it together," and be felt as pressure to stop crying. In the effort of supporting a complete surrender, allow face fluids to be natural and flowing without interruption; just have something nearby in case the Rockee requests it.

A note about body size:

Different body shapes and sizes will fit together differently, but I have held bodies four times my size and been held by people half my size, so just let go of previously conceived notions about how bodies are supposed to fit together, and go for finding a place of support and holding. Cooperation and presence ought to allow any two people to participate in this practice together.

Take turns rocking:

Get into pairs.
Take some time to find a rocking position that works for one of you.
After you have found your rocking, set a timer, or play a song. Rock until each person feels complete or to the end of the timer, song, or the cry. When complete, trade places.

Here are two possible variations for adult rocking:

- Sitting Up with Rocker and Rockee
- The Rocker sits with their legs in a V.
- The Rockee sits between the Rocker's legs, leaning into the Rocker's chest with one shoulder, and draping both legs over one of the Rocker's thighs. Depending on the relative size of each person's body, Rockee can either wrap their arms around the Rocker's neck, or tuck their arms into their own chest, whichever feels more comfortable and allows for easier relaxation.
- The Rocker then closes their legs around the Rockee's body, wrapping the thighs and low back in a diamond shape, and holds the Rockee under one or both armpits or wraps around their tucked arms.
- The Rockee gives all their weight to the Rocker, and the Rocker rocks steadily. A good starting point is 1-3 seconds for a rock, speeding up or slowing down as necessary to find a soothing and repeatable rhythm.
- You can move back and forth or front to back. You can alternate, just keep with one at a time for a minute or two at a time.

- Laying Down
- Lay down together, either in a spooning position, or with the Rockee laying however they are comfortable and the Rocker to their side.
- Laying down, the Rocker wraps one leg over the body, and possibly wraps an arm under the armpit and places their hand on the heart or belly. The Rocker gently pulls the Rockee to the Rocker's body, so that when the Rocker moves so does the Rockee.
- The Rocker begins to rock themselves initiating from the place

you have the most contact, which is often the hips or chest, as the Rocker rocks their own body they will bring the Rockee with them.
- For each rock, give about 1-3 seconds. As you do the first 5-10 rocks listen for a natural way their body wants to be moving in a repeated, rocking rhythm. Each body is is own world so it may be much much slower than you might think, or perhaps twice as fast, either way both of you relaxing and breathing will help.

What to Do with Yourself

You can provide the benefits of physical relaxation, the stabilizing experience of providing care, and the deep relaxation of being rocked, by rocking your own body. I will explain a couple of options you can explore to find ways to rock yourself.

In most spaces, it is easiest to do this lying down on a surface that offers some friction. A bed, a rug, or the earth are all good examples, whereas hardwood or tile floors might make it difficult. Once you are familiar with the sensation, it is easily applied to any position, and even micro rocking can be comforting.

Once you have found how you can rock yourself, set a timer and do it for 3 minutes.

Balls of Your Feet Method:
- Lay down so that the balls of your feet have something to push against when your feet are extended and your toes are a little pointed. Usually, the wall is the most accessible surface to touch your feet to, but laying in a bed with a baseboard or headboard will also work.
- Gently push off the wall or baseboard from the balls of your feet, without breaking contact with it. Stay relaxed so that your body does not slide along the bed or floor you are lying on. Your body will naturally return to its previous position.
- When you body bounces back, initiate the bounce again.
- You can also bounce your body by hooking your toes under a ledge, and flexing your feet to pull your body. It will return in the same way, and the same bouncing feeling will be accessible.
- If you are having difficultly check to see if your arms are tight, and try placing them on your body in a loving way, so they are not holding you still.

Heels Method:
- This method is ideal for spaces without a vertical surface to push against, like a green space outdoors, or a bed without a baseboard. Lay down and begin pointing and flexing your feet, using your heels as the point of contact that you are pushing against, so that whole body moves

back and forth along your spine.
- Keep as much of your body relaxed as possible, and only engage your legs just enough to get the movement happening with the heels of your feet.

ASK A NEW, PULL A NEW

1. Take a moment to clear you mind and focus on a new question
2. Shuffle the *Four Seeds Wisdom Path Oracle Cards* while repeating the question 3 times (aloud or silently)
3. Pull a new card

BEGGING FOR HELP

For most of us this is completely outside the notion of who we are allowed to be. It is an absurd idea to let the beggar beg. And yet, that is what I am inviting you to do. Say "Help" over and over and allow whatever else to fall out of your mouth. This may feel awkward and that is absolutely part of it. If you start to laugh, beg through it, don't fight, just don't let it stop you either. Same goes for crying. In the most surrendered way, this is a power pose. It's power comes from unapologetic authenticity and vulnerability, so be as you are while it happens. Allow yourself to be as yourself and to be changed.

Kneel with hands in a begging position and say aloud "help." You can reach up towards the sky or place your head to the floor. This is not a look-good-feel-special pose. This is a surrender, humbling, allowing yourself to be something that needs assistance. Honor the part of you that does need help.

This is sacred and precious. Give your tender sacred beggar space to exist.

What to Do as a Group

You can put on some music to hold a sound container since everyone will be speaking at the same time and it can help hold the sound space so its easier to focus on you, it is also powerful to do these things in silence together, so do whatever feel supportive. Everyone claim a spot standing up, sitting, kneeling or facedown where are not facing another person either towards the outside of the circle, in a line in front of an altar or agreed upon direction, or into a fire or natural element. Then do the do the speaking and communicating simultaneously.

Do this for one song or set a 5 minutes timer.

BIRTH THE WORLD

You can review the Instructions for Practices on page 310 and then do the following meditation.

Everybody (no gender exceptions) pantomimes giving birth to the world.
　　Put on some birth music and then release into the journey.

Close your eyes.
　　Imagine you are carrying the world inside you.
　　You can feel all its potential, its beauty.
　　You know that this is a miracle, and you are carrying it.

Slowly begin to deepen and speed up your breath.
　　Feel contractions through your body and your energy body.
　　It's happening.
　　Right now.

Let gravity help, I recommend squatting, or on all fours.

Use your breath and voice. Allow your jaw to relax and you let sound move from you.
　　Loud.
　　And quiet.
　　Raw and song filled. Make a path through your body with sound.

*You can play as being birth partners.
　　Examples: squatting across from each other holding hands, hold one another from the back, pressing and giving support to sacrum... get silly and sincere, and allow the body to guide you.

BLESS IT

Blessing is a power tool that can be used inside your being, in relationships, and in cultural processes. I recommend practicing inside your own being first, to get a very real and confident relationship with the practice. Blessing is not a judgmental practice, it is a radical acceptance and radical love practice. Blessing is about honoring, celebrating, supporting, nourishing, optimizing what is and fulfilling sacred and holy needs that a wound may have. Whatever you are being invited to bless, it is most potent when we surrender into the perspective that There Is Nothing To Fix (card teaching on page 104), only things to love. So love boldly with listening, offerings, and witnessing.
　　Here are 10 steps to make a blessing. I recommend that you do the

whole process at least twice to get a sense of the evolutionary power of blessings. When time space allows, you can repeat the blessing process until there is a true and honest feeling of completion. This repeated blessing process is a powerful way to unwind a tangle in our being.

Let us begin to understand the power of blessing by blessing ourselves:

1. Identify what is being blessed by asking your body, your self, what is in need of the blessing? Listen for sensations, images, words, a place in your body, a memory, and when you have identified the landscape move on to the next step.
2. Take in the landscape as much as you can, explore temperature, sensations, story, any elements. Really observe this place in you. Be attentive to details and nuance. Allow any judgments that come up to be included in the landscape. Really take in what is revealed.
3. Ask this place in you: "What do you need? What have you been holding out for?" Listen for a response. The response can be a sound, a feeling, a thought, an image, a knowing, a taste, a word, it can be anything, so trust what comes. If nothing in particular comes, then use the powerful word of "blessing."
4. Then offer yourself a blessing. There are many ways to do this, so trust yourself. If you need a starter, start with "I bless this. I offer the blessing of..."
5. Then shift your focus to be on the receiving end of the blessing. Get inside that detailed place in you that is being blessed.
6. Sense the blessing entering this landscape.
7. Choose to *accept* the blessing, allow it in all the way. Feel for it from the inside, feel it make contact with the landscape.
8. Observe how the landscape or feelings change. Notice the organic evolution that occurs as the blessing makes contact and washes through you. Be patient and breathe. You don't have to make it change, it will change just from the blessing, just watch and sense curiously.
9. Allow the shifting and evolving space to unfold. Like a ripple on water, let it move through. The landscape will shift and move and then it will settle.
10. Now take in this changed landscape, sometimes it opens and releases into more ease and pleasure, sometimes it reveals a denser or more painful aspect. Whatever it is, have the courage to let it be, let yourself *be* just as you are, and in this new landscape repeat the process of blessings from step 2-10.

"BLESS THE SHIT OUT OF IT!"

This is a humorous and communicative phrase to encapsulate how to bless things that we don't want in us any more. Things that are being felt as wretched, unjust, painful, unloveable, intolerable, downright insulting, or repulsive. This phrase helps me honor the fury I have about a circumstance by returning me to this powerful practice. This is great for things we can not control or circumstances we feel powerless to change. Accept them as they are, and then bless it. Bless it, bless it anyway, bless it in every which way, bless the shit out of it.

BUILD AN ALTAR

What to Do as a Group

Pick a place and clear it off

Place something down or dress up the spot to designate the area

Everyone walk around, outside and/or inside (up to host) and look for things that spark a sense of wonder, faith, reminding of self or a loved one, when you find something, ask it if it would like to be part of the altar you are building, if yes bring it, if no leave it. If it is your hosts object also ask the host.

Everyone gathers and arranges the space, creating the altar

Then open the altar by taking a moment in front of the space by calling in who and what you would like to be invited into the space and your practice and invite the altar to hold and support everyone and everyone's journey

Sing, speak out loud from the heart, ask for blessings, and enjoy!

Closing and Dismantling the Altar:

Take moment and give thanks to all those who have been present and supported

Bless and release all that has been present

Respectfully take things down, put them away, give them back, take them home with you (if it's your or has been given to you)

Wipe down the space and return it to a clean and open space. If things were moved to make the space, move the things back (unless the host requests otherwise)

What to Do with Yourself

First if you have an altar practice - dive in and commune. Blessings to you.
If you want more guidance here is a lovely way to start:

1. Go to your Altar or pick a place to build one
2. Take a moment to arrive, look, notice. What do you see?
3. Identify if there is clearing or cleaning needed. If there is, do it.

Examples of things you can do to clear objects or space

- Singing, toning, singing bowl, drums
- Smoke or breath
- Reiki meditation or energy practice
- Burning
- Moonlight or sunlight soaks
- Putting them in the sun
- Burying them
- Putting them in a moonlight cycle
- Rinsing them in cold water
- Thanking them for their work and verbally telling them they are relieved from the work
- Praying and asking for them to be cleared
- Hold them, breathing in and out of the object, and then gradually let go of your breath and feel its "breath" and taking 3 strong clearing exhales
- And many, many, many more options

1. Identify what you would like to bring to the altar and take moment with the objects or prayer charging them up
    - Charging and activating objects or the space is about two things. The first is about bringing them into their own full resonance and powerful being. You do this by clearing and celebrating the essence that is presence and inviting it's wisdom to bless you. The second is about asking them to join you in your journey and supporting your prayers and healing journey or the prayers you have for others. You can do this by holding an object while you think and feel about your prayers and intentions, sing or say a prayer out-loud, light a candle, place an offering to the object, such as a gift of incense or food at the base of a picture of sculpture or image.
2. Dress the space up how you are inspired, art, fabric, candles, and place the objects or written out prayers in the space
3. Open the altar by calling in all those you would like to honor and asking for help and/or speaking to what is present and alive for you in this moment.
4. Sing, breathe, sit, dance, be with the altar.

CLEAR OBJECTS AND TOOLS WITH RESONANCE

Clearing objects or the space is about restoring everything into an open and available state. If you think of the Altar as a working space, holding and filled with prayers and processes, clearing the objects or space is about relieving them from those responsibilities and restoring them to their natural resting space or making space for new prayers. Examples of things you can do to clear objects or space:

Singing, toning, singing bowl, drums
Smoke or breath
Reiki meditation or energy practice
Dancing and touching things with loving clearing focus
Physically cleaning things
Burning
Moonlight or sunlight soaks
Putting them in the sun
Burying them
Putting them in a moonlight cycle
Rinsing them in cold water
Thanking them for their work and verbally telling them they are relieved from the work
Praying and asking for them to be cleared
Hold them breathing in and out of the object and then gradually letting go of your breath and feeling its "breath" and taking 3 strong clearing exhales
And many, many, many more options

Charging and activating objects or the space is about two things. The first is about bringing them into their own full resonance and powerful being as it. It is also about asking them to join you in your journey and supporting your prayers and healing journey or the prayers you have for others. You can do this by holding an object while you think and feel about your prayers and intentions, sing or say a prayer out-loud, light a candle, place an offering to the object, such as a gift of incense or food at the base of a picture of sculpture or image.

CONSTRUCTIVE FEEDBACK

What to Do with Yourself

Write out or speak out loud the following prompts for getting feedback with your self and your wise knowing self

What to Do as a Group

Get into pairs and take turns following the instructions below

Ask if the person (self or other) is open to receiving some feedback
If yes, proceed.

1. Acknowledge what you know that is working.
2. Admit what you know that is not working.
3. Ask them what they notice or have observed or their thoughts about these things.
4. Share 3 alternative responses or activities to do instead (this is just the beginning of the process).
5. Ask for their ideas on those alternatives.
6. Thank them for the discussion.

COSMIC SHUFFLE

For traditional Cosmic Shuffle, go to your entire music library. Or, you can pick a particular playlist to work from. Take a breath and ask for divine guidance in selecting songs, asking for the Universe to select the best songs for the process and healing opportunity at hand. Hit the shuffle button.

Meet the songs with faith and curiosity. Don't skip songs and listen all the way through. Choose to be open to whatever is in service to you, which could be the lyrics, the vibrations, or the melody. Make a decision to accept the wisdom in the Cosmic Shuffle selections.

As the songs play you can move your body, sit still, listen to the lyrics or vibrations while mindfully doing a task at hand, or meditate with the music.

COSMIC SHUFFLE DANCE PARTY

Decide if you're going to do one song or a set of songs.

Use Cosmic Shuffle (page 322) or if you would prefer for your dance party pick a song or playlist you want. Then you are going to move, dance, stomp, mime, play, breath and shake through the song. This is a time to move your body and breath. Before you start say the Permission Invocation on page 307 and the words are printed here as well. Trust, play, celebrate, feel, and heal.

Permission Invocation
I give myself permission to experience healing.
I give myself permission to KNOW love.
I give myself permission to change.

I give myself permission to feel.
I give myself permission to receive all that I need.
I give myself permission to BE just as I am.
I give myself permission to heal.

Celebration Option: Pick a fun celebration dance song or use cosmic shuffle. DO the Permission Invocation and then dance around, jump up and down, stomp your feet, and say, "It's okay! I AM ON TIME!" for the WHOLE SONG. It's only one song, so go for it. Don't worry about being a good dancer, just let the goofiness wiggle about. Sometimes it helps to close your eyes.

Offering Style: After saying the Permission Invocation, speak aloud or in your mind that this dance and music is an offering, and that each and every movement is a gift of thanksgiving and recognition for whatever you are making an offering to.

Sensual and Sexual Edition: After saying the Permission Invocation add, "I give myself permission to explore, discover, reveal, and free my sensual and sexual self." Do Cosmic Shuffle or pick the sexiest song you can think of. Then be sure to explore sensual and sexual expressions. For example, get into those hips with circle motions and thrusting. Caress your own body, lick your lips, get on the floor, and move slowly.

LITTLE CHECK-IN

Get a stuffed "Little". This can be a doll or stuffed animal. Preferably something you like to hold so you can tend to your Little literally. This helps engage the experience of expressing things through the doll that may be harder to embody, and allows you to embody the caregiving and response. It's just useful, trust me and try it out, and see for yourself.

Your "Little" is you. Your inner little person. Tend to the doll or object with sincerity. Talking and asking, listening and acting out. You get to be both the grown up with perspective, wisdom, kindness, context, and the Little, the innocent, honest, vulnerable, precious, lovable you. Be both.

Below are prompts for checking in. Ask and answer. Allow it to be a playful and sincere conversation. PLAY and get real. You will get the most out of it if you surrender into the imaginative zone. Allowing it to be both silly and profound.

What to Do as a Group

Find an object in space the be your Little for this exercise. Then get a piece of fabric to swaddle and wrap your Little so that it snug. Then cuddle it and do one of the following:

Do the Fear/Little Meditation on page 237 and then at the completion of the meditation do a check in with your "Little" in person.

What to Do with Yourself

Do the Fear/Little Meditation on page 237 and then continue the conversation with your little everyday.

This is a daily practice, get your "Little" and then for the next 3 weeks do a morning and evening check in with your Little.

Morning:
  How are you feeling?
  Listen to your Little (give voice to your Little)/Answer as the adult
  What do you want to do today?
  Listen/answer
  What do you need?
  Listen/answer
  Is there anything you want me to know? I'm here to listen.
  Listen/answer

Evening:
  How was your day?
  Listen/answer
  What was the best part? What was the worst part?
  Listen/answer
  Do you have any questions about how the day went for me?
  Listen/answer
  Did you try to tell me something or ask for something today that I missed? What was it?
  Listen/answer
  What do you need right now?
  Listen/answer

DECLUTTER

This practice is the physical manifestation of: "I am willing to let go of who I have been to become who I am." Decluttering is a practice of being conscious of the items, tools, and things that are taking up space in your life. Among our possessions, most of us have both useful and inspiring things, and also burdensome and complicated things (sometimes an object might even be all of these). This practice is to support you in appreciation and enjoyment of that which you have, and also support your conscious creation of your life as you grow and move forward. Decluttering what you have is often an essential step to make space for what you are longing for or wanting now. By practicing sorting, keeping, housing, and stewarding belongings, many people become more discerning about what they take in in the first place. Knowing you will be touching something, and making decisions about it over and over, encourages confident decisions about what you accept into your life. This physical practice is grounding and helps hone the subtler and etheric aspects of life as well.

What to Do with Yourself

Pick an area or theme. Examples: Top of a dresser, your clothes, papers, books, digital files, apps, etc.

Choose to either set a timer or commit to an area of decluttering, knowing that you may complete it in one session, and that you also may need to return to it multiple times.

Take a moment to center. Breathing into your body and feeling your spaciousness and your congestion. Make the decision to make space in your being, make space in your life.

Here is the process of sorting I most frequently use.

Ask for guidance on what to keep and what to give away. Ask your mind or body to "SHOW ME KEEP" and then listen and feel. Then ask "SHOW ME GIVE AWAY" and then listen and feel.

Alternately, ask the question: "Did I use this thing in the last year?" Pick an amount of time that works for you. Past month? Past 3 years? What counts as enough to justify having it be useful to steward and house daily? If the answer is "no," consider letting it go.

Alternately, ask the question: "Do I *love* this?" If that answer is "no," consider letting it go.

You are allowed to keep anything you called to keep, *anything*. And you are allowed to let go of anything you are called to let go of, *anything*. Many times we think, "I don't want this, but it was given to me by so-and-so," or "... but it is so valuable," or "... but I'm *supposed* to keep it." The point is, if you are called to keep it, you can. If you feel obligated to keep it, give yourself permission to let it go, connect to the freedom of your autonomy and your authority to make this decision now, and then listen again to hear your true alignment. If a thing is not yours, you can give it back to whom it belongs, or ask them what they would like you to do with it.

Gather all of the items in one place, and then begin one item at a time. (I often do this with my eyes closed when sorting clothes, completely surrendering to my body's wisdom and trusting the feeling. I invite you to do it however *you* are inspired.)

Placing the things you want to keep in a Keep pile, and place the items you are releasing in a Give Away pile.

Put the Keep stuff away in places where they belong (make new places if needed) so everything has a home.

Give Away stuff gets dropped off, trashed, donated, recycled, sold, etc. No matter how it is released, it is an offering you are making. By making this offering, you create space for what is true and in alignment for you now and what is coming in.

Practicing this sorting and listening will hone your ability to make discernments in all areas of your life, and it will get more and more fine-tuned the more you do it. So if it's hard, just do it more.

A share for when this feels harder or more emotionally loaded:
I have done this since the early 2000s now, and of all the things I have released and returned as offerings, only five things ever cross my mind with a longing or question. When I think of it like that, and I think of how much I have let go and how much lighter and more spacious I feel, those five things become even more precious to me, and I offer them again in memory with gratitude and wonder. If they were the cost of all that spaciousness and functionality, then it was all worth it. And this has helped me discern and keep the things that are precious as well. Sometimes we lose things on purpose and sometimes we lose them by accident, and space is made.

What to Do as a Group

Everyone pick something they can declutter right now.
Some options are:
- Physical things people may have with them: pockets, car, purse, bag
- Digital items: emails, who you are following on social media, apps on your device, files, calendar, notes or digital to-do lists

Then each individual follow the instructions for What to do with Yourself above. Then set a timer for 15 minutes - *DECLUTTER!* Make space for you!

DEEP CLEAN

These are ways in which a surface layer clearing just doesn't address the nitty gritty of ourselves. A deep clean helps us see clearly by looking closely and literally cleaning up the corners and harder to see spots, the stubborn grim and the layers of dirt.

Here are some often missed places and ways to deeply clean your space:
Declutter a particular room or type of item (Declutter instructions on

page 324)
 Clear surfaces of miscellaneous items and then clean
 Launder any fabrics (curtains, shake out rugs, cushions)
 Scrub window sills, inside shelves, closets, floor boards, underneath furniture, windows panes, picture frames, mirrors
 Sweep an area twice
 Dust
 Mop
 Polish or oil wood
 Reorganize and arrange furniture, art, or tools

DISCERNMENT PRAYER

This is a prayer and practice to help sort out what is your real and true connection, from what is your medicine, your ideas, or wounds which you might be projecting onto another person, and thus giving away your power. It's about claiming your power while honoring the love.

A lot of healing practitioners out there will talk about "cutting cords." This can be helpful. That being said, I have found it to be incredibly temporary if you do not change your internal relationship to the external relationship. This is a part of my version of "cord cutting."

This is a sacred path of allowing the true connection of love between you and a loved one. It invites healing for yourself, and releasing projections you've made of them. It's a space to allow any soul or energetic conversations that need a space to occur to occur.

This can be great for a current or past relationship like an ex, friend, co-worker, family member, or partner, alive or if they've given up their bag of bones. It is especially designed for those to whom you are feeling that unhealthy and stubborn attachment to or feelings of regret, which at times can feel like obsession, with a particular person. It can also be applied for an identity attachment to yourself.

- Acknowledge there is both a true connection that is blessed and sacred and a powerful projection of your own medicine, wounds, power, peace, etc., with this person. "I acknowledge there is a sacred and true soulful connection between _____ and me. I also acknowledge that many of my thoughts or dreams or feelings about them are not actually about them, but are my own self and my own needs, power, and medicine that I have attached and projected onto this person."
- Create a scheduled time once a month for this Monthly Ritual*. Put this on the calendar and treat these appointments with respect.

(I.e., rescheduling if you can't make it, etc.) This is a time where you can consciously be with any of the mysterious connection, blessings or messages that may be happening between the two of you on a soul level.

Now, right now say this prayer and commit to doing this practice:

Discernment Prayer: "By the power that I AM and the divine wisdom and love that I am, I summon the forces within me and those who walk with me to hear and bless and bring forth my prayers. Thank you in advance for your love and assistance. I retract and unhook my attachment from the being of _____, energetically, physically, mentally, emotionally, spiritually, and in all other known and unknown ways- knowing that our true and real connection is not based on or changed by any of these attachments, and our true interconnectedness cannot be broken or damaged, for we are in perfect and divine relationship, as I am with all things. I invite the untangling of my projections from our shared soulful connection. All energies, thoughts, discontents, gratitude, forgiveness or misgivings that is rightfully between _____ and I gather at the scheduled time for clearing and optimizing the true and real thread between us. I call all my power, my medicine, my joy, and all known and unknown energies that are truly mine that have been projected onto _____. I invite you and bless you in your wisdom and thank you for all your attempts to reach me in the ways made available to you. Know this, from now on, all visions or thoughts, etc., of _____ will be treated as symbolic medicine for me to digest and be with for my own healing and enlightenment, and all actual relationship things will take place inside the time designated and held in blessed sacred sanctuary for whole healing there."

Complete the following prompts: As I say these prayers I am aware... I am grateful for... I ask for blessings of the hardest part of this, which I already know will include... I can feel in my own body... I ask and call in blessings to these very places, knowing my sensations are my body's song of healing.

Closing: Be with me as I walk into this new way of being. Bless this journey of self-knowledge and compassion. Thank you for the guidance I know you will provide and the healing you are. I thank myself for this practice, potent wisdom, embodied love, and ... Thank you for all I have already learned, healed, become, and am becoming. I love you sweet divine. I am blessed by this very prayer and acknowledge that you receive it.

Your preferred way to close a prayer: !!!

Monthly Ritual:

- Open the ritual: "I have arrived to honor our soul connection and for the next 15 minutes I am open to sharing and receiving honest, blessed, mysterious and true communion on a soul level."
- Then sit for 15 minutes and notice, feel, communicate, out-loud, visions, ideas.

FOLLOWING THE THREAD

There are so many things you could focus on in life, today. How do you ever pick?

This practice is about listening deeply to your soul. Your deepest knowing and guidance.

Listening for the request there.

What does your soul envision for you?

What action does it want you to take?

What is the thread of you that weaves your sacred life divinely?

When we have many things we need to attend to, it can make it difficult for any single thing to come to completion. This practice is about identifying one thing and making it your priority with the understanding that you can only do so much in a day for that one thing, and the rest of your day and time is flexible and open for the myriad of other things that make up and life and could be addressed.

Once you identify the one thing which your soul wants you to be attending to, you then listen on a daily basis to what you ought to do for that Thread today. It may take 15 minutes, it may take 4 hours. Usually it's a thing or a focus. If you do that thing, the rest of your day will feel more spacious and you will know that you are honoring your Thread each day.

This is about allowing a singular thread to reveal itself, and making a practice, everyday. Ask your soul how it wants you to tend this vision today, then do that thing. You will know it is your guidance with practice. Most often it will be a singular action, rarely more than 2 actions.

They key is to ask and then **DO IT** (or them).

Then live the rest of your life however you feel so inclined. This allows creative energy to go in many directions while also getting the results of priority and daily action. It's not an *"Either, or"* it's a *"Yes, and"*. Relax and trust that all is unfolding.

Ask yourself, your soul, "What do you want me to do?" Do it. Then live your life in ease. Visions come to be over time space, with the steps happening one step at time. If you are clear on what it is, and do one step at a time there is no reason to fret or be concerned about needing to be or doing more. Do your part and watch the magic of your life unfold.

Careful, some days the message will may very risky or challenging things like: *"Rest."* Do that, too.

What to Do as a Group

Identify what your thread is. You know, it is write there, what is the one thing that is always in the back of your mind and front of mind that wants to be taken care of and maybe even complete?

If you can't identify it write about it, talk about it, meditate.

Set a timer for 5 minutes. Take this time to get clear individually or with each other.

Set another timer for 5 minutes. Everyone individually listen for guidance on one thing to do today for to follow your Thread?

Set another timer for 5 minutes. Do it right now. If it will take more than 5 minutes schedule when you will do it and put it in your calendar or set an alarm.

What to Do with Yourself

Identify what your thread is.

Ask yourself, your soul, "What do you want me to do?"

Do it.

Then live your life that day knowing you are on track for your should work becoming manifested.

Do this practice everyday. It will support both the completion of a vision and the peace of mind that comes with confidence.

FINANCIAL TRANSPARENCY

I recommend a combination of a tracking system for your spending as well as a Spending and Savings Plan spreadsheet.

There are many online and offline systems for tracking how your money is coming in and going out. Inside your bank or credit union they may offer an online bookkeeping program. This system works easiest if you use a debit or credit card regularly, if you use cash, and sometimes checks, you will have to enter it manually, because it will load your previous transactions from your cards, and then track card spending from there automatically. You can load bank accounts, student loans, retirement funds, and other financial aspects, if you can log in online you can often get them tracked here as well.

1. Using a system, or by inputting your own receipts, review how you spend your money. Notice, not how you think you should, but

how you actually do!
2. Input your average money spent over the past three months into a spending plan or budget ledger or spread sheet (Online I have linked a program and google spread sheet templates to start you off).
3. Then enter other costs that you know about that may not have appeared in the past three months automatically.
4. Then enter your known income.
5. Notice if there is a difference between what you spend and what you make. Review the amount you have been spending on things and if you would rather rearrange that money being spent. For instance, do you see that you spend more after work getting food than you want, and you could trade that money to get a massage once a month and pack an after work snack? Or do you see that you can both buy an after work snack and get some self care without damaging your savings fund?
6. Make a space in your spread sheet to see deeper prosperity by listing resources that were spent or received without money exchange. Such as gifts and their estimated value, invisible labor like a friend helping you clean your house, or borrow a truck, or hold a lot of emotional space for you.
7. MOST IMPORTANT PART - return to your tracking system on a regular basis, an ideally weekly, to see how spending is lining up with your estimated spending. Are you spending more or less, in the upcoming weeks are you all set up to say yes to that inspiring invitation you just received or would that yes benefit from a mindful and perhaps different kind of spending?
8. Once a month, or every other month, sit down with the tracking of actual spending and the spending plan you have been using. Make the spending plan reflect the reality of spending, by modifying because of over or under spending. Let your numbers tell the story of your behavior.

THIS IS SO MUCH MORE EMPOWERING THAN I COULD HAVE EVER IMAGINED!

GO AHEAD - GET HEADY CONVO

Set a twelve minute timer, during this time have a freeform conversation about the concept presented. The timer is meant to be a container to give space and to remind you to bring it back in and move forward, and you are invited to have the conversation to satisfaction and completion as you all collectively feel called. When practicing individually have a conversation aloud with yourself. If it helps, do it in the mirror.

GO SWIMMING IN LIVING WATER

All water is a blessing. Cleansing, nourishing, resetting.
   Water Is Life.
   Living water is that which has not be domesticated and has even more vitality to offer in its presence.
   Give thanks to the water, offer a gift, and then ask for its blessings.
   Go sit by living water if you can't get in it.
   Go put yourself in water. Ideally living water: RAIN! River, Creek, Ocean, Lake, Pond, Hot Springs, etc.
   If Living water is out of reach, go to running water, a sink, a bath, a shower and offer prayer to the water blessing and honoring it, offer it healing and then step in or rinse with it. Commune and healing together.

GROUP PROCESS FORMAT

This is a format for addressing or processing things as a group. Professional, personal, familiar, creative process. It is tried and true and can quickly and easily be adjusted for the particulars of your circumstance.
   Some things to note. The repetition of the process is what makes it the most effective. The structure allows those who are participating to lean into the support of the group and be held accountable as well.
   At first they will take longer, after a few times their length will usually cut almost in half, usually running about an 45-min to an hour. Once everyone gets in the hang of it, it will be an upswing of joy and connection. Then things will go well and people may think that it is not longer needed to meet and do the whole process. That is not the case, keep going. It's like taking a shower and feeling awesome and saying your so clean you never need to shower again! Then the next phase is that as people are held in exposure of their commitments and personal vulnerability there can often be a little push back on the intact of being known and seen on a regular basis. It can get a little tough a few months in. Keep going, there is smooth sailing not too far off. Once people build trust in the process and the people, the process itself will support the evolutionary growth that is being facilitated.
   On to the nitty gritty.
   Step by step.

Standing Agenda

    1.   Pick a facilitator

2. Check-In (place to share what is happening, anything that needs to be acknowledged to be present, a space to speak from the heart, and a chance to make any requests about needs or desires for the meeting) a sense of belonging is one of the most rewarding parts of working or living in community and the check-in is an essential part of maintaining one of the most valued experiences. Though at times it may feel unnecessary, I stand by that even if its shorter if it essential to optimal function and satisfying productivity to always have a check-in.
3. Review Agenda see if anything needs to be added
4. Check in about any time constraints, and if any items needs to be prioritized
5. Go through items one at a time. Facilitator checks-in before moving on to next agenda item by asking "is everyone complete with this?" "anything else on this" "can we move on" and gets a confirmed yes, by nods or verbal agreement

Agreements for the Meetings

- No cross talk or interruption of each other. One person speaks until they are finished
- While someone is talking, people may raise hands or signal to the Facilitator for comments or clarifying questions. The facilitator then calls on people once a person is finished
- General respect, no name calling, belittling someone else concerns due to irrelevance or emotionality
- *Vent fest -- in the spirit of honesty and needing to be heard, this is a space for people to voice things that seem like non issues, but have been on their mind. This is not a discussion. This a chance for a vent. If something seems bigger it can get added to the agenda later on. The intention of this space to give a space to voice little things that don't need to be changed just shared. *Put this in the middle of the meeting, not too early on or too close to the end if you can. This came from house meetings living in community when we needed a space to just say the things that were't really agenda items, but would build up over time if there wasn't a designated space to just get them out. These are not personal comments about other people, they are statements about experience or preferences. Sometimes it comes with a request, other times it's just to have it be known, and no one is expected to do anything different.

<u>Sample Agendas</u>

Money+Resources Care Meeting

Call meeting to order
   Check-in
   Review Agenda
   Upcoming bills
   Review spending and saving
   Review spending and savings plan/budget
   Review non-monetary resources, invisible labor, gifts, and other items
   Upcoming expenses
   Updates or alterations to spending and savings plan
   Call meeting to a close

Community Meeting

Call meeting to order
   Check-in
   Review Agenda
   Food
   Cleaning
   Vent Fest
   Bills
   Upcoming events, birthdays, parties, travel
   Call meeting to a close

Work Meeting

Call meeting to order
   Check-in
   Review Agenda
   Accountability check-in past action items
   New assignments
   Issues or events by name
   Depending on the work environment *Vent Fest
   Review action items and timeline
   Call meeting to a close

What to Do with Yourself

Invite your people to implement a group process format to support an aspect of your shared life.
   Or schedule or do this process solo with a project you have in mind.

What to Do as a Group

Make an agenda, it can be sincere and reveling or completely functional and made up, inspired by one of the agendas offered at the bottom and do a practice meeting now.

As a group decide the the length of the meeting and then the facilitator gets to practice keeping that agreement happening. Have fun, and listen to each other.

HABITS FOR FEELING YOUR FEELINGS

Either read to yourself and do each of the things or have one person read each step and everyone does them together.

- Round or Dome the soft part of the roof of your mouth, your soft palate
- Relax your jaw
- Place your tongue at the back of your top teeth or front of the roof of your mouth and let the mouth be slightly open, close your lips (or not)
- Drop your Grounding Cord
    - Imagine a rope dropping from your center down between your legs reaching into and plugging into the earth, then take a breath and image your pelvic floor opening and softening towards the earth, and allow a 6-12 inch channel opening and connecting down the path of the rope. Allow that channel to connect your heartbeat to the heartbeat of the earth. The cord is big enough to let your heaviest and biggest load go do to the earth
- Soften your belly and relax your muscles
- Open your hands and palms
- Breathe with your diaphragm at the base of your lungs and your pelvic diaphragm
- Make space in your joints by breathing and allowing them to soften and expand open
- Name the physical sensations you are having, focus on the feelings first and allow the named emotion to come after the feeling is felt
- Breathe, repeating and returning to any of the suggestions for 2 minutes

HABITS FOR COMPLETING GOALS

Make a list

Review your list
Complete the things on list
If things are not getting completed do two things
Decide if you don't want to do it or want to do it differently
Make the step into smaller steps
        Example: Instead of "get a job", List all the steps that make that up
draft a resume
edit resume
send resume to friend for feedback
Confirm my references
Identify 5 jobs I want to apply for
Apply to them within 5 days of finding them
Set alerts to follow up after application is sent
Set start dates and completion dates
Trust your intuition about what is the next step to do
Use your wisdom for identifying priorities
Give yourself the time it takes, meaning if it's taking "too long," keep going and give yourself more time next time

Notice if you are doing the following, are they useful? If not, interrupt or shift them into more useful things:

- **#1 *Give Up Bully Yourself*** for not completing things-you are wasting precious life force
- You are precious. Completing your goal takes courage, focus and support. Be on your own encouragement team.
- Are you using your faith as an excuse for not taking action you *know* and have been guided to do?
- Use your faith as the fuel to take the risks and have courage to do the things you *know* you need to do.
- If you are making excuses to not do something, consider why and how you are doing it
    - For example, are you blaming others for you not making time space to do what you say you are committed to doing?
    - Are you saying you are sick and don't feel well so you don't have to say no to people who you have a hard time saying no too? Or do you need more rest and struggle with taking care of your base and necessary needs?
- Own your responsibility and power to make time and prioritize the things you say you want and are committed to
- Focus on what needs to be done now
    - Let go of worrying about how things that need to get done later will get done now

HELP THROUGH THE CRACK

Sit quietly for about 1-2 minutes feeling for the place that is longing for guidance, relief, healing, and/or change.

Focus on that sensation and then relax your muscles and joints.

Soften your eyes, let them gently close or go out of focus.

Search your being to find the crack or thread that's open to change.

Then relax your jaw, turn your palms up and say aloud, volume doesn't matter, "Help."

HOW TO ACCEPT A COMPLIMENT

1) Some one gives you a compliment: "wlekjrq ;l43j58u(*U8 AU98ah"

2) Your response is "Thank you." Or some variation of acknowledgement and accepting the offer.

The art of receiving a compliment is a complex one that requires self knowing so as to only take in what you really want. This is another layer of the art which is receiving the offer for something without taking it in.

You see, compliments aren't really about you most of the time anyway. They are an expression of what someone else is seeing or observing, a societal or cultural expectation, a moment of affection. There are many reasons for giving a compliment.

Some compliments are spot on and meet our longing to be seen and known, whereas other compliments are totally off and not even really commenting on us personally, and are instead are actually commentary on their own projections. There are also compliments that speak so deliberately to a longing that we have not cultivated the courage to accept.

So initially, it's this, so simple, "Thank you." No deflecting, no changing the subject, not even returning a compliment, just "Thank you."

Then decide if you wish to let what was offered in as nourishing truth or let it roll off the surface as rain droplets returning to the earth.

What to Do with Yourself

Write out or speak out loud a compliment and then accept it.

What to Do as a Group

Get into pairs and take turns offering and accepting compliments.

Compliments are their own wonderland of personal preference. People's desires about what feels good to have commented on really varies. So play with this:

Person who is going to give the compliments ask the person receiving compliments these questions before offering you commentary:
- What is something that people say to you that you think they think is a compliment but you do not like?
- What compliments do you get and like and want to believe yet struggle to take in?
- What compliments do you wish you got?

Then offer them a compliment.

Person who is receiving then take a deep breath in, make eye contact if you can, and say "thank you".

Person giving the compliment say, "My pleasure." "You are welcome" or some such acknowledgement.

Then switch roles and begin with asking questions.

And both have given and received take a few moments to talk about your experience, about giving, receiving, the compliments in specific, feelings, physical sensations, or thoughts.

HOW TO MANIFEST WHAT YOU REALLY WANT

You are an immensely powerful cocreative force with the universe. You are an Origin Source Point!

You are a powerful origin point of existence, and anything you desire is coming into being.

Because, I know you can call anything into existence consciously and unconsciously I want to share with you the most kind version of manifesting I know. It will help you call into your life that which will bring you true joy and satisfaction, in the place of what can feel like a cruel magic trick of getting what you asked for but it being entirely not fulfilling. So, here's how to manifest what you really want rather to what you *think* you want, 'cause it turns out sometimes they don't match up. Follow these steps and you'll be set for getting your heart's desires met even better than you could ask for yourself!

I recommend doing each step in its entirety as you go. Do it with a partner or write it down - get excited! It can take 5 minutes or 20 depending how deep you're willing to go. The more excited you are, the louder the call to the co-creative universe.

This is essentially two stages of this process. Imagine you treat the magical resonating field of the universe's waiting room. In the first phase you are in the waiting room, and here is where you get clear before you step in the broadcasting station. When you first arrive, you may think that you go in and ask for what you want, but upon arriving you are informed to enter into the broadcast room you must leave all words, and all images outside. That the machine will read the vibration of your being when you go in. You can not put in words or images.

This means that you need to get clear and have a strong vibrational experience of what you came to call into existence.

These steps 1-5 are preparation and clarity exercises to get you into a vibrational connection with what your sacred desire is. Step 6 is the process of stepping into the broadcasting room and sending it forth. Here we go!

1. Ask: What do you want? It's alright to admit you want -- you have permission to want it really intensely. Take the time to get brave and kind to connect with the world of desire inside you. So really, what do you want? You can do it now... Take the vulnerable risk and say it out loud, draw a picture... Excellent - now - Dream even *bigger*, like if you had a magic wand, and it could be everything, out of this wold anything - what would it look like then? Yeah! That version.
2. Describe your awesome vision in detail. What does it look like? What are you wearing? What does it smell like? It's okay if it would be different in an hour. Do this unabashedly right arm this moment, you'll see why it's not as important if the image or words change soon. Be thorough in the imagination. What would you hear? How do you feel there? Who else is there? Get specific. What do you see? Yes! Even *more* nitty-gritty! Don't hold out for what you think is possible! The Spider Queen (story for another day) taught me, "I double dog dare you, to think of something that is IMPOSSIBLE in the LIMITLESS UNIVERSE." So go ahead, and name how would it be if it could be exactly what you wanted! Even if gravity doesn't exist there. Truly go for it. Is it so clear you can taste it? It's okay if it's not what you thought you would dream up. It's okay if the shape of it changes the next time you think of it. In fact, it most likely will. That's a good thing -- it indicates that you're wishing from the present moment, and that's where you have the most power.
3. Sweet! We're getting closer! Now, notice how you are *feeling* connecting with that dream. Articulate exactly how you feel when this dream is happening and is fulfilled. The you that "got it all." What are your body sensations? How does your heart feel? What

are your thoughts? What is the experience of having that want met? *Who are you when you get it all?* How would you describe that state of being? The more particular you are, the better the chances of getting the heart of your desires understood.

4. This is the most abstract part until it is experienced, and then it is very concrete. As you feel into the feeling, shift into a receptive state of being, and ask to be shown the vibrational state of the sacred desires, true heart's longing, the core of vision fulfilled. Then be curious and sense beyond while still feeling the senses you can, feel with your whole being the vibrational state.

5. Now shift perspective, enter into the understanding that what you truly want is to vibrate this way, and be that person. Enter into acceptance that your most powerful creative self is not the physical check list but the experiential state inside and through you life. Could this want and desire field really be about how you want to experience this incarnation and you think this is a way to have that experience? If the answer is "yes," or even "it's possible," continue to step 5.

6. Connect with the vibrational state of being. Allow those feelings, emotions, physical and mental activities to move as waves that have become a coherent frequency. Then stepping into the broadcasting center of your universe, become the speaker amplifying and ending those coded frequencies out into the correlative cosmic field. Invite a kindness purification to weave with you bringing the best and most loving version into your experience of life. Be the speaker, a resonating star, gemstone, a cosmic wellspring of life force. Let go of al preconceived notions of what will bring this vibrational expense into you life, say yes to the true fulfillment of your being, and beam and sound forth. Echoing and expanding into the great love of the cosmos. Resonance will attract those frequencies to you and you to it. Creating an articulated manifestation.

7. Take a deep breath, and let it go. Walk boldly, and as patiently as possible into your life knowing it is ini the creation process and is now beginning. Get curious and go have some fun with confindence your call into creation has occurred.

I AM WILLING TO ADMIT

Truth-telling and shame-clearing are two of my favorite healing techniques, and they happen to be highly effective. This is an exercise you can use to clear the heaviness of secrets or internal voices with yourself or in relationship.

Relationship is anyone or thing you relate to! Including but not limited to family, friends, colleagues, plants, animals, work, community members, lovers, and partnerships of all kinds. This can be done, in a group, in a pair, with ourselves, or at the altar. The prompt and response is the same.

The Sharing Prompt for this exercise is: "Even though I'm afraid I'm willing to admit..."*

When the sharing is complete the listener/s say the Listener's Response:

GROUP OF 6+ people say "We honor you.

We hear you.

We see you.

Thank you.

We love you."

Groups 3-5 Pick one of the following responses to say after the person sharing completes their share.

1. "I honor you."
2. "I hear you."
3. "I see you."
4. "Thank you."
5. "I love you."

*"**I believe**" **Variation** is done in the same format, be it group, pair, or solo, and is modified in one way. The Sharing Prompt is modified to be: "Even though I'm afraid I'm willing to admit that I believe..."

What to Do as a Group

Groups of 3-8:

Stand in a circle.

One person steps into the center and completes the Sharing Prompt three times complete the prompt with different or the same phrases as they are called as they speak their truth.

Group says the Listener's Response.

Then the person steps back in the circle.

Go around the circle twice.

Pairs:

Sit across from each other.

Each person goes alternately with the Sharing Prompt, starting each turn with "Even though I'm afraid I'm willing to admit..."

You each complete the prompt once per turn, but taking many turns back and forth.

When you both feel complete,

Each say the Listener's Response one at a time (ideally looking into each other's eyes) "I honor you. I hear you. I see you. Thank you. I love you."

What to Do with Yourself

Get settled and perhaps set upper self up in front of your altar with oe without a mirror if you have one. (Not needed and can be *really* helpful.) Repeat the Sharing Prompt "Even though I'm afraid I'm willing to admit..."
    At least 10 times... do it until you feel emptied, complete.
    Place one hand on your heart and say the Listener's Response out loud "I honor myself. I hear myself. I see myself. Thank you. I love myself."

INTERNAL BODYWORK

*Advanced practice internal bodywork

This practice is meant to bring connection and awareness to a space that most of us are not even aware that we have lost awareness. This is intended to bring a point of contact that allows you to reestablish an ownership and presence of your own self that inspires healing, balance, well being, wholeness, and access to your power by accessing your self.

It's different to connect to our bodies with more curiosity and listening than agenda or bossiness. It's a powerful and impactful way of being that can change everything. Internal genital massage also in the simplest and physiological way increase circulation, general health, and optimal health for earthful living and greater pleasure. So whatever your goal, it's good for your health.

Outer and inter-genital bodywork and deep perineum (that's the space between the genitals and the rectum) work can be felt very deeply inside, energetically an physically.

What to Do as a Group

As a game, you can do this exercise without doing internal work by everyone doing steps 1-5, placing your hands on your own root.
    As a deep healing ritual, this practice can be done in a group. One way to ensure people are their entirely by choice is by agreeing to do it ahead of time, that way people can come if they want to. When setting up the ritual space:
    set up an altar and invite people to bring their own objects of offerings
    Everyone brings their own materials, blankets, sheets, and cushions to

feel supported

Begin by opening the altar and saying prayers blessing the space and healing, and reclaiming of the body.

Go around the circle and do a check in sharing why they are here

Remind each other that there is no wrong or right way, that this is a time to be supported in connecting to your own body away from other peoples agendas, you don't have to go inside your body or touch any part of you want, and at the same time it is a safe place for you to touch your own body which belong to only you.

Review the instructions and any supplemental materials

Either have one person sing songs or play music or drum, or play some healing music to support people dropping into the connection with their own body

What to Do with Yourself

You have do this as curious and lighthearted as you want, or as deep ritual as you desire.

You are setting yourself up to make connection with your body and come into deeper awareness and true relaxation of your core.

Follow instructions.

Session are often about 15-20 minutes if you go inside the body or work the tissues around the genitals. You can go longer or shorter, just listen to your body.

1. Have a lubricant that you like, you can use oils from the kitchen, coconut oil, sesame oil, or cocoa butter, shea butter, or a standard lubricant you like.
2. First placing your hand over your pubic bone breathing into your pelvic floor.
3. Sending 5 breaths from your lungs and heart down and out through your root.
4. Breathing 5 breaths deeply into your root nourishing and filling the bowl with breath.
5. When you feel connected tell your body out loud, or silently, clearly "I am here to offer support and listen and help you clear tension, bringing us into balance and connection with ourself." Then ask, "Is there anything you want me to do or hear before we start?" Listen here for any specific guidance.
6. After hearing and acting on the message or not hearing any, gently and confidently enter or press on your own genitals with 1 or 2 fingers (you can use a tool, I recommend, if possible, starting with your hand to be able to get a sense of the tissue and sense the

7. Listen to your body's response, are you open and ready? Tight and resistant? At ease and curious? All of them? Something different? Move with curious listening, and listen for any specific guidance from your tissues and your intuition.
8. Explore different depths of touch. You can usually press harder than you think. But remember in bodywork rarely is there *TOO deep*, just *too fast*. Feel for tight muscle knots and dense feelings. The balanced and healthy bowl feels supple, responsive and dynamic. So increase pressure with your breath and notice places that are, numb, sticky, sore, hurt, hot or cold. Invite spirit guides, your own wisdom or a divine essence to join you in listening and support the healing and balancing of your bowl.
9. Let your body and soul relax and unwind, allow this process to be one of connection and remembering. It is your body, you are always allowed to touch it.

For more specific and in-depth information about practicing on yourself. You can find supplemental supportive materials for self practice in the App at **sophiawiseone.com/member-access/.** I recommend reading "Wild Feminine: Finding Power, Spirit, and Joy in the Female Body" by Tami Lynn Kent. If doing this is intimidating but know it would be helpful, I check the resources page online to help you find a practitioner. This work is too intense for many people to do alone, whereas others feel incredibly empowered and comfortable doing this. Blessings on us all.

LEARN SOMETHING NEW

Learning something new is a vulnerable task. It requires being, at least in some ways, not good at something for a moment, so times many moments. It's also informative about how we process under stress, how we make decisions, and how we have changed since last we learned. It grows us.

If you are in a group, take a moment to see if anyone has a skill to share and teach right here and now.

Learning something new can include a new form of study, a new field, new terms with vocabulary and philosophy; from math, to money, to biology, to art history, to business, to a new language, to anything that interests you. It can also be a body thing: hand games, a new dance or dance form, marital arts, or a new sport. Or a new skill like building things with wood, or metal, or with a program or your hands or a tool. Or you could learn a new instrument, your voice, percussion, wind, or string.

You can go back to something you used to know and learn it better from the beginning or you can start with something you have never done before.

Just learn something.

The one thing that all these things have in common is if you want to learn it, you are going to have do it or something related to it, with continuity for many days over a good period of time.

You can study via books, internet, and youtube. You can go take a class or course, you can sign up for a training program, or you can explore and learn on your own.

What to Do as a Group

Does anyone in the room have something you can teach us right now? A simple hand game, how to draw something, how to sharpen a knife, a photography tip, cooking knowledge? Some one here has something to share. Share your knowledge with your group, right here, right now.

What to Do with Yourself

Pick something new and go for it with commitment.

RECORD A STORY AND LISTEN TO YOURSELF

1. Get something with which you can record audio
2. Think of a story of when you learned something new, or made a mistake, or gave apology, or was *SO HAPPY*
3. Record yourself telling the story
4. Play the recording and listen to yourself speaking, use Pro-Active Listening techniques on page 352 techniques to really listen to yourself all the way through

INVERSIONS

Shoulder Stand, Legs up the Wall, Hand Stand
   Get your head and heart below your feet in some way
   Set a time for 10 minutes
   Breathe and let gravity do the work or giving your heart a rest and your system a reset

<u>Legs up the wall</u>
   Lay down on the floor
   Put your bottom against the wall and swing your legs up the wall, place a cushions under your knees to support them if you are a distance from the wall

Upside-down

Sit sideways on a couch or solid chair

Swing your legs around so they are up on the top of the furniture and allow your head shoulders to come off from the chair/couch towards the floor

Stay for just a few minutes, until the head has had enough

IRONIC TO SINCERE "THANK YOU" PRAYER PRACTICE

This was first shared with me as Sufi practice and since then has appeared in a number of spaces and traditions in their own way. What I share here is the practice I have developed that is influenced by the combination of those experiences:

There are times in our anger or frustration where there appears nothing to be grateful for.

Start there.

Using your voice and body, speak in the tone and expression of rage and disbelief, and speak of the things you are hateful and angry towards and yet start every new sentence with the words, "Thank you for..."

All the things you would like to start with "Fack you for..." you say "thank you," and then rant, curse, wail, wave, but don't stop until you actually start to feel grateful for something. I mean entirely-honestly. The hardest part about this practice is it will only work if you are honest about all the things you are so hurt by. You can't back down when you feel tired or spent, you have to keep going until you are actually grateful, not because you should be, but because you feel it. This may take 15 minutes to a half hour. Set yourself up to pound something with your arms.

I first did this practice outside in the rain and pushed into the soft wet earth. If possible, try *that* sometime.

There is a video in the App at **sophiawiseone.com/member-access/** on self-care and safety notes on how to pound while caring for your body's wellbeing, so you don't injure yourself or anyone else.

NATURE BATH

Focusing on and consciously absorbing, soaking in the natural world elements. Sounds, smells, sights, textures, the overall feeling of nature. Sit and look at a singular natural element, close your eyes and take in as much sound as you can. Bathe in nature. Get to nature for 20 minutes in one of the following ways:
- Take a barefoot walk on the earth be it grass, mud, sand, stone
- Take yourself somewhere that either is plant filled nature or

- reminds you of wild nature, and take a walk
- Go outside and walk around and feel the air and look at the sky
- Hug a tree
- Sit, smell, feel, see, listen with a bouquet or a singular flower
- Look at picture of nature landscapes while listening to nature sounds

"YES" AND "NO"

This is done in partners when in a group. When practicing individually, imagine a partner and do the vocalizations aloud. You may be practicing saying and hearing "no", "yes", or both. When practicing both, do both practices in their entirety.

"No"

In this exercise you will be given multiple opportunities to say, "no" and hear "no." Through rehearsing in different dynamics you expand your potential landscape of comfort. I encourage you as partners to take risks. Allow the positioning and implied circumstance or acted out circumstances to be edgy. That will help you build confidence in your "no." At the same time, if the position or circumstance is too intense or moves too fast for a no, replay it and turn it down until you get a no, and consider doing it a few times increasing intensity if the person is up for it. This is a trust exercise so stay present and attuned to your partner.

1. Get a partner, Partner A and Partner 1
2. Partner A and 1 think of one things they have a hard time saying no to.
3. Partner 1 share where you would like to confidently say no. The options are limitless from emotional manipulation to violent acts to micro-aggressions. Decide a scenario and make a physical position and cue line for the no, decide the position and prompt for the three distances:
    1. Physically touching
    2. Just at arms length distance
    3. Over 6 feet away
4. Move through all three positions with Partner A doing the positions and Partner 1 voices "No". When inspired you can add, "Stop". You can say more words, and remember the focus of this exercise is to vocalize you "no".
5. Repeat by having Partner A moving through positions, 1-3, and then 3-1, and then a third time 1-3 ending with the boundary "No"

and "stop" from at a distance.
6. That is three rounds from close to far, far to close, and then close to far again. This is so the closing practice is the declaration of the boundary at the first sign that there needs to be a boundary
7. Repeat Steps 2-5 switching Partner 1 and A roles
8. Check-in about the experience

<u>"Yes"</u>

1. Get a partner, Partner A and Partner 1
2. Partner A and 1 think of one thing they have a challenging time saying "Yes" to, that they want to say "yes" to.
3. Partner 1 share where you would like to confidently say yes. The options are limitless from subtle to overt pleasing and desired positions. Decide a scenario and make a physical position and cue line for the yes, decide the position and prompt for the three distances: Meaning three positions in which clearly one person is being prompted to say yes.
    - Physically touching
    - Just at arms length distance
    - Over 6 feet away
4. Move through all three positions with Partner A doing the positions and Partner 1 voices "Yes." "I want this."
5. Repeat by having Partner A moving through positions, 1-3, and then 3-1, and then a third time 1-3 ending with the distant position of something wanted "Yes" and "I want this" from at a distance
6. That is three rounds from close to far, far to close, and then close to far again. The closing practice is the declaration of the wanting and saying yes to something at first sign
7. Repeat Steps 2-5 switching Partner 1 and A roles
8. Check-in about the experience

NOURISHMENT PRACTICES

Pick a way to nourish by feeding yourself food or drink. Below are three examples of ways you feed yourself.

<u>Drink nourishing tea</u>

    Make your favorite cup of tea.
    Thank the tea.
    Give yourself permission to receive all the tea has to offer, all the wisdom, the medicine, the nourishment
    Drink it.

Notice it while drinking it.
Thank the tea at the final sip.

How to Make an Infusion:
- Pick a tea that infuses well (not all do) for instance nettles are very nourishing.
- Put quart of water on to boil
- Add 1/4 cup of tea bring to a simmer for 20 minutes
- Let sit for 8 hours
- There is your infusion
- Appreciate, drink with awareness receive, and enjoy

Nourishment: Food High in Fat

I was told once that fat in food is the energy of Mother Love. That breast milk is at least 60% fat. That the war on fat in our foods is a war on being nourished and loved. Fats are good. They are essential for brain function, hormonal balance, and mood regulation. Eating fat regulates blood sugar and can help lead to a more stable and trustworthy appetite. Processed and toxic things in our food are concerns which can be carried in fats, so quality fats and foods are something to be mindful of.

So eat food with fat and be fed.

Nourishment through freshness

Food from scratch with lots of freshness can bring a whole additional level to the process of being fed. So make a meal and make sure it has raw vibrant elements. Be fed with aliveness.

PENDULUM PRACTICE

A pendulum is a device that is weight at the end of line. When used as a divination tool is it guided not by gravity or forced swinging but by the subtle forces. This is a complete practice unto itself that, for some people, is their main tool for divination. I invite you to explore this and see if it might be an additional tool or something to further pursue for your tool basket of accessing information.

This can be radically different with an actual crafted pendulum, that being said a necklace or something that hangs and has a weighted end can be used. You hold it between two fingers or suspended between fingers.

What to Do with Yourself

Sequence when using a pendulum for consulting:

Identify who you are asking for guidance (Ancestor, Your Higher Self, Divine, Spirit Guide, etc.)
    Hold the Pendulum
    Ask Pendulum "Show me yes"
    "Stop"
    "Show me no"
    "Stop"
    "Show me unclear"
    "Stop"
    "[Insert who you are asking] are you available to answer my questions with this pendulum?"
    Watch Pendulum
    When you get the yes, go ahead and ask away.

What to Do as a Group

Using a pendulum on the body:

Get into pairs and have one partner lay down
    Place the pendulum above about 3 inches from top of the head
    Take a few breaths and observe what movement occurs
    After noticing what is happening, then try adding an intention There is a great power in observation and invitation. The invitation I offer you to practice with the body "I invite you to bring this place into harmony with itself"
    Then move the pendulum down the body repeating the process at each point: forehead, throat, heart, solar plexus, below belly button, pubic bone, between the feet.
    You can do this over any part of the physical or invisible bodies.

PLAYERS CHOICE

Just do you - do a practice of your choosing from this book or one you already have an know. You can find the list of practices in the book listed in the Table of Contents.

PROFESSIONAL ASSISTANCE

This is a time to schedule an appointment with professional.

There are things that can be helped with good intentions and best efforts and there are things that can get worse without proper support. When you are provider, be sure to take the best care of yourself by letting someone who is coming to you for support know when what they need is out of your realm of knowledge. And take care of those offering you support by getting the help you need from someone who is trained and capable of giving it to you.

Acupuncturist, Herbalist, Therapist or Counselor, Chiropractor, Communication Specialist, Bodyworker, Private Yoga Instruction, Sex Specialist, Medicine Caller, Naturopathic Doctor, surgeon, dentist, trainer, and/or an physician. There are so many people who have dedicated their life to having answers and insight in the thing that is ailing you.

Below there are guidelines for finding a therapist and then help center hotlines below.

- Picking a Talk Therapist (these steps can be applied to any therapeutic relationship you are adventuring into):
- I've been told talk therapist's efficiency breaks down like this: 1/3 make you worse, 1/3 make you better, and 1/3 don't make a difference -- so please shop around.
- Make sure they have additional training or experience with recovering from trauma and, in particular, has practice for activated or trigger states of trauma (our culture as a whole is recovering and navigating trauma) and any other specific elements you are navigating that you know about.
- Part of getting to that 1/3 who make you better is finding the right fit, you ought to be able to tell within 2 sessions if you are making progress. Progress means your uncomfortable stuff is getting touched and found and you are feeling supported and respected while learning to navigate or gaining insight into those uncomfortable pieces.
- Interview your therapist in your first session too - to get a sense of what they are looking for and how they work, so that you can trust the process you are working on together, they maybe the professional practitioner and yet you remain the authority on your life and your needs baring specific diagnosis.
- Find a practitioner, if possible, who does not find your story interesting, ideally you want your case to be old news. They can find you personally interesting, just ideally not your circumstance. When possible you want to work with someone who has walked through this journey many times with success before.
- You do not need to like your therapist, *and* you do need to trust and respect them, and to get the best results, once you pick a therapist that has met your personal criteria for respect and trust, *listen to and implement their advice.*

When it comes to finding bodywork, same things apply except that instead of needing trauma experience you want them to have general experience with their clients seeing a change in their body. You want to know they have techniques they feel comfortable with for resetting the systems in the body. It often takes a second session to confirm if you like a practitioner's work because the first session everyone is getting their bearings. Be sure to speak up about what is not pleasing to you. It will make them more effective. You will actually get better therapeutic results if you let them know certain kinds of pressure or techniques are uncomfortable and what feels good.

This is a list of hotline and resource centers, I am not endorsing them personally, I share them here as a reference, a starting point. They are resources and it's best to start somewhere.

- A national 24-hour, toll free confidential suicide hotline for LGBTQ youth. www.thetrevorproject.org/ 1-888-989-2455
- The National Domestic Abuse Hotline www.thehotline.org 1-1-800-799-7233 1-800-787-3224 (TTY)
- National Suicide Prevention Lifeline 1-800 273 8255
- Alcoholics Anonymous https://www.aa.org/
- Narcotics Anonymous https://www.na.org/
- National Sexual Assault Hotline RAINN www.rainn.org 1-800-656-4673
- The Childhelp National Child Abuse Hotline 24/7 https://www.childhelp.org/hotline/ 1-800-4-A-Child (422-4453)

PRO-ACTIVE LISTENING

What to Do with Yourself

Review the exercise as it is done in a group and then go and do Record a Story and Listen to Yourself practice on page 345 using the recording as your partner.

What to Do as a Group

Get into pairs.

1. The first sharer speaks for 2 minutes about anything on their heart or mind while the listener does not speak: no interjections, no questions, no comments, sits with open body posture, facing the person, looking at then with no arms or legs crossed.
2. Then, with a silent transition, trade roles and do it again.
3. Then with the same rules, each person gets one minute to share about the experience they just has.
4. Set a timer three minutes, share a free flow conversation about the overall experience.

PRAYER PRACTICE

One is the Altar and the other is the Pray-er. This practice was created when my students asked me to share with them how to pray out loud. One of the key elements to praying out loud is the experience of someone actually, very literally, listening. Speaking your truth and getting vulnerable in the presence and support of something is the mystical combination. Feeling a little foolish or self conscious is often a good sign early on that you are getting somewhere good and real. So this exercise was birthed. One person is the listener, and the other the heart pourer.

Things to consider when praying for others:
- Make sure they want it. This stuff works and is powerful. Without permission you are meddling in someone's space that you do not have permission to be in.
- I do not recommend praying for specific outcome, especially for others. Do you really want to assume you know what is best? Even if it seems obvious, such as healing from a disease or ending of painful relationship. I don't. I have had people "pray for me" with an agenda, and I felt it, and it felt presumptuous, controlling, paternalist, egoic and about them, not me. So check your intentions and ere on the side of best care and experience possible for the person without deciding what that is.
- My most common way of praying for another is by identifying the part of myself that carries the same thing and then pray to have that part of me healed and then offer the resonance or dedicate the healing to them *if* they want it.

What to Do with Yourself

When doing this practice the "altar" can be anything, a shower wall, a plant, a gorgeous altar set up, an old picture, the point of the practice is to connect to talking to something that is listening. Don't overthink it, just set your self up and then go through the steps, the praying itself will take care of the rest.

What to Do as a Group

Get into pairs

Altar Person:
> You become the Altar, the sacred witness and channel and reflector of love and wisdom
>
> Sit in an open posture: hands open, sitting up, eyes closed, LISTENING with your whole body. Still. Receiving.

Pray-er Person:
> You are the Pray-er, you will pray out loud

Remember honesty is your most powerful tool when praying
Speak to Divinity through the space created by Altar

You are offered this format:
1. **Naming/Calling In [give thanks]** This is where you acknowledge who or what you are praying to or set the space for sacred or healing communion
   - Chanting or singing a song is a common way of setting the space
   - Name and honor the Divine as you feel called
   - This can be anything, if you do not have a faith practice you can try one of these for the call in:
     - "I call upon wisdom, compassion, kindness, and love. Be with me and hear me. I ask you to join me here and be with me in this time and space. Thank you for hearing my invitation and I welcome you here."
     - "I call the wisest and best part of myself. May this time bring us together, that I may be my best self by the end. Thanks."
     - "I call upon whatever mystery that may happen to care about my experience right now. If there is anything that unconditionally loves me or cares, I am here trying something new, seeing how it goes. Thank you for giving this an honest run with me."

- Call on Spirit or do the Calling The Directions practice on page 220.
- If you have deep faith and you don't know how to Call In or Name try one of these:
    - "I call upon the beauty and love of the cosmos. The mystery that creates and absorbs all existence. That which knows me, is me, treasures me, and guides me. I call upon you here. I ask your presence to be here, be felt, be known. I love you and am grateful to call on you. I welcome you into my space and consciousness. Hear me. Know me. Thank you for listening."
    - "Dear Goddess/God/Universe/[insert specific divine name]/Beloved/mystery. I call upon your love and presence. I ask you to hear me, know me, see me, and be with me here. Thank you."
    - "Dear _____ I give thanks and praise to your wonderment, that which is beyond understanding, articulation, and comprehension. I call to you with appreciation for all you have given me. I feel you each and everyday and am grateful for your loving presence in my life."

2. **Coming Clean/surrender [give thanks]**
    - THIS IS SO IMPORTANT! This is where you come clean, speak your mind, spill your guts. Name your struggles, don't worry about poetry or sounding nice, this is where you establish intimacy and share what you are carrying close to your heart.
    - Share fears, doubts, dreams, longing, pains, aches, confusion, excitement, ideas, and inspirations.
    - Sharing your secrets is an offering.
    - This is where you can share that you have not been feeling great, or have no faith. This is where I would say things like, "I don't feel your presence, I can't feel your love. I feel lost, and alone, and full of doubt."
    - This is also where you share what you are feeling FABULOUS about. You precious joys and dreams that you keep close to your heart. This is where I would say things like, "I feel the power of the cosmos flowing through me. Time is bending and I know the truth of who I am. It is precious and powerful and I am grateful for all that I and others and you have done to bring me to this experience." Or "I feel so f-ing amazing. I am so in love and I haven't told anyone. It's so tender and precious and powerful, I

feel a little bit like I am losing my mind in the best way possible."
- They do not have to be secrets, just speak from your heart, share what's on your mind, and just put it all out there.

3. **Asking [give thanks]**
    - This is where you get vulnerable enough to ask for what you want, really, really want.
    - Aim to get to the core feelings of what you are longing to experience. *(See How to Manifest What You Really Want on page 338 for more clarity on getting to what you really want)
    - You can pray for a change in circumstance as well as a change in your own being.

4. **Offer it up [give thanks]**
    - *This is essential!* This is where you offer all your confessions from you coming clean as well as what you have asked for.
    - This is where you surrender your ideas about what you think you need and specific outcomes and make space for what will really serve your deepest truest longing and all others' wellbeing as well.
    - Hand it over and make space for this or better with as little expectation as you can muster.
    - Some examples:
        - "Okay now you have heard it all. Take everything I have shared and make it into something beautiful and better than I can imagine it."
        - "I hand all my dreams into the wisdom and purification of real love. Not sentimental or self imposed importance, really, really please do whatever you need to do. I am willing to change, to give it all up, to become what I need to be in truest service of love. "
        - "I know I have a lot of ideas about what should happen, know this, they are ideas, and honestly, desires. More important that my desires is my wholeness. I ask that you hear and bring forth that which is really my truest self, my most whole version of life, and that I may be of service and remember my own sanctity and honor the sacredness of all other things."

5. **Give thanks**
    - Give thanks for everything you can honestly.
    - Make an offering.*

*Check out Instructions on page 278 for more info on offerings.

REVERSE THE QUESTION

Flip the subject with the object, change what to how, how to what, who to why, why to what, how to why, should to why would , etc.

In whatever way you can, reverse, inverse the question and see what happens.

Examples:
   How can I be with this person?
   What experience do I want to be having when relating with this person?

Why is this happening to me?
   What is happening?

What am I going to do about the dog?
   How is the dog?
   Or
   How is the dog getting care?

Should I leave?
   Why would I, do I stay?
   Or
   What do I need to stay? What do I need to leave?

SAVORING

This too shall pass.

Savoring is not just about food. It is about taking in the details of sensation of an experience. Practicing with food can be a very effective place to begin seeing opportunities to savor. Practice with food and then apply the same sequence to hugging, taking a shower, accepting a compliment, starting your car, opening the mail, and feeling joy, excitement, grief, irritation. You see, all of these moments will come and then be gone.

Savoring is an art of recognizing that this experience will pass, no matter how sweet or sour, mundane or monumental. It's your life and then your life will be something else. It the practice of *not* missing your life, and instead soaking it up.

Individually or in a group, take 10 minutes to eat something delicious, such as an orange, or chocolate, or drink a cup of tea.

1. Set a timer.
2. Start with looking at it: light, color, variation.
3. Think about what it is, how it got there: where and how it was planted and/or grown, harvested and prepped, made or crafted, shipped or traveled, and sold or gifted. Consider the journey it took to get to you.
4. Then touch it, feel the texture, the temperature, the weight.
5. Then smell it, first breathing in the smell through your mouth and nose, and then with your mouth closed just your nose.
6. The take a very small bite and feel the flavor hit different parts of your mouth, notice the rest of your body, chewing and/or swallowing when you choose.
7. After the timer goes, sit for 1 minute in silence, then go around and share about your experience.

Bonus Round
What to Do as a Group

Feeding each other. This is done without words.

1. Make 1 plate of tasty things, fruit or sweets, or savory things that the people present can eat.
2. Sit in a circle (after everyone washes their hands). One person starts with the plate (for groups larger than 8, you can make multiple plates and start them spread out around the circle).
3. The person with the plate shows the plate to the person to their left so they can visually take in the splendor.
4. The giver then feeds the food to the receiver by hand.
5. The receiver then accepts the plate and turns to their left and becomes the giver, repeat steps 3 & 4.
6. After completing one round in the circle, do a second round. Either in the same direction or changing directions. It is important to do the circle at least twice because the first time it's new and second time you can experience it differently. You can do as many rounds as you want until you feel done, everyone passes, or the plates are empty.

SELF SWADDLING

Many of have had the experience of wanting something to hit, push against, shove, or destroy. Some of us have done this in unconscious and painful ways for yourself and others. This is a way to tend to that urge that is respectful and healthy. Many of us have also had the desire to be held in our rage lovingly, maybe you don't even know you would like that, so many of us have been shamed and shut down around anger that to know that you could be supported in this feeling may be brand new.

This exercise offers both the loving support and the space to express in kind ways.

Swaddling is known to be soothing to most nervous systems, the equal pressure simultaneously activate the parasympathetic nervous system.

At the same time, we often hold our anger in with inside tension that is energetically and physically costly to our selves. Giving yourself time space to express and press that stuck feeling, sensation, and pressure out through conscious action is often transformative.

Follow the instructions below, and know that everyone has their own experience, and oddly enough even this is something that you get better at with practice. Be gentle and brave with yourself, trust your power and urges while also being kind and providing that loving space to yourself as well. You are creating a space to both be free and express and to hold and tend yourself.

1. Make a safe space for noise.
    - Tell housemates or family members you might be loud and it's okay.
    - Turn on loud music very loud (make a playlist or pick an album or crank the radio).
    - If you are concerned that if you go towards these intense emotions they will never end, set a 30 minute timer.
    - If you are concerned of being seen in such vulnerable state, it can help to put a sign on the door or lock the door to feel protected.
2. Get a BIG blanket or two blankets staggered to make it longer (different kinds of blankets will swaddle differently, the squishy ones with give will be tighter around but you need many layers to give resistance, a heavier or quilted blanket will give you a firm resistance to push again, but may be tricker to get that snug feeling, so if you do it and want a different kind of snug try changing the blanket).
3. Stand and bow to The Rage (Yours, mine, ours, *the* Rage) you are here to give it healthy respectful space to do its healing magic.
4. I would recommend calling on help in some way. An opening prayer, asking for the presence and guidance of your spirit guides, opening your altar. (This is not required to have the exercise work, I just find it to be more supportive.)

5. If you're using it, turn the music up.
6. Start on one end of the blanket and wrap it around you tucking it under you body and then roll over and over until you are entirely swaddled
7. Breathing deep into your pelvic floor, softening your throat; then press and push and yell and scream against the safe resistance of the blanket. Rage darling, rage.
    - The rage and anger will likely come in waves, between the waves maybe waves of grief, fits of laughter, or bouts of fatigue, breathe into your pelvic floor imagine yourself having a sacred tunnel in your core that allows all your letting go to flow out, and all you need to flow in.
    - Give yourself AT LEAST 3 rounds of raging with grieving, resting, or laughing in between.
8. Lie in stillness for the length of at least one song or 3 minutes after the last come down wave. Breathing and blessing yourself and the space. As you breathe, honor and welcome blessings into your mind, body, emotions, and spirit.
9. Stand and bow to The Rage and the feelings that you experienced move through you.
10. Closing and gratitude to any other support you called in.
11. Drink water. Live your life :-)
12. You are sacred, holy, and loved.

SENSITIVITY SCANNING

Get into pairs, triads or do this with yourself.

Everybody take a brief moment to stretch and breathe, coming into your body, feeling into your feet and hands, stretching up and bending down.

Stand across from your partner.

One person will be scanned and the other will scan, or you are scanning yourself.

The person being scanned close your eyes and relax.

The person scanning start one foot above the head and then slowly scan down the body to the feet. Keep the hands off the body about 6 inches.

Repeat the scan a second and third time, exploring closer and farther from the body 3 inches to 1 to 2 feet off the body.

After the scanning is complete, tell the person being scanned to opens their eyes.

First let the person who was scanned share what they experienced.

When the person who scanned shares keep the following things in mind:

Share what you felt or sensations when you were hovering over certain areas of the body: tingling, warm, cold, buzzing, wanted to move my hand quickly, stay, etc. Focus on the sensation not the story. If you are the scanner avoid things like "your heart is..." "Wow your _____ is really blocked/stuck/open/full/hurt..." Stick with the sensations you experienced using statements that start with "I", "I felt...", I noticed", "I wanted to...".

Remember, everyone's experience is real, and they do not have to be the same to have them be accurate. It's like listening to a song. Some people hear the lyrics, some people hear the bass, it's all there. If you stick with the sensations of your experience and not prescriptive descriptions of "what it means" then you can avoid language that assumes one person is right.

Rotate to the next person until everyone gets a chance to be scanned and scan.Rotate to the next person until everyone gets a chance to be scanned and scan.

After you have done it with eyes closed if you want you can play around and do it again with with eyes open and discuss while it's happening.
Play!

TAKE A BATH

What to Do with Yourself

Fill bath to preferred temperature
  Give thanks to the water
  Add things as a blessing to yourself and blessing to the water, such as:

- Epsom salt is detoxing, and will pull stuff out
- Sea or mineral salt is nourishing and feeds the body and spirit
- Oil -- examples are olive oil, coconut oil, sesame oil, hemp oil, other bath oils
- Flower petals or herbs -- examples are lavender, roses, rosemary, holy basil
- 3 drops of an essential oil

Light a candle, or turn lights down low
  Put on relaxing music, or silence
  Have relaxing book or journal nearby with a towel to dry your hands in case you want to read or write
  Lightly stretch and breathe into your body in the warm nourishing water

Take a couple minutes to breathe and give yourself permission to experience the relaxing or healing potential of the bath
Enjoy!

What to Do as a Group

You have a number of options here:

- The group can run a bath and bless the water for the person who pulled the card, now or at the completion of the game
- Everyone can share what they have at home or where they can go take a bath
- Everyone can mediate for 12 minutes and imagine going to healing baths and soaking
- Everyone goes to hot springs or a bath house right now
- Make foot baths in pots and buckets with what you have on hand, or take chairs into a bathroom and soak your feet together in the bathtub and take a foot bath together
- Take a bath together
- Some other bath magic you decide

TOUR OF THE PELVIC BOWL

Everyone get comfortable to listen to or read this reading:

I want to invite you on a journey around the landscape of the pelvic bowl where we will be discovering ourselves, our wisdom, our wounds and the power they hold up for us to take.

One could definitely call this an advanced practice. Many choose to do Pelvic Floor work because it's the "final frontier," the one important place that hasn't been listened to and healed. And isn't that funny? The base, our root, is the last place we tread when we want to change, even though everything sits atop it? I presume it's because when it comes to reconnection, most of us need to work our way down from our heads.

From transforming body-based physical ailments (pain during sex, menstrual issues, hips and knee problems), emotional struggles, and imbalances to spiritual evolution, being in satisfying intimate relationships, creative and joyful living, and manifesting like a pregnant woman, this potent packed journey has limitless healing potential.

Let's begin exploring some knowledge about this incredible center of peace and healing, our foundational place.

I offer this first, ROOT teaching:
You are made of space and matter.
You take up space and you matter.

Let's take a walk around the pelvic bowl.

Here we will be exploring the pelvic bowl quadrant by quadrant. Tami Lynn Kent first taught me the process of mapping the pelvic bowl into quadrants (you can learn more about her brilliant teachings in her book *Wild Feminine: Finding Power, Spirit, & Joy in the Female Body*). As we wander through the landscape, think of the pelvic bowl like a medicinal herb garden where each section grows its own medicine. Each plant has its own specific strengths, needs for tending, and sensitivities. And each garden has its own perfect balance and unique variations. What follows is the integrated knowledge from my studies, as well as the personal experience of healing my own bowl and facilitating others' healing...

Proclamation

This information is not meant to tell you what your own body is telling you. It is intended to help inform you so you can open up and start a deep and sincere conversation with your own self. That is sacred communication, and no one knows better than you.

The Left Quadrant ~ Intuition & Nurturing

Oooooo. Ahhhhhhh. Yeaaaaaah.
Oh to melt into divine love and be rocked endlessly.
I see walls of roses.

The left side is often associated with the Feminine. A foundation question here is, "How was your mothering?"

The left side is where I often hit a clusterf%$#@ of tissue. Mothering is not about your birth mother necessarily; it's about the tending of your creative, intuitive, feeling, needing and evolving self. If there is a person connected to the left side of your bowl, it's the person (or persons) that emotionally tracked you when you were little. The one(s) who saw and tended your emotional, physical and deep soulful needs and nurtured them. Or, as most humans in our imperfection, the one(s) who missed and/or disregarded those needs. Most often a combination of the two.

In this part of the pelvic bowl we often find the areas of neglect, the stories about how we are not worthy, uncared for, or forgotten. We find the places where our subtle and potent selves needed attention and nurturing and didn't get it properly. If you were hungry, lacked enough fat in your diet, or had poor nutrition, the left side of your bowl is a place that this wound might show up.

Here is where I have felt and found my need for deep care, for having my emotional needs anticipated (also where I get my super powers for anticipating the emotional needs of others), and for connecting to the Great Cosmic Mama (the mama of even the sun and our earth mama, and our spinning clusters of galaxies). Here is where I find my need for sisterhood. To have others feel not just for me when I am upset or unhappy, joyful or blissful, but with me.

COM = with.
PASSION = feeling and sensuous experience.

Here is where I find compassion. (Technically compassion is often translated to mean "suffer with." I find that definition limited but also accurate.)

Here is where I have held many of the memories from past lives or lineages of being hunted, burned or sacrificed because of the wisdom I carried.

Here is the land of Wisdom, the landscape of experience and trusted KNOWING (not to be confused with thinking), of embodied and sensual experience. As my left side has become more balanced it has shown me deep imagination and dreams, the magic of rhythm and cycles, powerful inspiration, the beauty of growth and connection, and the productivity of non-linear, orb-like, shape-shifting growth. As I dive deeper into this space, ecstasy, pleasure and desire find me here too.

Here is the place that can be so open and so full it radiates wholeness.

The Right Quadrant ~ Manifestation and Protection

Oh! Wow! What a kind, glorious and majestic side of myself!
SO SOLID! So Firm! So Clear! So Holy!

The right side is repeatedly revealing itself as the masculine space in me. The land of magic, autonomy, and SPACE. This refers to both outer and inner space.

The Cosmic Papa, the Divine Masculine, the rowdy cowgirl, the go-get-it-done-er, the make-it-happen-er, and the ultimate protector. The right quadrant is responsible for ensuring you are safe, you are respected, you are strong. It looks after your physical well being, the use of your body, the building of your muscles, the alignment of your bones, and all of your doing. It also brings your ideas into materialized reality!

Found in the right quadrant are issues with structure and plans, follow through, and spacious flow.

Over and over again I've been shown a common imbalance here: the exhaustion of trying to get things 'right.' This is the area of my body that attempts to be or do things 'right' and is suffocated by it.

In these knotted tissues, I have found the lack of a 'father' presence. Fathering is not necessarily about your biological father, it's about the space or energy of those (including yourself) who were responsible for making sure you were and are protected from the emotional, physical, spiritual, and soulful abuse of this world. It's about those who were entrusted with insuring that you brought your inspirations into materialized or manifested form. This protection and successful manifestation is something that ought to be provided to us as wee ones, and as we grow we become adept at providing this for ourselves and offering it to others.

Thus, the right is the constricted, exhausted side of constantly fighting for our OWN.

The right side teaches us to stand our ground, to share our voice, and to do and act as we are inspired and called to be.

When balanced, this is our torch-in-hand, our guiding light illuminating the path.

When out of balance, this is the torch that burns down our home, sanctuary, body. We have been culturally dominated, across gender and bodies to BE a particular something, be USED for something, and to PRODUCE something. That control, abuse, and resistance can wreck the right side.

One of the most common places we have not been protected, no matter the gender, is our root, our genitalia, and/or our sexuality.

The Right Side is where I have found the cosmos spinning inside of me, the magician who can materialize a miracle in an instant, and a light so bright all is illuminated and all action is clear. Here, I AM READY.

The right side represents your internal container, and like a bowl, if it has a crack, it leaks. Viewed through the lens of masculine and feminine, the right masculine side is the sturdy container for your flexible, fluid, feminine aspect.

The feminine reminds me of a putty-like substance, radiant, vibrating, healing, alive, soft, malleable, and responsive. It likes to be more liquid, solidify for a moment or two and then change again.

Fluid takes the shape of the vessel that contains it. So it is with this partnership of container and substance in the pelvic bowl.

If your right side is wonky, if your container is leaky, busted, weak, or too small and tight, i.e if you lack a safe internal container, this is what it might look like in your life:

1. Your feminine aspects overtly leaks out (or if the space is too small, spills out) -- you are experienced by the world as subtly or majorly dangerous, untrustworthy, emotionally volatile, up and down, unstable, unpredictable, and/or needy. (Anyone remember me in my 20s?)

2. These aspects of your flexible, dynamic, feminine self solidify and stiffen to create the uber-firm boundaries and safety you need in lieu of a healthy container -- we can do this so much that we are experienced by others as cold, distant, controlling, and/or stubborn. (Sound like anyone you know?)

I imagine the right side more like an orb and less like a bowl when the two are sides are aligned; In a sweep of sci-fi sound effects, the right side's container whoooommms round, holding and protecting the ever-evolving left side substance, which expands inside the container beyond "sides" and dances freely.

With an intact container, the dynamic, fluid self can melt and form and melt and form, which means you can be your dynamic and fully creative, expressive, and extraordinary self. This strong, loving container maintains that you are always (in all ways) respected, given the necessary space, listened to, supported, and able to successfully manifest yourself and your dreams. YOU ARE SAFE to be your ever-changeable self.

The Right Side loves a job well done, clarity of role, and the mark of clear success. It loves boundaries and directness. It loves to make a safe space/house for the Creative.

The Anterior or Front Quadrant ~ Fear and Flow

YES.
I AM HERE.
HERE WE GO.
I take up space and I matter.
I impact my life and I fill my own world.

This quadrant is about the impact and effect you have on your life. It is about the space you take up for yourself, space just for you. It's the song of pleasure and joy.

A collapsed or tangled front side may show up as anxiety, fear, or a lack of self expression. You may find that you're awesome at responding to things; problem solving during a crisis, or showing up for someone else when they need something. You can do a good job if someone else tells you that you need to do it. What's hard for you is to do what you want. You may have a hard time acting on your own ideas or desires, like that dream project you've always wanted to make happen. If you do act on your dream/desire, you may have a hard time seeing it through to completion or to its fullest expression because of overwhelm or shut-down stemming from fear. This is the home of pleasure and enjoyment of your life and of yourself (embodiment).

The anterior quadrant is about vulnerability, intimacy, your own power, and PLEASURE! It's the landscape of being seen, visible, and recognized, and enjoying it!

It's a powerful place to work with intimacy issues, and that good old (ancestral) wound of witch burning and/or being hunted because of your awesome valuable knowledge and being.

When I first discovered the potential of the front of my pelvic bowl, I was learning and experiencing vulva healing, a healing practice from Tantra yoga that addresses the interior of the vaginal walls and the potent energy centers therein. The practice is similar to, yet not exactly like, Holistic Pelvic Care™ and thousands of years older. I was astounded at how aware I could be and how much sensation and sensitivity I could have in the front and in front of my body, both physically and energetically. I was amazed at how long I had lived without even knowing I was missing awareness there; I didn't know there was anything there to be noticing!

If you want to stop just reacting or responding to life, and instead want to bring forth your dreams, wishes, wisdom, gifts, and joy into the world, the front of your pelvis is a very good place to explore and inhabit.

NOW....

Both the adventure and challenge of the anterior is that it often holds both the pain of our fear, as well as the feeling of fear itself. You may find that just bringing your focus to the front of your body can be a hazy or anxiety producing experience.

When we feel fear we can get caught in a haze, and then switch automatically into an autonomic nervous system response of either fight, flight, or freeze:

1. Feel fear
2. Feel hazy or disoriented
3. Experience fight, flight or freeze

Either in milliseconds or over the course of days, if not interrupted, it leads us to continuously function from our unconscious coping mechanisms.

For example, when I'm scared I often experience freeze. My unconscious patterns sometimes create mental instead of physical freeze; instead of literally standing catatonic in panic, I can't complete a thought or get clear and I can't get much done.

Behind this fear, however, is FLOW!

Awesome, synchronistic, easeful flow -- an energy to meet and greet the world! An energy that flows outward from you. An energy that reaches out and engages, instead of one that responds or reacts.

The breath is especially important when exploring the front pelvis. Breath is the only thing we need to carry us consciously through feeling fear to connecting with flow, instead of dissociating and abandoning ship.

Here's the key Body-Wisdom ingredient to working with the front quadrant of the pelvis: your lungs, intercostals (muscles in between the rib cage), and diaphragm are the essential body partners to this zone.

Here's the thing about working with particular areas of body and their wisdom: they are still always in deep connection, interconnection, and relationship with the rest of you. Isolation is in many ways an educational exercise and the healing comes in the unification of self with self. Body part with body part, soul with body, mind with action, heart with words, etc.

To truly support the healing of your anterior quadrant we need to take a brief visit to...

BREATHING HEADQUARTERS

One of the biggest dangers for bodywork, yoga and most healing practices is halting the breath. If you are not breathing with and through the journey, you compress and split yourself, which is literally counter productive to the expansive, unifying and space-making goals of healing, building strength, engagement, and flexibility.

So let's talk about breathing how-to's by reviewing some of these ancient, complex, and awesome practices in the most simple/rudimentary terms:

Hatha yoga = the yoga of posture and structure
　Vinyasa = the yoga of flow, movement
　Kundalini = the yoga of energy
　Pranayama = the yoga of breath

The point of this is to say that the study of breath is a kind of yoga in and of itself, and is as complex, full, and rich as any hatha or vinyasa class you've ever heard of. In massage school they taught us that the diaphragm and use of breath is long known to be the FASTEST way to access the unconscious, or connect the unconscious with the conscious.

It's the center for our pleasure and fear, and it is a powerful and sensitive area. Breathe. Remember, it's just you manifested into physical form. It's just you. Move slow enough to breathe, witness and love ourselves.

Posterior or Back Quadrant - Trust and Support

Oh sweet back, sweet place of knowing and relaxation.
Sweet place of trust, of the support that allows me to open.

Of my strength and steadiness that allows me to know I too am support and supported.

The posterior quadrant shows its bodily intelligence by revealing whether or not we are leaning back. Are we experiencing trust, receiving support, feeling safe while being supported, and more specifically, leaning into that support? Are we? Am I? Are you?

Are we steadily grounded in our root and engaged in knowing how well we support ourselves and how capable we are of supporting others?

When we do not experience what we are longing for the body grips. It braces and holds tight.

The brilliance is that this means of coping works. Let's pause and clarify what 'works' means. Coping cares about one thing, NOT DYING. If you are alive than your coping mechanisms are working 100% successfully. Congratulations! There is a big gap, however, between not being dead and thriving in aliveness. Tension, especially painful tension, is your body telling the story of your coping.

Note: There is also a turning point when coping mechanisms can take a turn towards proactive self-destruction, and the change can be either subtle or overt.

Regardless, compassionately seeing ourselves and our coping mechanisms is an important step towards positive transformation. So let's take a look.

Are you either:

- Coping (just trying to get through)?
- Self-destructing (making efforts towards death)?
- Thriving alive-ing (living your life with fervor, not waiting to be perfect, pursuing your passions)?

If you can't tell, learn to listen to your body. It knows the difference, and can guide you through to wholeness.

Take a deep, full breath. And another one. We all have places where these questions and ways of being show up. Sometimes it's subtle, sometimes it's debilitating. Often it reveals itself in the back of our pelvic bowl. So what's the good news?

Healing happens.

Another breath.

Let's keep going :-)

The ease or gripping in the posterior of the pelvic bowl often tells the narrative of either deep trust and relaxation that lead to incredible openness and whole-self generosity, or the exhaustion and overwhelming experience of being alone, unknown, unsupported and coping.

Guh.

Looking around the rear of your pelvic bowl gives you great capacity to find that which you long to lean into. In literal, external concrete ways it helps you manifest support. For example, someone to pick up when you call, a job that sustains you, or a partner who keeps their word. Or, it can represent the more subtle or esoteric support you might desire, like deep feelings of faith or a connection to something bigger than yourself. This is a space that knows what you want to push against for support, and in what ways you want to be able to let go, relax, and soften in connection.

I tend to bump into feelings of worthlessness and worthiness here:

Who am I? Who am I to say or do that or this? Who am I to be supported or to be trusted as support? Am I worthy to relax and have things be okay, or am I at my core bad and hence unworthy of support?

Or:

I am wonderfully made! Wholeness is my nature! I feel the conspiring of the universe on my behalf! This is fun and enjoyable!

In the posterior dwells feelings of doubting and blaming others, resentment, self-doubt and the self-control of "keeping it all together." When I stay with these feelings and questions, committed to kindly and slowly moving through them, they release.

As they release "YES!" is all there is to say. I experience a silent, body-vibrating sensation of, "Yes. Existence is safe." This experience of deep knowing leaves me feeling vulnerable, open, safe, and without words.

Posterior pelvic tension can sometimes show up as: hemorrhoids, vaginal tearing during birth, sciatic pain, a sense that you can not be trusted with responsibility, or discomfort with sitting for extended periods of time.

*　*　*

Making connection to your body and exploring it is really wonderful, it is the groundwork of embodiment and self-trust. The body, aka your Self, is always communicating as best it can with you. As you make more effort, time, and space to hear those messages, the body will begin to communicate differently as well. It takes this even deeper. Once you're connected, you can use the connection to get clear guidance for your life, from your bowl.

In Conclusion...

YOU ARE WONDERFULLY MYSTERIOUS AND BEAUTIFUL.

There is SO MUCH more to each area of the pelvic bowl and so many more aspects to explore. Each and every area is connected with other parts of the body and has immense innate knowings and sensitivities.

Related parts of the body include but are not limited to: the ovaries (testicles for some folks), womb (womb energy around the body in male bodied folks), bladder, rectum, fascia, and musculature.

Whenever you experience pain or unwanted body symptoms it is an opportunity to listen to what your body is trying to tell you. It's an internal phone ringing, with valuable information waiting on the other end:

Are you willing to pick up?

Do you know how?

Are you ready to listen?

The body's wisdom is an incredible guide to becoming your truest self. You are an infinite being and yet, right now, you have this body. It is your teacher. This body is your vessel and an expression of your divinity, therefore it's an incredible place to start conversations with sacredness.

WARRIOR POSE AND TEACHINGS BY GRACE PERKINS

Grace Perkins (my Mother) taught me much about the path of the warrior, and she joins us here to share about The Warrior archetype, the warrior pose, and The Voice of the warrior.

She joins us for this section of the book to share her teachings. Read her offerings and practice the pose:

THE ARCHETYPE: THE WARRIOR

First, let's acknowledge we all have courage within us. The warrior's job is to confront injustice. This always requires a measure of courage. There are ways to strengthen and refine this excellent attribute. Confronting injustice may involve broken boundaries within ourselves, in our relationships or in a larger social context. (This is not to be confused with the job of the soldier trained to follow orders to engage in physical combat.)

The first task of the warrior is confronting injustice is to "show-up" and hold the boundary. It is to draw a line to what is acceptable within ourselves and the society in which we live without judging others. For example if at a party where a disrespectful comment is made about another's looks or religion, etc. and the thought arises, "I should say something - but what?" the choice may be to confront the person (fight) or go home with their negative remark stuck in your throat (flight). Rather than those reactions, it's possible to choose to respond with a phrase that establishes a boundary. A simple phrase such as "No, that has not been my experience." This has the ability to set everyone free. This action protects your integrity without judging another and gives you the ability to hold a "just" boundary.

THE PRACTICE: THE WARRIOR POSE

The intention in yoga is to combine physical strength, the light of the spirit and the focus of the mind into a healthy organism.

The warrior pose is done by moving feet to a lunge position and drifting the front knee into a bend that places the knee to just come in line with the big toe. Rock the body gently to establish that both legs are equally engaged and release the tailbone bringing the hips into line.

Pressing the hands together and centering them at the breast bone, allow them to rise above the head.

Press the shoulder blades down and back. Draw the arms as close to the ears as you can.

Observe in front of you by looking straight ahead at the vista. See the ceiling and floor, light and shadow, colors and what is at the edges of your vision.

In a strong voice say, "NO!" holding the boundary. Pressing the hands together: draw this power back to the center of the chest. Do a little dance. (This is to relieve the drama, as in, "shake it off!")

Repeat the lunge using opposite leg forward and the voice -"STOP!"

Repeat two more times using "NOT IN MY HOUSE!" "NO APOLOGIES!"

Many yoga tapes and books illustrate the warrior pose and its many variations.

It is important to vocalize in this practice as the voice creates commitment in the cellular body.

THE VOCIE: NO! STOP! NOT IN MY HOUSE! NO APOLOGIES!

The first voice comes from the first lesson people learn in a self-defense class.

The second and third voices come from interviews Oprah had with Maya Angelou during which Oprah remarked that if someone said anything derogatory when at her house she would say to the person, "STOP, NOT IN MY HOUSE" and ask them to leave. This can also be a personal thing that happens in one's own self in which case "STOP!" and don't leave, just get a cup of tea.

The fourth voice is to stand in your truth and don't be tempted to apologize.

It is an action that excuses the other person and says "Please still like me."

Hence the dance at the end.

This is a practice. If you do it enough, you will be strong and centered and courage will fill you up. You don't have to take the warrior stance, it has you and will hold you.   Blessings.

WE ARE WHOLE, TOGETHER CIRCLE

Sit in a close circle so you can touch the person on either side.

Place your left hand on your own body in a reassuring and loving way.

Place you right hand on the back of the person to your right in a loving and reassuring way.

As a group take 5 deep breaths and then either sing a song together or listen to one.

Medicine Song recommendations: I Am Whole Just As I Am (p 176), We Are In This Together (p 180), or Peace Now (p 179).

WIND PRAYER

Spirit of the Wind

   You are the breath of the planet

   Giving breath to me and all I love

Your movements can cool a hot day, bring water to a drought, put out a flame or fuel a fire, lift the earth and move her and you can carve and smooth her mountain tops.

You link all breathing beings by moving between us, carrying our gifts to each other, our carbon dioxide to the trees and their oxygen to us just to name one thread you weave.

Wind you bring evolution of thought and expanded perspectives.

Thank you for all that you are and all that you carry, wisdom and vision beyond my experience.

I turn to you with gratitude and wonderment and ask for your blessings on me and my journey at this time.

Bring to me your peace of breath, your power of breath, your inspiration of song, and your limitless expansiveness.

UNWINDING GROUP EXERCISE

This practice is rooted in the understanding that through compassionate companionship things change and unravel on their own. Through mirroring, acknowledgment, support, affection, protection, space holding, all sorts of contact, and witnessing we change. We don't need to be made to unravel, we will unwind our tensions when we are held and supported in non-judgmental deep respect.

What to Do with Yourself

Review the exercise and dream of, or invite, who you want to do it with. Right now go and practice the Organic Movement Meditation exercise on page 204.

What to Do as a Group

Do this exercise with the person who pulled the card going into the center first. If the group wants to do other people you can do so one person at a time as time and energy allows.

1. Make a circle.
2. One person goes into the middle and closes their eyes and thinks of themself in their worst or most vulnerable state, or of the burden they are carrying at the moment, and takes a deep breath

allowing their body to tell the story of this part of them, making a sculpture or posture of this feeling.
3. The group sits, with open body posture,[6] taking in and appreciating this bold share
4. Each person looks to observe for a place where the person could use physical support. A space to connect and meet them where they are.
5. Once an observer sees a clear place they would like to offer acknowledging support to the person in the center the person goes in and does it. This may be a hand placement, or a back for the person to lean against, or a posture that isn't physically touching but visually cueing or inviting. (Be mindful of this so that the person offering support is holding all of their own bodyweight and does not require the person in the center to change.)
6. It is the job of the person in the center to accept that support and then relax or soften in whatever way that support organically encourages, the person who comes into the circle stays present and shifts in whatever way is needed.
    - (For example, the supporter won't come and open crossed arms, though in response to the supportive hand on the person in the center's body, they may naturally unlock their arms and open them.)
7. When the point of support has shifted and the posture is still again, another person can move into the circle and now offer support to this shifted and different posture.
8. People move in offering support slowly, one shift at a time, until the person in the center comes to a significantly different position and state of being (it doesn't need to be ALL good, just stay with it until their is an unwinding or a completed or distinctly shifted sensation for the person in the center.)
9. When the person in the center feels complete say verbally that you are complete or finished or nod and do a gentle squeeze on each of the people so they know you are done and don't feel like talking.

---

[6] Palms open, body open, eyes observing and taking in what you see, leaning slightly forward or neutrally. Do your best to not cross your arms, if you need to hold yourself or protect yourself, place one hand on your belly, and one on your heart, or turn the body slightly on angle away from what you are looking at, and yet, keep the focus on them, while breathing deep.

www.ingramcontent.com/pod-product-compliance
Lightning Source LLC
Chambersburg PA
CBHW040419100526
44589CB00021B/2756